I0118535

The Bloody Century:

True Tales of Murder

in 19th Century America

Robert Wilhelm

Copyright © 2014 **Robert Wilhelm**
All rights reserved.

ISBN: 0692300678
ISBN 13: 978-0692300671
Night Stick Press
Boston, Massachusetts

For Anne and Tom

CONTENTS

i

INTRODUCTION

It may seem arbitrary to label the nineteenth as America's "bloody century" when all of her centuries have seen a fair amount of blood, but a murderous atmosphere pervaded nineteenth century America unlike any before or since. It is not a matter of statistics—the per capita murder rate declined throughout the century—it has more to do with public interest and private attitudes toward the crime of murder. Murder stories flourished in the new republic as pamphleteers and newspaper publishers began printing the lurid details of sensational murders, and, as if responding to the growing need for sensational copy, many otherwise law abiding people began to see murder as a solution to their problems.

The English tradition of selling broadsides—one page printed documents—commemorating executions continued in the new world. At first they were transcriptions of sermons or ballads written about the murder, but the American versions grew into multi-paged pamphlets, summarizing the details of the crime and usually including the condemned man's confession or, less often, his protestation of innocence. As the century progressed, the pamphlets continued to grow in size, adding court transcripts, portraits of the killer and his victim, and sometimes illustrations of the crime itself. By the end of the nineteenth century, specialty publishers were producing books of a hundred pages or more on prominent murder cases, precursors to the true-crime literature that flourished in the centuries that followed.

Newspapers, before the 1830s, were primarily aimed at the upper classes, with shipping news and market prices for merchants and political news for party members. When technical advances drastically lowered printing costs, "penny press" newspapers included subjects appealing to a wider audience, such as sports, entertainment, and crime—especially murder. The investigations and prosecutions, in New York City, of the Helen Jewett murder in 1836 and the Mary Rogers and Samuel Adams murders in 1841 were followed closely by readers throughout the country. The trend spread rapidly until it was rare to find a newspaper anywhere in America without at least one murder on the front page. By the end of the century, the "yellow journalism" of Pulitzer and Hearst gave murder reporting another boost, by sending first class writers like Julian Hawthorn and Nellie Bly to cover murder stories all over the country. American readers followed the daily reports as if they were serialized mysteries.

Illustrated magazines which gained popularity in the mid-1800s, would also publish murder stories. *Harpers Monthly Magazine* printed illustrations from the Smuttynose murders in 1873. *Frank Leslie's Illustrated Newspaper* was on the verge of bankruptcy in 1857, until a series of articles on the Harvey Burdell murder sold enough copies to save the publication. Illustrated murder reporting was a staple of the *National Police Gazette*, a men's magazine found in every barber shop in America.

For the most part, these were not stories of hardened criminals for whom murder was a way of life, the killers were ordinary Americans, of every class and occupation, who had concluded that their lot in life could be improved by the death of someone in their circle. It was an era of second chances; some traveled west to start a new life, others looked for their second chance through more violent means. Harvard professor John White Webster thought he could relieve his debts by killing his creditor. Frankie Silver and Roxalana Druse murdered their husbands to escape abuse, while Henry Green and Adolph Luetgert got rid of their inconvenient wives. Jealousy drove Daniel McFarland to murder his rival and Laura Fair to murder her lover. Greed drove the Knapp brothers to plot the murder of their rich uncle.

Then there were the murders committed for no reason at all. While still in his early teens Jesse Pomeroy tortured and killed two young children and could not explain why. Thomas Piper murdered two young women before senselessly killing a five-year-old girl in a church belfry. Theo Durrant, who also did his dirty work in a church belfry, murdered and mutilated two young women from the Christian Endeavor Society which he led. Lydia Sherman and Sarah Jane Robinson poisoned their husbands and children in murder sprees that went on for years. And of course, the infamous H. H. Holmes systematically tortured and killed an estimated 230 men, women, and children.

In telling these stories I have endeavored to stick to accepted facts and current prevailing opinions. In some cases this means contradicting long held beliefs and cherished traditions, such as the murder of Naomi Wise, which has been preserved by songs and stories that are completely wrong. In other cases it means giving short shrift to popular alternative theories, such as the dozens of unfounded suppositions regarding the Borden murders. Where credible alternative theories exist, I have listed them, but the stories themselves are all based on currently accepted facts and no more. I have also avoided any social or psychological analysis of the situations and people involved, opting instead for concise telling of what I believe are fascinating stories in their own right. Many, if not all, of these stories are worthy of book-length treatments and quite a few have already been the subject of contemporary books. Those interested in learning more about a particular case can find them listed in the chapter notes.

All of the stories in The Bloody Century have been posted on-line, in a rougher form, at Murder by Gaslight (www.MurderByGaslight.com), and represent the best of the blog's first five years. They are presented here alphabetically by the victim's last name. The titles, for the most part, come from sources contemporary with the murder—newspaper headlines, pamphlet titles, nicknames given to the case by reporters and other writers, quotes from those involved, and lines from songs. The songs themselves, along with poems and bits of verse associated with the murders are also included. Most of the illustrations were taken from nineteenth century murder pamphlets, newspapers, or magazines.

The days of America's distant past, the time of gaslights and horse drawn carriages, are often viewed as quaint and sentimental, but a closer look reveals passions, fears, and motives that are timeless and universal, and a population inured to violence, capable of monstrous acts. A visit to the bloody century may well give us insight into our own.

Samuel Adams

1. THE CORPSE IN THE SHIPPING CRATE

On September 17, 1841, an expressman picked up a crate on Maiden Lane in Manhattan and delivered it to the New York dockyard, where it was loaded aboard the packet *Kalamazoo*, scheduled to leave that afternoon for New Orleans. Inclement weather kept the *Kalamazoo* in port for a week, and sailors started complaining of a foul odor coming from the hold. The stench was traced to the crate, which was opened, revealing a decomposing

FINDING THE BODY OF SAMUEL ADAMS

human corpse. John C. Colt, a mild-mannered bookkeeping instructor, who had arranged the crate's delivery, was prosecuted for the crime in what would become one of New York City's first sensational murder trials.

Date: September 17, 1841

Location: New York, New York

Victim: Samuel Adams

Cause of Death: Blows from a hammer

Accused: John C. Colt

Synopsis:

John C. Colt came from a family of achievers. His father was a successful Hartford, Connecticut, businessman, his older brother James was a judge in St. Louis, and his younger brother Samuel was a gunsmith who invented the Colt revolver. But John took a long time finding his place in the world, and in his early life he was a bit of a rolling stone. At fourteen, he was apprenticed in a store but soon, at his own request, he was sent back to school. Before graduating he ran away to Baltimore, where he taught

1

mathematics at a girls' academy. He worked for a while as a surveyor. He joined the navy but didn't like it and was released at his father's request. After he apprenticed at a law firm for a year, he entered the University of Vermont. He went west and engaged in land speculation, then to New Orleans where he taught chemistry and bookkeeping. Bookkeeping was the trade that stuck, and in Cincinnati John Colt published a book on bookkeeping that is still read today.

Colt moved to Manhattan and seemed ready to settle down. He rented an office in a building on the corner of Broadway and Chambers Street that also housed a school of bookkeeping and penmanship, and the office of printer Samuel Adams. In 1841, Colt began living with a beautiful young woman named Caroline Henshaw.

Samuel Adams, who had been printing Colt's book in New York, called at Colt's office on Friday, September 17, 1841, and the two had a heated argument over the exact amount of money Adams was owed. The argument quickly escalated and soon they were exchanging blows until Colt received a blow that caused his nose to bleed. Colt then struck Adams with his fist and they began grappling. Adams grabbed Colt's neck handkerchief and twisted it until Colt could scarcely breathe, while at the same time pressing him hard against the wall and table. Colt reached for a hammer that was on the table and began to fiercely strike his adversary on the head until Adams finally let go and fell over. In Colt's words:

> *I then sat down, for I felt weak and sick. After sitting a few minutes, and seeing so much blood, I think I went and looked at poor Adams, who breathed quite loud for several minutes, then threw his arms out and was silent. I recollect at this time taking him by the hand, which seemed lifeless, and a horrid thrill came over me, that I had killed him.*

The blood pouring out of Adams began to pool on the floor. Colt was afraid it would leak through the floorboards into the apothecary below, so he mopped up the blood with a towel and a bucket of water he kept in the office. Other tenants of the building rushed to the office to investigate the commotion, but Colt ignored their knocks on the office door. He cleaned up what he could, then went to the City Hotel to seek counsel from one of his brothers who was staying there. He met his brother but seeing that he was engaged in conversation with two gentlemen, he left without telling his story. He next thought of going to the magistrate and confessing all, but he did not want to submit his family to public scandal. Back in his office, Colt considered setting a fire to consume the body along with the building, but rejected this plan after realizing the innocent lives that would be lost.

He finally came up with a plan he thought was foolproof. He disposed of all items that would identify Adams, then packed his corpse into a shipping crate. He worked late into the night packing the crate and cleaning the floor and walls of his office. He dumped the bloody water into the gutter outside, then left the office and stopped at a bathhouse to clean himself and his clothes. When he returned home, he told Caroline he was late because he had met a friend from Philadelphia.

The next day he hired an expressman to deliver the crate to the pier where he arranged to have it shipped to New Orleans on the packet *Kalamazoo* and from there to St. Louis. Colt returned to his office, thinking his problems were solved.

They might have been solved if rain hadn't kept the *Kalamazoo* in port for a week. The body began to decompose, and the sailor complained of the odor in the hold. The odor was traced to Colt's crate and it was opened revealing the rotting corpse. The shipping clerk remembered Colt, as did the expressman who led police back to his office. Adams's disappearance had been reported by the press, and it was ascertained that he was last seen alive in Colt's office.

It turned out that Colt's actions the day of the murder had not been as clandestine as he thought. Asa H Wheeler, a teacher at the bookkeeping school, had heard a noise that sounded like "the clashing of foils," then a violent fall to the floor coming from Colt's office and went to investigate. He looked through the keyhole and saw two men's hats on the table and one man bending over something. He sent a student after a police officer who sent word back to keep watch, but that he would not dare break down a locked office door. Others had heard the sound of scrubbing coming from the office, and the sound of hammering; several had seen the crate addressed to St. Louis via New Orleans.

When Colt was confronted, he confessed all. John C. Colt was arrested for the murder of Samuel Adams and sent to The Tombs—the New York City jail.

Trial: January 21, 1842

Because of his confession, John Colt's guilt in the murder of Samuel Adams was not at issue in his trial. What the prosecution attempted to prove was that the murder was premeditated. They had expert witnesses testify that the wound on the head could have been from a ball fired from a gun. It would have produced a round hole, as was found in the skull, and the sound may have resembled the clashing of foils.

The defense attorney called the defendant's brother Samuel to the stand to demonstrate that the power of a cap and ball pistol—the type the prosecution claimed Colt used—was insufficient to pierce the skull. In his demonstrations the guns had a loud report but were only able to penetrate a few pages of a book. In one experiment he caught the ball in his hand.

Samuel Adams's severed head was brought into the courtroom to be examined by the defense's physicians in front of the jury. They concluded that the wound was consistent with the hammer the defendant claimed he used.

Caroline Henshaw was called to testify to Colt's behavior the night of the murder, and to his general good character. The prosecution objected because they lived as husband and wife and if they had actually been married, her testimony would not be allowed.

In the end, the defense's most compelling testimony was the statement written by John Colt and read in court by his attorney. He explained in detail exactly what happened in his office that day, what thoughts went through his head, and why he acted the way he did, but it was not enough for the jury. They found John C. Colt guilty of willful murder.

Verdict: Guilty of willful murder

Aftermath:

After a failed appeal, John Colt was sentenced to be hanged on November 14, 1842. John Colt and Caroline Henshaw requested that they be allowed to marry before the execution. The request was granted, and several hours before the scheduled execution, they were married, with Colt's brother Samuel and John Howard Payne, composer of "Home Sweet Home," serving as witnesses. After the ceremony the couple was allowed a few minutes alone.

Just before the hanging was to take place, a fire broke out in The Tombs and it was feared that the prison would burn down. The execution was forgotten while firemen scrambled to put out the fire. Once the fire was under control, authorities hastily prepared for the execution. A clergyman went to Colt's cell to console him but found him lying dead with a dagger in his heart.

There were rumors following the event that Colt's friends had set the fire and during the confusion he had escaped, leaving the dead body of another in his place. There was no proof to this claim; the only thing Colt had escaped was the gallows.

Rose Clark Ambler

2. THE RAVEN STREAM CRIME

Rose Ambler said goodnight to her fiancé at the Raven Stream Bridge in Stratford, Connecticut, the night of September 2, 1883 and started walking home alone, as she usually did. She was never again seen alive. Her body was found the next day, beaten and stabbed, the circumstances of her death a complete mystery. The case had numerous suspects, and everyone in Stratford had a theory as to who was guilty, but none of the evidence seemed to fit together and none of the accusations would stick.

ROSE CLARK AMBLER

Date: September 2, 1883

Location: Stratford, Connecticut

Victim: Rose Clark Ambler

Cause of Death: Beating, Stabbing

Accused: William Lewis

Synopsis:

Rose Ambler was visiting with her fiancé, William Lewis, at his father's house the evening of Sunday, September 2, 1883. They were to be married on Thanksgiving and would move into a new house that Lewis was having built. Around 9:30 p.m., Rose started walking back to her parents' home, about a mile and a half away. Lewis walked with her as far as the Raven

Stream Bridge, but Rose declined his offer to walk her all the way home. She knew he had to get up early the next morning for his job peddling vegetables and felt safe walking through the peaceful neighborhood outside of Stratford.

That night, Preston Hodges, who lived not far from the bridge, was awakened by a violent thunderstorm. Around 11:00 p.m., he heard an intense scream; at the time he thought it was an owl screeching. The following morning the body of Rose Ambler was found beaten and stabbed lying near a wall in a meadow between the bridge and Hodges's house.

It was first thought that she had been raped. Rose was not carrying any money and there did not appear to be any other motive for the crime. The first suspect was Boston White, a young black man with a bad reputation in Stratford. A group of angry citizens broke into his house and demanded that his mother show them Boston's clothing so they could check for bloodstains. They found no blood, and Boston White had an alibi; he had been sleeping in a stable several miles away, a fact that was verified by the stable owner. He knew Rose Ambler, as did most residents of Stratford, but he had no connection with her. In fact, there had been no evidence against Boston White other than his race and reputation. He was soon dismissed as a suspect.

An autopsy revealed that Rose had not been raped, forcing investigators to look at her rather complicated personal life for a motive. Rose Ambler (nee Clark) had, at age eighteen, been engaged to a sailor. He went to sea and was away so long that Rose stopped waiting and married Norman Ambler, a farmer who lived near Stratford.

Rose and Norman Ambler were divorced several months after their marriage, and it was rumored that she had been abused by her husband. In fact, the marriage ended because Rose was cheating on Norman with his cousin and business partner, William Lewis. He had been living in the same house with them; Rose fell in love with Lewis and he returned her affection. When Norman learned of the affair, he sent Lewis away. Norman and Rose began quarrelling, which led to separation and divorce. Rose left him to marry William Lewis.

Rose Ambler was usually described as pretty, or even beautiful, but this was disputed by a New Haven newspaper that said she was "…hardly up to the average in good looks…She was, however, intelligent, and was highly esteemed and universally liked." William Lewis knew that she was also fickle and flirtatious. Lewis, who was described as "…an ideal Connecticut countryman, with oiled hair, bushy blond whiskers, and blue flannel clothes," was also described as extremely jealous.

Norman Ambler was jealous as well, and still bitter over the loss of his wife to Lewis. The two men met shortly before the murder and reportedly

Ambler told Lewis, "You will never marry this woman; either you or she shall die first."

Coroner's Inquest: September 4, 1883

A day after the body was discovered, Deputy Coroner J. A. Joyce began a closed-door inquest to investigate the murder of Rose Ambler. While the coroner was taking testimony, the Stratford police, assisted by Pinkerton detective J. S. Wood, continued to look for evidence. A reward of $300—later raised to $1,000—was offered for information.

The first suspect to emerge from the inquest was Norman Ambler. A witness testified to seeing him in town that day, and his threats against Rose and William Lewis were well known. But since the divorce, Ambler had been living at the home of Henry Hatch in New Milford, forty miles away. Hatch swore positively that Ambler was home in bed the night of the murder.

Boston White was brought back in to testify, this time to be asked about a companion of his, a white man named Michael Heslin. There were three deep scratches on Rose Ambler's neck, and Heslin was known to be missing a finger. Edward Bertram testified that he saw Rose Ambler walking with a man Sunday night. Miss Julia Roberts saw a man behaving strangely near the bridge that night. Neither could identify the man they saw but both knew Michael Heslin and could swear that it was not him.

Another suspect was an unnamed man staying at a hotel in Stratford. There had been complaints from women claiming that he had been harassing them and some believed that he was the unidentified man seen with Rose that night.

Though the detectives had ruled out William Lewis as a suspect, he was rapidly becoming the prime suspect of the inquest. Bloodstains were found on the lap robe in Lewis's carriage, and some fibers found on Rose's clothing matched fibers from the lap robe. Though it had rained the night of the murder, Rose's clothes were dry; the coroner suspected that Lewis had murdered her in his barn then wrapped the body in the lap robe before dropping it by the wall. Witnesses testified that he and Rose had been heard quarrelling, and it was speculated that he either had second thoughts about the wedding, or he had killed her in a fit of jealousy. But William Lewis had a solid alibi as well.

The inquest went on until September 29 and reached no conclusion. There was not enough evidence to charge anyone with murder, though it was stated that the jurors "think suspicion points toward" William Lewis. No one was ever charged for Rose Ambler's murder and the case remains unsolved.

Aftermath:

Speculation as to what really happened the night of September 2, 1883 continued for years. Most theories involved Rose having a romantic relationship behind Lewis's back and was either killed by her new lover or by her jealous fiancé.

William Lewis remained the prime suspect in public opinion. Reverend M. Houghton of the Church of the Messiah in Stratford made headlines when he preached a sermon against William Lewis saying, "Lewis's actions show him to be a man of low animal instincts, and just the type of individual to execute such a horrible deed."

The unsolved murder of Rose Ambler prompted many comparisons to previous unpunished murders in Connecticut—most notably those of Mary Stannard in 1873 and Jennie Cramer in 1881. Mark Twain commented, "He killed a woman in Conn. No matter—it is a crime they do not punish there."

The national magazine Puck placed the blame on the rural character of Connecticut at the time:

> *Now, we do not believe that the murders committed in Connecticut are any more mysterious in their essence than the ordinary crimes committed in other states. The trouble is that there is no adequate machinery of law to deal with them…You cannot trust the untrained minds of a lot of excited countrymen to study out the immediate and urgent necessities in such a case as the Rose Ambler murder, which is now throwing an interesting gloom over a small Connecticut community…By the time that the medical examiner and the coroner have had their fight out, and the inquest—which is no inquest, but really a trial—is concluded, any murderer of average intelligence has had time to either escape or to cover up his tracks.*

Maria A. Bickford

3.   THE SLEEPWALKING DEFENSE

The morning of October 27, 1845, the body of Maria Bickford, a beautiful young prostitute, was found murdered in her room in Boston's Beacon Hill. Her throat had been cut from ear to ear and her bed had been set on fire. The prime suspect was her consort, Albert Tirrell, who was seen arguing with Maria the day before. Tirrell was represented in court by prominent attorney and former US senator, Rufus Choate, who used a three-pronged defense: maybe Maria Bickford had cut her own throat, maybe someone else killed her, or maybe Albert Tirrell killed her while sleepwalking and was not responsible for his actions.

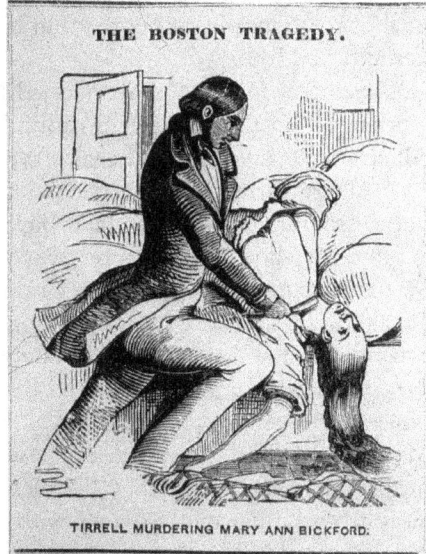

THE BOSTON TRAGEDY.

TIRRELL MURDERING MARY ANN BICKFORD.

Date: October 27, 1845

Location: Boston, Massachusetts

Victim: Maria A. Bickford

Cause of Death: Slashing

Accused: Albert J. Tirrell

Synopsis:

Maria Bickford was born Mary Ann Dunn in Bath, Maine, and in her teens, moved with her family to Bangor, Maine. There she met, and at age sixteen married, James Bickford, a shoemaker. They lived modestly but happily for three years until 1842 when several of Maria's friends convinced her to visit Boston with them. She was captivated by the fashion and liveliness of the city and returned home a changed person. Maria became dissatisfied with her humble condition and told James she wanted to move permanently to Boston.

9

At the same time, an attractive young man living in the same boardinghouse caught Maria's eye and she began flirting with him. That October she ran off with him to Newburyport, Massachusetts. In the words of James Bickford, "Ere she became acquainted with this man, she was one of the most virtuous of her sex, but his insinuating plausibility quickly drew her into a whirlpool of vice."

Her new lover soon abandoned Maria and she turned to prostitution, working in brothels first in Boston, then in New Bedford. There she met Albert Tirrell, and the two began traveling together.

Albert Tirrell was married with a child when he met and became hopelessly infatuated with Maria Bickford. He was the son of a prominent Weymouth shoe manufacturer who had served for twelve years in the Massachusetts state legislature. Upon his father's death, Tirrell inherited $8,000, a sizeable fortune in 1844, and within a year and a half, he had squandered it all on Maria. He bought her whatever she desired and when they travelled, they stayed in the best hotels. They rented a furnished a house in Boston that Maria ran as a "house of assignation" under the name Maria Welsh. But the relationship was deteriorating; Maria wrote to her husband in Maine that Albert Tirrell was abusing her and she wanted to get away from him. After a quarrel with Maria in June 1845, Tirrell broke up the household. Not long after that, he was arrested for adultery and lascivious cohabitation.

In October 1845, Maria Bickford was living in a disreputable boardinghouse on Cedar Lane in Beacon Hill. On October 26, Albert Tirrell, out on bail, visited her there. The owners of the house, Joel Lawrence and his wife, saw Maria and Albert arguing that day. Around five o'clock the next morning, the Lawrences heard a shriek then a heavy thud coming from upstairs, then they heard someone rushing down the stairs and out the door. When they went to investigate, they found Maria Bickford on the floor with her throat cut; her windpipe and jugular vein were severed. Several fires had been started in the room, and Maria's face and hair had been burned. The walls were splattered with blood, and a bloody razor was found at the foot of the bed. Some articles of men's clothing were in the room, along with a letter initialed A. J. T. to M. A. B.

About five thirty that morning, Albert Tirrell went to a nearby stable and requested a horse to take him to Weymouth, explaining that "he had got into a little difficulty and wanted to go to his wife's father." From Weymouth Tirrell traveled through Vermont to Canada. In Montreal he wrote his family that he was bound for Liverpool. The boat he took had to turn back because of bad weather, so in New York City he booked passage on a boat for New Orleans. Authorities in Louisiana had been alerted and on December 5, they boarded the boat and arrested Tirrell.

Trial: March 24, 1846

When Albert Tirrell was a fugitive, public opinion in Boston sided with Maria Bickford and everyone was anxious for the capture of her killer. But by the time of Tirrell's trial, the public had turned against Maria and now viewed her as an evil seductress who took advantage of Albert Tirrell.

Circumstantial evidence against Albert Tirrell was quite strong, but when Terrell's family hired a high-powered defense team led by noted orator Rufus Choate, it became obvious that facts alone would not decide the case.

The prosecution presented testimony from the Lawrences and other residents of the boardinghouse who knew that Tirrell had spent the night with Maria Bickford and left her room before dawn. The defense questioned witnesses who tarnished the reputation and credibility of the Lawrences and their boarders, and though much of the testimony was disallowed as hearsay, it made an impact on the jury. They also brought in witnesses who knew Albert Tirrell and swore he was a good, upstanding man before becoming infatuated with the harlot Maria Bickford.

Choate and fellow defense attorney Annis Merrill offered alternative scenarios for Bickford's death. First, that she killed herself. They continually echoed the testimony of the coroner, who stated that suicide was "the natural death of the prostitute." Second, they postulated that someone else had killed her. A fireman had testified that Joel Lawrence had, at first, tried to keep him out of Maria's room; was he trying to hide something? Finally, they introduced numerous witnesses who knew that Albert Tirrell had suffered from somnambulism all his life. Relatives and friends told anecdotes of Tirrell walking in his sleep. One cousin testified that as recently as September 1845, Tirrell had pulled him out of bed brandishing a knife while in a sleeping state. If Albert Tirrell killed Maria Bickford, it was while sleepwalking and he was not responsible for his actions.

On March 27, Rufus Choate gave his closing arguments before a packed courtroom. He told the jury he did not intend to take up much of their time, then he talked for five hours straight before breaking for dinner. After dinner he spoke for an hour and a half more. Choate was famous for his rapid-fire approach to oratory. There is no definitive record of his speech because, as one stenographer put it, "who can report chain lightning?" The *Boston Daily Bee* quoted Choate at the climax of his argument:

> *How far does the testimony lead you? Did any human being see the prisoner strike the blow? No. Did any human being see him in the house*

11

after nine o'clock the previous evening? No. Did any human being see him run from the house? No. Did any human being see him with a drop of blood on his hands? No. Can anyone say she did not take her own life? No. Can anyone say that on that night he was not laboring under the disease to which he was subject from his youth? No. Has he ever made a confession of the deed? To friend or thief taker not one word.

On Saturday, March 28, the judge spoke for an hour and a half giving instructions to the jury that were generally favorable to the defense. He spoke of Maria Bickford's depraved character and referred to somnambulism as a form of insanity. The jury retired to deliberate then returned two hours later with a verdict of not guilty. As in the trial of Richard Robinson for the murder of prostitute Helen Jewett ten years earlier, the packed courtroom greeted the verdict with "a roof-shaking hurra" and spectators broke into applause.

Verdict: Not guilty

Aftermath:

Albert Tirrell still had to stand trial for arson, also a capital crime in 1846. Using similar arguments, Choate won Tirrell an acquittal on this charge as well. Tirrell pleaded no contest to the charges of adultery and lascivious cohabitation, but the judge would not dismiss them. Albert Tirrell was sentenced three years hard labor in the state prison.

Following Tirrell's acquittal for murder, Rufus Choate was besieged by criminal defendants anxious for his services. Choate turned his back on private practice for a time to become Massachusetts' attorney general, but he was never able to escape the reputation of introducing the sleepwalking defense. On his death he was critically eulogized by attorney Wendell Phillips as the lawyer who "made it safe to murder."

Andrew Jackson Borden and Abby Durfee Borden

4.   LIZZIE BORDEN TOOK AN AXE...OR DID SHE?

Either Lizzie Borden got away with murder in August 1892, or someone else in Fall River, Massachusetts, did. Lizzie was acquitted of the axe murder of Andrew and Abby Borden and no one else was ever arrested for the crime. The Borden murder case has been cold for more than 120 years, yet criminologists—professional and amateur—continue to pore over newspaper accounts, police reports, and trial transcripts looking for the real killer. There have been many theories, but the case remains unsolved.

LIZZIE ANDREW BORDEN

Date: August 4, 1892

Location: Fall River, Massachusetts

Victims: Andrew Jackson Borden
                     and Abby Durfee Borden

Cause of Death: Blows from an axe

Accused: Lizzie Andrew Borden

Synopsis:

About 10:45 on the morning of August 4, 1892, Andrew Borden returned home from his daily errands in downtown Fall River. About half

13

an hour later, his daughter Lizzie found him dead on the couch in the sitting room. She called out to their maid, Bridget Sullivan, who was in her upstairs bedroom. Andrew had been hacked beyond recognition, his skull crushed by hatchet blows. Shortly after, while Lizzie was being tended to by neighbors and the family doctor, Bridget Sullivan went upstairs and found Lizzie's stepmother, Abby Borden, on the floor of her bedroom, in the same state as her husband. Doctors determined that Abby had been murdered first, an important fact since had Andrew died first, his estate would not have been inherited by Lizzie and her older sister Emma.

The police concluded that the murder was committed by someone within the Borden home. Only Lizzie and Bridget Sullivan were home at the time, and Lizzie became their prime suspect. At the inquest on August 9, Lizzie gave testimony that was confused and contradictory. Two days later she was arrested for murder.

Lizzie and Emma had grown apart from their father and stepmother to such an extent that the family never dined together. Emma, who seldom left home, was out of town on the day of the murders.

John Morse, brother of Andrew's first wife Sarah (mother of Lizzie and Emma), was visiting the Bordens that week. Andrew had decided to divide his property among relatives while he was still alive. He was in the process of transferring a summer home to John Morse. The daughters felt this property should be theirs. This was thought to have been Lizzie's motive.

Trial: June 5, 1893

Police had found a hatchet with a broken handle in the basement, but it showed no sign of blood. Forensics experts testified that it was not the murder weapon, as it would have taken the killer too long to clean it so thoroughly. Andrew's body was still warm when it was discovered. Similarly, it was argued that it would have taken too long for Lizzie to have changed her bloody clothing and returned to "discover" the body.

A neighbor testified to seeing Lizzie burn a blue dress in the kitchen stove, claiming it was covered with paint. She also testified to seeing Lizzie in a blue dress the morning of the murder. A few days prior to the murder, Lizzie had tried to buy prussic acid, a deadly poison, from a local druggist but her request had been refused. This fact was excluded from her trial.

Lizzie had a powerful defense team that included former Massachusetts governor George Robinson. Though there was compelling circumstantial evidence against her, with the murder weapon successfully challenged, the prosecution had no physical evidence. The defense was able to cast doubt on all of the prosecution's case.

14

Verdict: Not guilty

Aftermath:

After the trial Lizzie and her sister Emma used their inheritance to buy a much larger house in Fall River, which they named Maplecroft. They lived together there until 1905 when, after an argument over a party Lizzie had thrown for actress Nance O'Neil, Emma moved out. Lizzie remained in Maplecroft until her death in 1927. During the time at Maplecroft, she changed her name from Lizzie, the name on her birth certificate, to Lizbeth, the name on her gravestone.

Though Lizzie Borden was found not guilty by a jury of her peers, the public has never been satisfied with the verdict. The story is incomplete, and there is a need to know more. If Lizzie did it, how did she hide the evidence? If she didn't do it, then who did? In the hundred and twenty years since Lizzie's acquittal, dozens of authors and media producers have been working to satisfy that need. Here are a few of the theories put forth—it should be remembered that these are all pure speculation, not based upon fact:

•   Bridget Sullivan was angry over being asked to clean windows on an oppressively hot day. She had been sick with food poisoning the previous day. Perhaps she snapped under the pressure and killed her employers.

•   John Morse had been out of the house when the murders occurred. He could have been hiding in the basement then, alone or with Lizzie's help, killed the Bordens. It has been speculated that Emma was also included in this conspiracy.

•   Lizzie did not get any blood on her clothing because she removed them and committed the murders in the nude. Then she hastily redressed, careful not to get any blood on her dress.

•   William Borden, an alleged illegitimate half-brother of Lizzie and Emma, committed the murders out of revenge after his father failed to submit to his extortion demands.

Verse:

This well-known anonymous rope-skipping rhyme was originally sung to the tune of "Ta-Ra-Ra Boom-De-Ay:"

Lizzie Borden took an axe
And gave her mother forty whacks.
When she saw what she had done,
She gave her father forty-one.

Allen Britt

5.   HE DONE HER WRONG

"Frankie and Johnny were lovers," the old song goes. "He was her man, but he done her wrong." In truth, they were lovers, but his name was Allen, not Johnny, and Frankie Baker was Allen Britt's woman, but yes, he done her wrong. He was her pimp, and he abused her. When Frankie caught Allen cheating with Alice Pryar on October 16, 1899, she shot him in the bedroom of her St. Louis apartment. By that evening a local songwriter had composed a ballad that would immortalize the story of Frankie and Al Britt, and provide the framework for a century of misinformation.

FRANKIE BAKER

Date: October 16, 1899

Location: St. Louis, Missouri

Victim: Allen Britt

Cause of Death: Gunshot

Accused: Frankie Baker

Synopsis:

In his 1927 book *Read 'Em and Weep: The Songs You Forgot to Remember*, Sigmund Spaeth wrote:

> *But everybody that knows anything at all about "Frankie and Johnnie" is likely to have a version of his or her own, and there is nothing so rabid for righteousness, so bristling with self-defense, as the dyed-in-the-wool Frankie-and-Johnnie fan.*

In the early twentieth century, the origin of "Frankie and Johnny" was the subject of heated debate among folklorists. Carl Sandberg claimed the song was widespread before 1888, Leonard Feather said it was sung at the Siege of Vicksburg in 1863, others linked it to Frankie Silver, who was convicted in 1832 of killing her husband. But the song "Frankie and Johnny" never appeared in print before 1925.

17

Today there is almost universal agreement that the song is based on the 1899 murder of Allen Britt by Frankie Baker in St. Louis, Missouri. Frankie, in her midtwenties, was a prostitute, famous in the black "sporting area" of St. Louis for her beauty and flamboyant elegance. She wore diamond earrings "as big as hen's eggs."

Allen Britt was Frankie's seventeen-year-old pimp. Britt was well known in St. Louis as a ragtime pianist. The night of October 15, he was playing for a cakewalk at the Phoenix Hotel. Frankie went to the hotel to hear him play and caught him in the hallway making love to an eighteen-year-old prostitute named Alice Pryar. They began arguing in the street outside the hotel, and Frankie begged Allen to come home with her. He refused and she went home alone. Around three in the morning, Allen entered Frankie's apartment and the fight continued. When he pulled out his knife and started to attack her, Frankie grabbed a pistol she kept under her pillow. She shot him once in the chest.

Allen was taken to the hospital and Frankie was arrested. The police took her to the hospital, where Allen identified her as the shooter. Though Allen Britt didn't die until three days later, the evening of the murder, "barroom bard" Bill Dooley was performing a ballad he wrote called "Frankie Killed Allen."

Trial: November 13, 1899

In many versions of the song, Frankie is executed, sometimes in the electric chair, but in reality, the coroner's jury called the killing justifiable homicide in self-defense. She was still required to stand trial and on November 13, 1899, she was acquitted by Judge Willis B. Clark.

Verdict:　Not guilty; justifiable homicide in self-defense

Aftermath:

As the song grew in popularity, in St. Louis and beyond, it went through a number of changes. First, the name Allen Britt became Albert and the title of the song became "Frankie and Albert." Then Albert was changed to Johnny, possibly at the request of Allen's parents, who were unhappy about their only son being remembered this way, but more likely because singers found the phrase "Frankie and Johnny" more pleasing than "Frankie and Albert." The name "Alice Pryar" became "Alice Frye" or "Nellie Bly"— more familiar and easier to sing.

As the popularity of the song grew, a number of different versions developed and there have been at least 256 recordings. Popular singers sang the published, somewhat sanitized version of "Frankie and Johnny." African American songsters like Leadbelly and Mississippi John Hurt sang grittier versions and continued to use the title "Frankie and Albert." White country performers, like Charlie Poole, sang their own versions.

In St. Louis, people began singing the song when they saw Frankie on the street and a year after the murder, she fled to Omaha, Nebraska, to escape the humiliation. The song had already arrived in Omaha, so she moved again to Portland, Oregon. There she worked as a prostitute and was arrested several times. Around 1925 she gave up prostitution and opened a shoeshine parlor.

In 1935 the movie *She Done Him Wrong*, starring Mae West and Cary Grant, was released, and Frankie was hounded again by reporters, autograph seekers, and folks who would stand outside her house and gawk. In 1938, Frankie sued Republic Pictures for damages but lost; she couldn't convince the all-white jury that Mae West's character was based on her. In 1942, she sued Republic again when they released *Frankie and Johnnie* starring Helen Morgan. She lost again.

Frankie Baker was later admitted to a mental hospital in Portland where she died in 1952. But her story, though somewhat less than accurate, will live forever.

Ballad:

Frankie and Johnnie

Frankie and Johnnie were lovers,
Oh, Lordie how they could love!
They swore to be true to each other,
Just as true as the stars above,
He was her man, but he done her wrong.

Frankie and Johnnie went walking
John in his brand new suit.
Then, "oh good Lawd," says Frankie
"Don't my Johnnie look real cute!"
He was her man, but he done her wrong.

Frankie she was a good woman,
And Johnnie was a good man,
And every dollar that she made
Went right into Johnnie's hand,
He was her man, but he done her wrong.

Frankie went down tn the corner,
Just for a bucket of beer.
She said to the fat bartender,
"Has my lovinest man been here7"
He was her man, but he done her wrong.

"I don't want to cause you no trouble,
I don't want to tell you no lie;
But I saw your man an hour ago
With a gal named Alice Bly,
And if he's your man, he's a-doing you wrong."

Frankie looked over the transom,
And found, to her great surprise,
That there on the bed sat Johnnie,
A-lovin' up Alice Bly.
He was her man, but he done her wrong.

Frankie drew back her kimono;
She took out her little forty-four;
Root-a-toot-toot, three times she shot
Right through that hardwood floor,
She shot her man, 'cause he done her wrong.

Roll me over easy,
Roll me over slow,
Roll me on de right side,
'Cause de bullet hurt me so.
I was her man, but I done her wrong.

The judge said to the jury
"It's as plain as plain can be
This woman shot her lover
It's murder in the second degree
He was her man, though he done her wrong.

This story has no moral
This story has no end
This story only goes to show
That there ain't no good in men
They'll do you wrong, just as sure as you're born

Carrie Brown

6. "OLD SHAKESPEARE"

CARRIE BROWN

Inspector Thomas Byrnes, head of the detective bureau of the New York City police at the end of the 19th century, had no love for mystery. For Inspector Byrnes, solving crimes was a simple matter of applied common sense and diligent police work. In 1888 with London in terror and Scotland Yard baffled by the Whitechapel murders attributed to "Jack the Ripper," Inspector Byrnes told a reporter that if someone committed such murders in New York, police would have him "in the jug in thirty-six hours." When Bowery prostitute Carrie Brown was found murdered and mutilated on April 24, 1891, the headlines screamed, "Jack the Ripper has come to America." And, true to his word, Inspector Byrnes had a man in custody the next day. Never mind that it was the wrong man. Whether or not Jack the Ripper killed Carrie Brown—as some theorists still believe—there is no question that the Ripper influenced the investigation and prosecution of her murder.

Date: April 24, 1891

Location: New York, New York

Victim: Carrie Brown a.k.a. "Old Shakespeare"

Cause of Death: Strangulation

Accused: Ameer Ben Ali

Synopsis:
On April 24, 1891, the body of Carrie Brown was found in room thirty-one of the East River Hotel on the waterfront of East Side Manhattan. Not merely murdered, she was slashed open and disemboweled. She was found

naked from the armpits down and her clothing was wrapped around her head as if the killer wanted to cover her face as he worked. The body had multiple stab wounds, and an "X" had been carved on her left buttock. There was blood everywhere and the weapon, a sharpened, wood-handled table knife, had been left behind.

The New York City newspapers were quick to point out the similarities between this murder and those in the Whitechapel section of London three years earlier; the killer, still at large, was known as "Jack the Ripper." Inspector Thomas F. Byrnes, head of the detective bureau and acting superintendent of police, quickly and unequivocally stated that this murder was not the work of London's Jack the Ripper, but Byrnes knew he was under intense pressure to find this killer. He had previously asserted that a series of Ripper-like murders would be impossible in New York City. In an effort to avoid the hysteria surrounding the Whitechapel murders, he personally headed up a massive investigation to find Carrie Brown's killer.

Carrie Brown was an aging prostitute—at least fifty-seven years old; some sources say over sixty. In her youth she had been a successful actress and her habit of quoting the Bard when drunk had earned her the nickname "Old Shakespeare." In 1891 she was living the subsistence life of an East Side whore, turning low-priced tricks hoping to make enough money for whiskey and a place to sleep. When a choice had to be made, drink took precedence and more than once she had spent the night behind bars in Blackwell's Island for being drunk and disorderly.

The afternoon of April 23, Carrie told her friend and fellow prostitute, Alice Sullivan, that she hadn't eaten for three days. Alice bought her a cheese sandwich at a nearby saloon, and that evening they both had corned beef and cabbage at a Christian mission. They separated then to ply their trade. Alice last saw Carrie Brown around eight thirty with a man she knew as Frenchy. She was later seen with another man, Isaac Perringer, who was also known as Frenchy. The housekeeper at the East River Hotel, Mary Minter, saw Carrie with her last customer of the night, who she described as "…about thirty-two years old, five feet eight inches in height, of slim build with a long, sharp nose, and a heavy mustache of light color. He wore an old black derby hat, the crown of which was much dented."

He and Carrie checked into the East River Hotel, registered as "C. Nicolo and wife." They went up to room thirty-one carrying a candle and a pail of beer.

Around two in the morning, his work finished, the killer left room thirty-one, locked the door, and took the key with him. Trailing drops of blood, he started down the stairs. About halfway down he changed his mind and went back upstairs all the way to the roof. He then climbed to the roof of the building next door, the Glenmore Hotel, another East Side flophouse. He then went down the stairs and into the lobby and asked the night clerk, Mr. Kelly, for a room.

Kelly later gave a description of the man that matched Mary Minter's description of Carrie's last customer. He noted that the man's hands and clothes were smeared with blood and added that the man had a pronounced German accent. He wanted a room but had no money, so Kelly sent him away.

The next day, when a hotel employee made the gruesome discovery, a frantic message was sent to the Oak Street Police Station. Several detectives and quite a few reporters hurried to the East River Hotel, to the most horrifying crime scene any of them had ever seen.

Mary Minter and Mary Healy, who had also been drinking with Carrie Brown the night before, were taken into custody for questioning and protection against the killer returning to silence the witnesses. They told police about seeing Carrie with a man called Frenchy and, with little else to go on, the police began rounding up suspects named Frenchy.

Apparently this was a common nickname in the East Side and police and the press took to calling them by number (e.g., "Frenchy No. 1," "Frenchy No. 2"). As they were brought in, they were shown to the witnesses but were not recognized. Inspector Byrnes began losing faith in his witnesses' information, saying, "The people depended upon to give it were a drunken lot, without enough intelligence to remember how the man looked."

In the end all of the Frenchys were released except Frenchy No. 1. His real name was Ameer Ben Ali, a French-speaking Algerian, who had been staying in room thirty-three of the East River Hotel, across the hall from the murder scene. Though it hadn't been seen by reporters that morning, the police claimed there was blood on his door and doorknob, both outside and inside.

Trial: June 24, 1891

The prosecution of Ameer Ben Ali relied almost exclusively on the blood evidence. The state's team of expert witnesses:

> ...*together made microscopic, stereoscopic, and chemical examination of the blood spots on the mattress upon which the murdered woman lay, the spots on the bed tick in the room which 'Frenchy' slept, and the spots upon his clothing. He found traces of intestinal matter in all but six of the pieces upon which there was blood. In the scrapings of Frenchy's fingernails, traces of the same matter were discovered.*

23

In cross-examination, the experts were not able to state with certainty that the blood was human or even mammalian. The defense had its own experts who said the blood evidence was circumstantial at best.

Ameer Ben Ali's own testimony was seen as excited and contradictory and he was not believed. The case was given to the jury on July 3, 1891. At one point during the deliberation, the jury was polled at eleven for first-degree murder, one for second degree. With everyone anxious to be done by the 4th of July, they returned a unanimous verdict finding the Bin Ali guilty of second-degree murder.

Later, one juryman expressed the opinion that the jury had been "packed" and the verdict had not been fair.

Verdict: Guilty of second-degree murder

Aftermath:

Inspector Byrnes was a pivotal figure in the development of the New York City Police Department—he led the transition of policemen from thugs with badges and sticks, to effective crime investigators. But his methods were tough and not always just. He was also tainted by his close association with Tammany Hall. At his retirement Byrnes was worth $350,000, a small fortune at the time, earned on a salary of $2,000 per year. He found it increasingly hard to fight reformers like journalist Jacob A. Riis and in 1895, the newly elected New York City police commissioner, Theodore Roosevelt, forced him to resign.

In 1902, after eleven years in Sing Sing prison, Ameer Ben Ali was released. The work of several journalists, including Jacob Riis and Charles Edward Russell, convinced Governor Benjamin Odell that the blood evidence had been, either accidently or deliberately, tampered with. The evidence taken to court was not what was seen by reporters on April 24. The governor officially declared Ameer Ben Ali to be "innocent of the Carrie Brown murder."

Another possible suspect emerged in 1901 when a Crawford, New Jersey, farmer told of a farmhand, a Danish man, who was absent the night of the murder. He left soon after, leaving behind a bloodstained shirt and a key similar to those used at the East River Hotel. But ten years after the fact, this information could not be trusted or acted upon.

The murder of Carrie Brown remains one of New York's great unsolved crimes.

Priscilla Budge

7.   A BALANCE OF PROBABILITIES

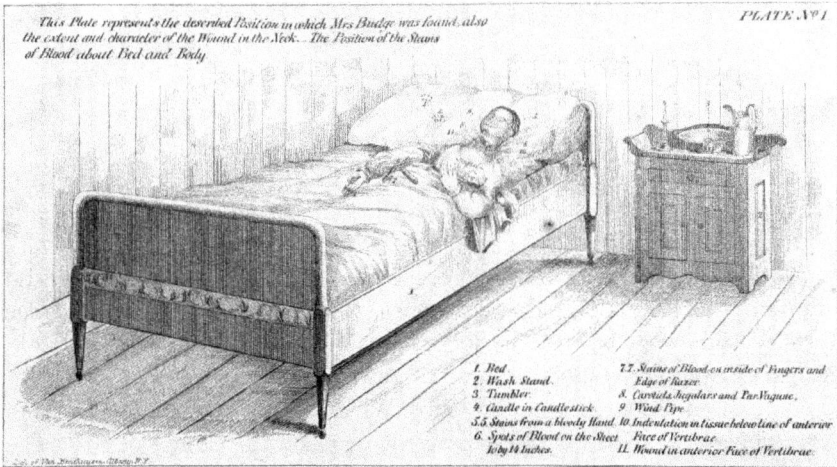

This Plate represents the described Position in which Mrs Budge was found, also the extent and character of the Wound in the Neck. The Position of the Stains of Blood about Bed and Body

PLATE N°1

1. Bed
2. Wash Stand.
3. Tumbler
4. Candle in Candlestick
5.5 Stains from a bloody Hand.
6. Spots of Blood on the Sheet 10 by 14 Inches.

7.7. Stains of Blood on inside of Fingers and Edge of Razor.
8. Carotids Jugulars and Par Vague.
9. Wind Pipe
10. Indentation in tissue below line of anterior Face of Vertebrae
11. Wound in anterior Face of Vertebrae.

SCENE OF PRISCILLA BUDGE'S MURDER

The morning of December 11, 1859, eleven-year-old Priscilla Budge carried a cup of tea to her mother's bedroom, where she found her mother lying on the bed with her throat cut. Mrs. Budge was known to be mentally unstable and her husband, the Reverend Henry Budge, immediately declared that his wife's death must have been suicide. The coroner's jury agreed, and Mrs. Budge was soon buried—a quick conclusion to an unpleasant event. But as it turned out, it was not the conclusion, just the opening argument of a debate that would go on for years.

Date: December 10, 1859

Location: Lyons Falls, New York

Victim: Priscilla Budge

Cause of Death: Slashing

Accused: The Reverend Henry Budge

Synopsis:

In 1849, Reverend Henry Budge and his wife Pricilla came to America from England with their three-year-old son, Henry Junior. Ten years later,

25

they were living in Lyons Falls, New York, with six children, ranging in age from two to thirteen. Though she had help from her eleven-year-old daughter, also named Pricilla, Mrs. Budge appeared to be breaking under the strain of raising six children. The children would later testify that their parents were constantly arguing, and Mrs. Budge would berate her husband for coming home late and spending too much time away from the family.

Mrs. Budge had grown up in a wealthy family in England, but was disowned by her father after she married Henry. She had never really adjusted to her lot as the wife of a poor preacher in a strange country. Her relationship with her husband had grown cold and by 1859, Mr. and Mrs. Budge no longer slept in the same bedroom. In addition to constantly fighting with her husband, Mrs. Budge was prone to fits of "derangement."

On December 10th, Mrs. Budge wrote a letter to her sister in England and gave it to Emma Gould, a neighbor girl, to mail. Young Pricilla Budge was not sure what was in the letter, but she had gleaned enough from hearing her mother read it aloud to know that "it was not right." She went to Emma and asked her for the letter. When Emma refused to give it to her, Pricilla told her father and he went to talk with Emma. Rev. Budge persuaded the child to give him the letter and told her "that his troubles had been as they were for eleven years, and that he would not endure it six hours, were it not for his children."

The next morning Mrs. Budge was found in her bedroom with her throat slashed. Mr. Budge never went into the bedroom himself but relied on the neighbors to describe the scene. He said it must be suicide and told them to look for the weapon. They found a straight razor lying near her hand.

A coroner's jury was convened, and Mrs. Budge's body was examined. The court ruled "death by suicide," and Mrs. Budge was quickly buried.

As the months passed, persistent rumors circulated about the Budges' marital problems and of Rev. Budge's possible infidelities. To fan the flames of suspicion, Hon. Caleb Lyon, a former US congressman from New York who would later be governor of Idaho Territory, published a pamphlet that included a long poem accusing Budge of adultery and murder. There were also a number of inconstancies in the physical evidence and descriptions of the crime scene, which led the district attorney to exhume the body for further examination.

Having been underground through a cold winter, there was very little decomposition in the corpse. The body was examined by a team of physicians led by Dr. John Swinburne, who would later be mayor of Albany and a US congressman from New York. What they found appeared to contradict the notion that Mrs. Budge cut her own throat.

The wound was five and a half inches long and as deep as the vertebrae. Though an artery was severed, there had been no spurting of blood, as would have occurred had it been cut while she was living. In fact only about a quart of blood was found outside the body—much less than if the artery was cut with the heart still beating. The nature of the cut was not consistent with a razor slash; it appeared to have been made by stabbing into the right side of the neck and up through the left. It was also deep and strong enough to slice part of a vertebra, which would have damaged the razor. The razor at the scene was not damaged, and it had surprisingly little blood on it. Her lungs were filled with fluid, which would be consistent with asphyxiation, but not with a cut throat. Swinburne concluded that Mrs. Budge had been strangled to death, then cut in the throat with a sharp weapon after death to make it look like suicide.

A second inquest was held, and Dr. Swinburne was on the witness stand for twenty-two consecutive hours. In the end, the Reverend Henry Budge was charged with the murder of his wife. Budge's attorney went before a judge on a writ of habeas corpus, and Budge was released on the grounds that the second inquest was illegal. A month later the case was brought before a grand jury of Lewis County, but only eleven of the twelve jurors were in favor of indicting Budge. The following September the case was again brought to the grand jury, and this time they indicted Reverend Budge for murder.

Trial: August 1861

The prosecution called witnesses, including Budge's own children, to testify to the ongoing marital difficulties between Mr. and Mrs. Budge. The defense countered with witnesses who testified to Mrs. Budge's insanity. But the bulk of the testimony consisted of detailed medical opinions as to whether or not Mrs. Budge was alive when her throat was cut, and whether, given the position of the body, it was possible that anyone else could have cut her throat. The medical testimony went on for weeks until, during the testimony of Professor Valentine Mott of New York, Budge's attorney moved that the charges against his client be dropped. Judge Allen ruled that, while the circumstances made a strong case for judicial investigation, the defense had shown qualifying circumstances, such as how the fluid might have gotten into the lungs without asphyxia. He added:

> *It is not for me to say that the case shall close. There are circumstances that might be forcibly urged to the jury; but it strikes me that, as the case stands, it is only a balance of probabilities, in which it would be unsafe to*

convict; and in view of the fact that these doubts have arisen, the prisoner is entitled to the benefit of them, and should be released.

The case was abruptly sent to the jury pro forma, and by the direction of the judge, the prisoner was acquitted.

Verdict: Not guilty

Aftermath:

According to a biography of Dr. Swinburne:

> *When the case was so abruptly brought to a close, Dr. Mott, who had been interrupted, it was said, turning to Judge Allen, remarked sotto voce, 'I would like to explain.'*
>
> *'It is too late now,' said the judge.*
>
> *'But I do not believe that poor woman ever killed herself,' said the doctor.*
>
> *'Neither do I,' replied his honor.*

Though the verdict could not be altered, the case was, in effect, tried one more time. Following his acquittal, Budge sued Caleb Lyon for libel because the verses he had written charged Rev. Budge with murdering his wife, having criminal intercourse with other women, and other charges that held him up to ridicule and injured his good name. Budge wanted $20,000 in damages.

Caleb Lyon wanted to prove that he had good reason to think that Budge killed his wife, so the libel case ended up being a replay of Budge's murder trial. Many of the same witnesses were called, and Dr. John Swinburne handled the medical testimony, with additional evidence that was not included in the first trial due to Judge Allen's abrupt ruling. Lyon was found guilty of libel, but he was only fined a nominal $100 damages.

The trial also gave Swinburne the opportunity to publish a book, *A Review of the Case: The People Agt. Rev. Henry Budge: Indicted for the Murder of His Wife Priscilla Budge*, which included evidence from both trials. Swinburne never believed that the probabilities of the case were equally balanced and did not hesitate to assert that Reverend Budge had gotten away with murder. The book was well reasoned with detailed illustrations, including the following, which show four possible positions of the killer, refuting the defense's claim that, due to the position of the body and the arrangement of the room, no one but Mrs. Budge herself could have cut her throat.

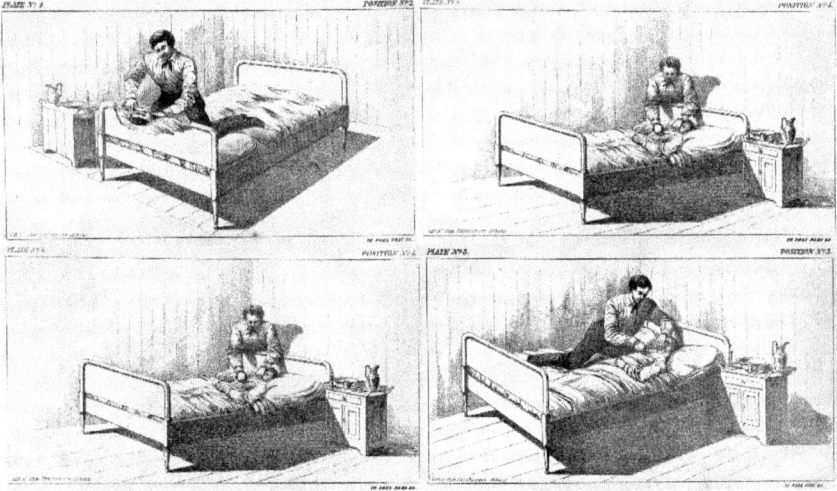

POSSIBLE POSITIONS OF THE KILLER

Dr. Harvey Burdell

8.   THE BOND STREET TRAGEDY

The townhouse at 31 Bond Street was, to all appearances, a model of staid middleclass Manhattan decorum. In 1857 it was a boardinghouse run by Mrs. Emma Cunningham with the dental office of Dr. Harvey Burdell on the second floor. But after Dr. Burdell was found in his office strangled and stabbed fifteen times, 31 Bond Street was shown for what it was—a hotbed of greed, lust, intrigue, and depravity.

HARVEY BURDELL IN HIS COFFIN

Date: January 30, 1857

Location: New York, New York

Victim: Dr. Harvey Burdell

Cause of Death: Strangulation and Stabbing

Accused: Emma Cunningham

Synopsis:

Harvey Burdell had come to New York City in 1834 to join the lucrative dental practice of his brother, John. They ran a successful office, catering to members of New York's high society, and together they published a dental handbook entitled *The Structure, Physiology, Anatomy, and Diseases of the Teeth, In Two Parts*. After five years working for his brother, Harvey left to establish a practice of his own.

In addition to his thriving dental practice, Harvey Burdell was successful in banking and real estate speculation. He was highly regarded uptown, but also well known in the Bowery, where he often went to gamble and visit brothels. Burdell was also known to service the dental needs of prostitutes working in his Bond Street neighborhood taking his fee in trade.

Sometime around 1854, Harvey Burdell met and began a whirlwind courtship with a young widow named Emma Cunningham. She was born Emma Hempstead in Brooklyn, New York, in 1818. Her father, Christopher Hempstead, was a poor but devoutly religious rope maker. Emma knew from an early age that she wanted more out of life and as a teenager, using her beauty and sexuality, began her social climb. She married George Cunningham, twenty-two years her senior, who inherited a successful distillery from his father.

In 1844, the Cunninghams moved to a townhouse on Irving Place in Manhattan and became part of upper middleclass society. But George Cunningham was not the businessman that his father had been and in 1846, a series of business reversals and foreclosures drove the Cunninghams back to Brooklyn. Amid their growing poverty, George and Emma had five children. Out of desperation, George Cunningham joined the gold rush to California in 1849. He failed at this as well and returned to Brooklyn, where he died in poverty in 1854.

Emma, now a thirty-three-year-old widow, inherited property and life insurance benefits worth $10,000. She knew the money would not last long if she lived the life she desired, so Emma, still quite attractive, went looking for another husband. She had several other suitors but set her sights on Dr. Harvey Burdell. The following August she joined Burdell at the upstate resort of Saratoga Springs. That fall Emma and Harvey were still together and Emma informed him that she was pregnant. Burdell persuaded her to have an abortion, and he may have actually performed the operation himself.

Around this time Burdell leased Emma the house at 31 Bond Street and she and her five children moved in. She ran a boardinghouse in the four-story building, with Dr. Burdell keeping his own room and dentist office on the second floor. Also living in the house was a tanner named John Eckel and an eighteen-year-old poet and banjo player, George Snodgrass.

By 1857 the relationship between Emma Cunningham and Harvey Burdell was strained, to say the least. Emma was intensely jealous of Burdell's twenty-four-year-old female cousin, Dimis Hubbard, who was a frequent houseguest. She was also, no doubt, aware of his trysts with female patients in his dental office. They had frequent arguments, and Burdell no longer ate at Emma's table, preferring to take his meals at the nearby Lafarge House.

About half past ten o'clock on the night of January 30, 1857, the man living at 36 Bond Street heard a bloodcurdling cry of "murder" but could not tell where it came from. The following morning, the boy hired to start the fire in Dr. Burdell's office opened the office door to find the doctor's mutilated body lying facedown on the floor in a pool of blood with blood spattered more than five feet up the wall.

The police examined the body and determined that Dr. Burdell had been strangled with a garrote and stabbed fifteen times with a long, slender knife. News of the murder travelled swiftly through the streets of New York and throughout the day, a morbidly curious crowd surrounded 31 Bond Street. The coroner was called in and an inquest that would last two weeks was begun in the house.

The police searched the house and questioned everyone living there, including some very observant maids. They learned quite a bit about the character of the inhabitants of 31 Bond Street. Emma Cunningham produced a marriage certificate proving that she was actually married to Harvey Burdell, though Burdell had requested that the fact be kept secret. The search of George Snodgrass's room turned up undergarments belonging to Helen Cunningham, Emma's fifteen-year-old daughter. The maids testified to Burdell's affair with his cousin, Dimis Hubbard, and to Emma's anger over the matter. They also testified that Emma was sleeping with John Eckel.

Witnesses from outside the house included Burdell's former business partner Alvah Blaisdell, who said Burdell had asked him to sleep at 31 Bond Street because he feared violence from Emma, John Eckel, George Snodgrass, and Emma's oldest daughter, Augusta. Dimis Hubbard herself testified at the inquest, claiming that her cousin had planned to end his deal with Emma Cunningham and replace her with another landlady. This was borne out by one of the maids, who related this conversation with Emma Cunningham:

> 'Who was that woman, Hannah, you were showing through the house today?'
> 'That was the lady who is going to take the house.'
> 'Then the doctor is going to leave it, is he?'
> 'Yes, ma'am.'
> 'And when does she take possession?'
> 'The first of May.'
> 'He better be careful; he may not live to sign the papers!'

The coroner also established that the knife wounds indicated that the stabber was left handed. Emma Cunningham was left handed. Emma Cunningham and John Eckel were charged with murder; George Snodgrass was charged as an accessory. All three were taken to the Tombs prison.

Emma Cunningham was not allowed to attend the funeral of her alleged husband—which attracted a crowd of more than 8,000 people—but she was allowed to pay her last respects. She was taken to see his body before the coffin lid was screwed shut and amid hysterical tears, that all present believed authentic, she said, "Oh, I wish to God you could speak, and tell who done it."

Trial: May 6, 1857

Before the murder trial began, the issue of the authenticity of Emma Cunningham's marriage to Harvey Burdell was taken up. Since Burdell died without a will, the outcome would have a significant impact on the distribution of his rather sizeable estate. Burdell's blood relatives had already begun maneuvering, and the matter was still unresolved when the murder trial began.

The trial drew enormous crowds, with every available inch of space in the courtroom occupied by spectators, with an especially high percentage of well-dressed women in attendance. Compared to the inquest, the trial of Emma Cunningham was very short, lasting only three days.

The prosecution's case was a rehash of the testimony presented at the inquest, telling the story now familiar to anyone who read New York City newspapers. They also did everything they could to thoroughly tarnish the reputation of Emma Cunningham.

The defense attacked the circumstantial evidence and did a hatchet job on Harvey Burdell, specifically his dalliance with Dimis Hubbard, the "kept mistress of her own blood cousin." Assuming the authenticity of Emma's marriage to Burdell, the defense asked why she would murder a husband with a steady and sizable income. They also posited many others who wished Burdell dead.

Though the judge did his best to suppress negative testimony on Burdell's reputation, the defense did their job well. The jury returned a verdict of not guilty.

Eckel and Snodgrass were never tried.

Verdict: Not guilty

Aftermath:

In the matter of Emma's marriage, Burdell's blood relatives hired prominent attorney and future presidential candidate Samuel Tilden to represent their interests. But it was Emma herself, and not Tilden's oratory, that defeated her claim. While still in the Tombs, Emma claimed she was pregnant with Harvey Burdell's baby. This fact, if true, would increase her claim on his estate from approximately one-third to 100 percent. Emma, in fact, was not pregnant, though she continued this claim after she was acquitted and released.

She realized that for her plan to work, she would need an accomplice. She confided in a Dr. Uhl, who agreed to help her fake the pregnancy, and to supply her with a baby to present as Harvey Burdell's heir. Dr. Uhl, however, went straight to the district attorney.

When the time came for Emma to "give birth," Dr. Uhl told her he had procured the baby of a woman who had become pregnant after her husband went to California. She now planned to join him and needed to give up the baby. In fact, the district attorney had gone to Bellevue Hospital and borrowed the baby of an indigent mother. Emma, dressed as a Sister of Mercy, carried the baby from Dr. Uhl's office in a basket.

The ruse was played out, with Emma faking delivery by screaming behind a closed door. But when Dr. Uhl emerged with the baby, policemen entered the room and charged Emma with fraud. The charge was eventually dropped, but it was enough to invalidate her claim of marriage in the eyes of the surrogate court.

After seeing that her daughters were taken care of, Emma left for California. She married again in 1870 and was widowed again thirteen years later. She moved back to New York, where she died in poverty. She is buried in Green-Wood Cemetery, a few hundred yards from Harvey Burdell.

Ballad:

The prolific ninteenth century New York State songwriter Henry S. Backus, known as "The Saugerties Bard" wrote several songs about the Burdell murder. This one was sung to the tune of Robert Burns's "Farewell."

Dr. Burdell, or the Bond Street Murder.

Awake sad muse, awake and sing, and softly touch the mournful string,
In solemn tones, in accents low, tell the sad tale of death and woe.
Must I in truth the story tell of deed so awful, wicked fell,
Alas! doth it to me belong, to sing this dismal, mournful song!

Let paler wax the orbs of light, that dimly shone that gloomy night,
Whilst I attempt the doleful strain, I would my harp were mute again.

Sad muses, lend your learned lyres, the awful theme a song inspires,
Assist while I the story tell, of the sad fate of poor Burdell!

The tragic deed transpired late, within the Empire City great,
And dark suspicions on two rest that murder rankled in their breast.
What though sure proffer does not appear, to candid minds the fact is clear,
The circumstances some think a shame, and exonerate Mrs. Cunningham.

And some, like Pootras, crow and cackle, and say no hemp has grown for Eckel,
To noose around his genteel neck, for crime t'would give a sudden check.
This fact is sure—Burdell is dead, at every pore his bosom bled,
Who did inflict the fatal bows? Some brutal fiends we must suppose.

Behold him lying in his gore, prostrated and dead upon the floor,
Then say who did the barbarous deed, what fiendish brutes caused him to bleed.
Fifteen stabs they did inflict, to make sure work we do expect,
Vile bigoted brutes, your fatal blows soon brought your victim bleeding low.

What though unseen by mortal sight, God of Justice will do right,
Ah! demons black will haunt thy soul, while ages ceaseless onward roll.
To Christ the Lord for mercy cry, repent, believe, before your die.
Repent, believe and be forgiven, or you can never enter heaven.

Anethe Matea Christensen and Karen Anne Christensen

9.   THE SMUTTYNOSE MURDERS

Life was hard on Smuttynose
Island, in the Isles of Shoals, off the
coast of New Hampshire; the
winter months were bitterly cold,
and the storms were devastating.
Maren Hontvet, her sister Karen
Christensen, and their sister-in-law
Anethe Christensen dreaded the
loneliness and isolation of the
island when the men of the house
were away fishing. The night of
March 6, 1873, with the men away,
the women were prepared to be
alone in the cold house, but nothing
could have prepared them for the
arrival, by rowboat, of a deranged
axe murderer.

LOUIS WAGNER

Date:	March 6, 1873
Location:	Smuttynose Island, Maine
Victims:	Anethe Matea Christensen and Karen Anne Christensen
Cause of Death:	Blows from an axe
Accused:	Louis Wagner

Synopsis:

In 1866, John and Maren Hontvet left hard times in Norway for the
promise of America. They spent some time in Boston but did not like the
city life and as soon as they could afford it, the Hontvets moved up the
coast and bought a house on Smuttynose Island, in the Isles of Shoals—in
the state of Maine, but geographically closer to New Hampshire. John

36

bought a fishing schooner and soon had earned enough money to send for his brother Mathew and Maren's sister, Karen Christensen.

Mathew was a great help, but John felt he needed another hand on the schooner. In the spring of 1972, he offered a job to Louis Wagner, a Prussian immigrant living in Portsmouth, New Hampshire, in exchange for room and board. Louis Wagner was down on his luck, working when he could for local fishermen. Though he was not happy to be working without pay, Wagner welcomed the stability this situation offered and enjoyed having two women to feed and take care of him. Wagner worked on the boat through the summer, though he was often laid up with rheumatism. That fall more relatives arrived from Norway, Maren and Karen's brother Even Christensen and his new bride Anethe. Louis Wagner's arrangement with the Hontvets ended soon after and he returned to Portsmouth.

On the morning of March 5, 1873, John, Mathew, and Even took the schooner to Portsmouth to pick up a shipment of bait arriving from Boston. The shipment was delayed and they sent word back to Maren, by another fishing boat, that they would be staying in town that night. In Portsmouth they ran into Louis Wagner and offered him a job helping them with the bait. He knew the shipment was late and they would not be heading home that night. Wagner accepted the offer, but when the bait did arrive, he could not be found.

Around eight o'clock that night, a rowboat was stolen from Pickering Wharf in Portsmouth. The thief rowed for five hours, through the bitter March winds, across ten miles of frigid sea from Portsmouth to Smuttynose Island. The man knew his way around Smuttynose; he docked the boat on the south side of the island and walked through the snow directly to the only occupied house on the island, the Honvets'.

Karen had been working at a hotel on Appledore, another of the Isles of Shoales, but that night she was visiting her sister. Because of the cold and their loneliness without the men, the three women stayed close together downstairs—Maren and Anethe in the downstairs bedroom and Karen on a makeshift bed in the kitchen.

The hinge on the kitchen door creaked as the intruder opened it and the family dog, Ringe, barked, waking Karen. She thought it was John returning from Portsmouth after all. The man was startled to find someone sleeping in the kitchen, and he sprang to life, grabbing a chair and raising it over his head.

Karen screamed, shouting, "John scares me! John scares me."

The man started beating her with the chair. Still thinking it was her brother-in-law, Karen shouted, "John is killing me! John is killing me!"

The screaming woke Maren, who opened the bedroom door and saw the dark form of a man standing over her Karen. He had paused for a moment and Maren was able to drag her sister into the bedroom and bolt the door. The killer pounded on the door; it would not keep him out for long. Maren persuaded Anethe that the only hope was to leave through the bedroom window. Anethe went through the window but only went a few paces before freezing with terror. The killer ran out of the house, grabbed the dull axe that was kept by the door for chopping ice, and ran toward Anethe.

Anethe now recognized the man and shouted, "Louis! Louis! Louis!"

From the bedroom window, Maren saw the man raise the axe and, with one blow, crushed Anethe's skull, killing her. The killer ran back into the house and started pounding again on the bedroom door. Maren tried to get Karen through the window but saw that her sister was dying, too. Maren's only hope was to climb out the window and leave her sister behind. As she went for the window, he burst into the room and rushed at her with the axe. She jumped out the window as he swung the axe, hitting the sill with so much force that the head of the axe broke off. From outside the window, she heard Karen scream as he finished her off.

Maren ran quickly looking for a place to hide. She was carrying the dog, afraid that if she let him down, his barking would give away her position. She first thought of hiding in the henhouse but rejected this idea as too obvious. She then ran to the dock, thinking she could escape the island in the killer's boat, but there was no boat there; he had come from the other side of the island. Finally she found an isolated section of rock. There, barefooted, in her nightclothes with only the dog for warmth, she waited until dawn.

In the daylight, not knowing whether the killer was still on the island, she hurried to Malaga, a small island connected to the north end of Smuttynose by a breakwater. From there she could shout to Appledore Island. She got the attention of some children playing on Appledore and was rescued.

Witnesses in Portsmouth said that Louis Wagner looked haggard that morning, as if he hadn't slept. He ate breakfast at his boardinghouse, then packed his bags and took the 9:00 a.m. train to Boston. When Maren told the story of the murders and accused Louis Wagner, a manhunt began. In Boston, Wagner bought a new suit of clothes and new boots, then had a haircut and shaved his beard. But he went straight to the North End neighborhood, where he had previously lived and was well known. By 7:00 that night, Wagner was arrested and on the train back to Portsmouth.

In Portsmouth, a crowd carrying torches was waiting at the depot when the train came in. He was hurried into a waiting police wagon, which was pelted with stones all the way to police station. Another crowd was waiting there, and a line of police carrying shotguns was required to guarantee his safe entry.

With Wagner safely inside the Portsmouth jail, the authorities needed to address some procedural matters. The Isles of Shoals are divided between New Hampshire and Maine, and while geographically closer to New Hampshire, Smuttynose Island is part of the state of Maine. Wagner had to be extradited to Maine, and he would run the gauntlet of the rock-throwing crowd once more. He was taken by train to South Berwick, Maine, then to the supposedly more secure prison in Alfred, Maine.

Trial: June 9, 1873

Louis Wagner's trial lasted nine days. The circumstantial evidence against him was strong. Before leaving Portsmouth, he had hidden a bloody shirt in the privy of his boardinghouse. Fifteen dollars and some change had been stolen from the Hontvets' house (Wagner had paid fifteen dollars for his new suit and boots) and among the coins was one of Maren's buttons. The button was found in Wagner's pocket when he was arrested. Witnesses testified that Wagner, at his lowest moments, said he would commit murder for money. He knew John Hontvet had money in the house that he was saving for a new boat. Maren Hontvet's testimony was compelling, stating without hesitation that the killer was Louis Wagner and relating Anethe's last words, "Louis, Louis, Louis."

But the most damaging testimony came from Wagner himself. His testimony was rambling and sometimes incoherent. He claimed he was working that night baiting trawls for a fishing boat. He could not remember the name of the boat, the name of the captain, or even the location of the pier. Then, he claimed, he went to a saloon, had two beers, then went to sleep outside. He could not remember the name of the saloon or its location. No witnesses were presented to verify any of his testimony.

Verdict: Guilty of premeditated murder

Aftermath:

Louis Wagner had been working on an escape plan since he arrived at Alfred prison, and he knew he had to act on it before he was transferred again. The night after the verdict, he picked the lock with the end of a wooden toothbrush and put a stool and other items under his blanket to make it appear he was sleeping soundly. Then, during the guards' regular 3:00 a.m. break, he made his escape.

Once again he was free, and once again did not know where to go. He was afraid to take to the woods, so he followed the roads. He was shown some hospitality by a local farmer but was captured at the farmer's house by a group of vigilantes and taken back to the prison in Alfred.

On March 26, 1875, Louis Wagner was hanged, along with a man named John True Gordon who murdered his brother's wife and child. Though Gordon begged for his life, Wagner remained silent. Louis Wagner strongly professed his innocence and never wavered.

Alternate Theories:

In spite of overwhelming evidence against him, Louis Wagner's steadfast assertion of innocence, together with the incomprehensible nature of his crime, have led some people to seek alternative answers.

- Maren Hontvet was the killer – As the only eyewitness, her testimony was given much weight, but she had more opportunities than a man in a rowboat from Portsmouth. An unsubstantiated rumor published by a number of newspapers in 1876 claimed that Maren confessed on her deathbed. The theory that Maren committed the murders was fictionalized by Anita Shreve in her 1997 novel, *The Weight of Water*.

- John Hontvet was the killer – In Maren's own testimony, Karen thought the man was John Hontvet, even as he was beating her with a chair. Perhaps John did the murders and Maren covered for him. For obvious reasons this story would be hard to substantiate.

These are just speculations, for the most part. Those who have looked at the case objectively believe that the state of Maine executed the right man.

Sarah Maria Cornell

10. THE MINISTER AND THE MILL GIRL

In December 1832, the body of a young, pregnant woman was found hanging at a Tiverton, Rhode Island, farm. She was identified as Sarah Cornell, a worker in a textile factory in nearby Fall River, Massachusetts. Evidence implicated Methodist minister Ephraim Avery, and the community was outraged that a man of the cloth had seduced and murdered an innocent mill girl.

THE MURDER OF SARAH CORNELL

But Sarah Cornell was far from innocent, and she had reasons to hate Reverend Avery that had nothing to do with her pregnancy. Could Sarah Cornell have planted evidence against Avery before taking her own life?

Date:	December 20, 1832
Location:	Tiverton, Rhode Island
Victim:	Sarah Maria Cornell
Cause of Death:	Strangulation
Accused:	The Reverend Ephraim Kingsbury Avery

Synopsis:

On Friday, December 21, 1832, John Durfee found the body of a young woman hanging from a cord tied to the roof of a hay stack on his farm in the town of Tiverton, Rhode Island, just across the border from Fall River, Massachusetts. Durfee sent for the coroner and when the news reached Fall River, local ministers and mill overseers hurried to the scene to help identify the body. Reverend Ira Bidwell recognized the girl as Sarah Maria Cornell, a member of his Methodist congregation. The identification was verified by John Smith, overseer of a weaving room at the Fall River manufactory where Sarah Cornell had worked. Sarah's doctor, Thomas Wilbur, also confirmed her identity and added that she was pregnant when she died. Dr. Wilbur speculated that she had killed herself in despair—she had told him

41

that the father of her unborn child was a married Methodist minister named Ephraim Kingsbury Avery.

An ad hoc coroner's jury first agreed with Dr. Wilbur's assessment and declared her death a suicide. She was hastily buried on Saturday; but by Sunday, new evidence came to light. In Sarah's bandbox a penciled note was found that read, "If I should be missing, enquire of the Rev. Mr. Avery of Bristol. He will know where I am. Dec. 20. S. M. Cornell."

An anonymous letter was found in Sarah's trunk, requesting a meeting with her on December 20. On closer inspection, the cord around her neck did not indicate suicide. While the loop was so tight it could not be cut off without cutting her skin, it was tied with a clove hitch, a knot that would not have automatically pulled tight. The body was exhumed and examined more closely. Bruises were found on her abdomen, suggesting that an abortion may have been attempted.

People of Massachusetts and Rhode Island, primarily Congregationalists, were suspicious of the rising Methodist Episcopal Church that some equated with Freemasonry. On Sunday the coroner declared that Sarah Cornell was murdered and a warrant was issued for the arrest of Methodist minister Ephraim Avery.

Sarah Cornell had been a tailor by trade but found she could make more money by working in the textile mills that were rapidly expanding throughout New England. Like many mill girls, she frequently relocated because of new opportunities and changing personal situations. Sarah had also gained an unsavory reputation that she had trouble outrunning. In Providence, Rhode Island, she was accused of shoplifting. She changed her name and moved to Jewett City, Connecticut, where she worked in the weaving room of a mill until she was dismissed after being seen leaving the building late in the evening accompanied by a young man.

During this time she had also converted to Methodism and several times had tried to become a member of the church, but her reputation had always stood in her way. In Slatersville, Rhode Island, she was admonished for lewd behavior and later, after a church trial, was expelled for fornication and lying. In Lowell she had a relationship with a mill clerk that ended with more rumors of lewd behavior. She travelled from Lowell, Massachusetts, and as far north as Dover, New Hampshire, but could not shake her reputation as a bad girl.

Sarah met the Reverend Ephraim Avery when he was beginning his assignment as Methodist minister in Lowell and asked him for a job as a domestic servant. Avery claimed that she was never hired, but another witness said she had been hired and dismissed after one week of service because Avery's wife did not like the attention her husband gave her. Sarah got a job as a servant in Lynn, Massachusetts, but was terminated on suspicion of theft. She returned to Reverend Avery and asked him to give her a certificate of good standing with the Methodists so she could join a church in another community. He gave her the certificate, but she did not leave.

She had gotten another mill job in Lowell. When the overseer confronted Sarah with the rumors of her loose behavior, she admitted to having an illicit relationship but claimed that she had reformed. The overseer agreed to let Sarah keep her job if she would confess her sins to Reverend Avery. When she did, Avery was unsympathetic. Rather than offering forgiveness, he began the process of another church trial against Sarah. Her confessions to Avery would guarantee that she would be expelled again for fornication.

Before the trial ended, Sarah fled to Dover, New Hampshire, got another mill job, and attempted to join a Methodist church there. Meanwhile, in Lowell, Dr. William Graves went to Rev. Avery to ask about Sarah's whereabouts. He had been treating her for gonorrhea and she left without paying the bill. When the minister of the Dover church contacted Rev. Avery about Sarah, Avery told him that she was guilty of fornication, theft, and lying, and he told him about the "foul disease" she had. His letter ended, "Now if you want her in your church, you may have her."

Sarah sent several letters to Avery confessing her sins and asking forgiveness but got no response. Finally she went to Lowell and confronted him in person, and he agreed to sign a certificate of forgiveness that would allow her to join a church in New Hampshire. But the day after giving Sarah his signature, he wrote to the minister in New Hampshire, revoking his forgiveness saying:

> *We should all of us here be opposed to her joining anywhere…Alas! Alas!! Alas!!! This morning direct information was brought that she had told a known, willful falsehood—her standing being as it is, I have not taken any pains to enquire into the cause.*

Sarah left New Hampshire, and after a few stops in Massachusetts, went to live with her sister and brother-in-law in Woodstock, Connecticut. She stayed connected to the Methodist church by attending classes but did not try to join a church. That summer she also attended a Methodist camp meeting where hundreds of people slept in tents and attended four days of prayer and services. She was seen there by Reverend Avery (who had since been transferred to Bristol, Rhode Island) and several other Methodist ministers she had known in Lowell.

That fall, Sarah became aware that she was pregnant. She told her sister, and then related what had happened at the camp meeting. She said she had approached Reverend Avery, asking him to return her letters of confession. In her sister's words, this is what Sarah said:

> *They sat down; some conversation followed about Avery having burned the letters. He said he had not, but would on one condition, and settle the difficulty. At that time he took hold of her hands and put one onto her bosom, or something like it. She said she tried to get away from him but could not. She said he then had intercourse with her, and they returned to the camp. He promised to destroy the letters, on his return to Bristol.*

Her sister also said that Sarah had been "unwell as females are" eight days before the camp meeting, confirming that the conception had happened there. Sarah was advised by her brother-in-law and his lawyer to move to Rhode Island, where, if necessary, she could sue Avery for support. Sarah moved to Fall River, Massachusetts, on the Rhode Island border—not far from the town of Bristol—where she knew she could get millwork. She stayed in Fall River until her death on December 20.

On January 7, the justices gave their opinions. Both agreed that there was not enough evidence to try Reverend Avery for murder, or even that it was murder and not suicide.

Fearing the inevitable negative public reaction, Avery fled quickly and quietly, travelling to the home of Simeon Mayo in the town of Rindge, New Hampshire. While probably not in any physical danger, Avery correctly assumed that the people of Fall River and Tiverton would not be satisfied with the ruling. Should they come after him again, residing in a state without a border with Rhode Island would complicate the extradition process.

The people of Fall River and Tiverton did not accept the Bristol ruling and issued another warrant for Avery on the grounds that he was held and examined outside the county where the crime was committed. Deputy Harvey Hamden began a search for Avery that took him to Lowell, Boston, and in a remarkably short time, to Rindge, New Hampshire. Hamden had obtained the proper Hew Hampshire warrants and in Rindge met with a deputy sheriff and a posse, who rode with him to Mayo's house. Mayo feigned ignorance but let the men into his house, where they found Avery. Though he had grown a beard and was wearing green-tinted spectacles, Hamden recognized him. Avery was arrested and taken back to Tiverton.

Trial: May 6. 1833

Ephraim Avery's murder trial was held in the city of Newport and lasted twenty-seven days. It followed much the same course as the previous hearing. Once again Sarah's words to her sister and her doctor regarding the father of her unborn child were not admitted. Medical testimony regarding questions of suicide versus murder and the exact age of the fetus was quite prolonged, with each side summoning experts to support their point of view. The defense provided witnesses who could seemingly account for every minute of Reverend Avery's time at the camp meeting and again attacked Sarah Cornell's morality and sanity. But the circumstantial evidence against Avery was so strong that the defense claimed not only that Sarah Cornell committed suicide, but that she first planted evidence that would implicate Reverend Avery.

In the end, the jury could not find enough evidence to convict Ephraim Avery of murder

Verdict: Not guilty

Aftermath:

Ephraim Avery left court for Bristol ahead of the public announcement of the verdict. He did not remain there long. By June 5, Avery was in Boston awaiting a Methodist church trial. He was acquitted by the church of the charges of murder and "improper connexion."

He returned to Bristol and tried to preach, but his congregation was now divided, with many opposed to his continuing there. He was burned in effigy twice in Bristol and at least four times in Fall River. After 1834 Avery was never again stationed in the New England conference of the Methodist church. His role gradually diminished and by 1837, he was dropped from their roster. Avery and his family eventually settled in Lorain County, Ohio, where he died a farmer in 1869.

Though the murder of Sarah Cornell brought national notoriety to the town of Fall River, Massachusetts, it would be overshadowed fifty-nine years later by another Fall River killing—the murder of Andrew and Abby Borden.

11.   FOUND DRIFTING WITH THE TIDE

FINDING THE BODY OF JENNIE CRAMER

When the body of beautiful, young Jennie Cramer was found on a sandbar in the ocean off West Haven, Connecticut, in August 1881, it was assumed that she had drowned, and had possibly committed suicide. But there was no water in her lungs, and a thorough examination of the body revealed that she had been poisoned. It was also revealed that she had been violently raped within the previous forty-eight hours. Suspicion fell immediately on Jimmy Malley, Jennie's current beau and nephew of the richest man in New Haven. The problem for the prosecution, and everyone since, was determining what exactly happened in the last two days of Jennie Cramer's life.

Date:	August 6, 1881
Location:	New Haven, Connecticut
Victim:	Jennie Cramer
Cause of Death:	Poisoning
Accused:	Jimmy Malley, Walter Malley, Blanche Douglas

Synopsis:

Jennie Cramer was the daughter of Jacob Cramer, a New Haven, Connecticut, cigar merchant, and his wife Christina. Sickly as a child—probably anemic—Jennie was pampered by her family and was the only one of the Cramers' three children who did not work in the cigar store. She grew up to be a striking beauty, with dark brown hair and dark blue eyes, and a fair and soft complexion. Jennie Cramer was universally known as "The Belle of New Haven."

At age fifteen, Jennie left school and, with her mother's blessing, devoted her time to her appearance and her social life. Jennie had many suitors, and Mrs. Cramer kept a sharp eye on the kind of men who courted Jennie, hoping Jennie could use her beauty as a means to rise in class. Jennie became a notorious flirt, very forward in approaching men who hadn't been introduced to her. She loved having a good time and staying out late and although she kept her virtue intact, she had a reputation as a "fast" girl.

In 1881, at age twenty-one, Jennie met Jimmy Malley, who was two years her senior. Like Jennie, Jimmy liked to dress well and have fun and he still lived at home with his parents. Jimmy worked in his uncle's department store and Jennie would stop in to flirt with him. Jimmy was soon infatuated with her. Jimmy Malley was especially close to his cousin Walter, son of Edward Malley, owner of Malley's Department Store and the largest taxpayer in New Haven. Walter was the opposite of Jimmy; shy and reserved, he preferred art and music to sports and social life. He had attended Seton Hall and Yale but graduated from neither. Walter showed no ambition and was a disappointment to his father.

Walter and Jimmy took frequent trips to New York City and there, at a brothel run by Lizzie Bundy, they met a young prostitute named Blanche Douglas. She was born Anna Kearns, but escaping first an abusive stepfather, then an abusive husband, she changed her name and joined Lizzie Bundy's house. She had only been there two weeks when she met Walter and Jimmy.

Walter fell madly in love with Blanche Douglas, spending two or three nights a week with her and writing her letters and telegrams when he was not with her. Blanche had no education, and Walter wanted to introduce her to art, literature, and the finer things. Against her better judgment, Blanche agreed to visit Walter in New Haven when his father was out of town. Blanche was overwhelmed by his wealth.

Meanwhile, Jimmy was trying to court Jennie Cramer, but she had refused to go riding with him without a chaperone. The solution was to go out together with Walter and Blanche, who was introduced to Jennie as

Walter's rich fiancé from Long Island. They would go riding together and go to restaurants and other resorts where young people gathered. The night of July 23, 1881, she did not come home until 4:00 a.m., and Mrs. Cramer was beside herself. Jennie told her that they had gone back to the Malleys' mansion and though she had tried to leave, Jimmy refused to escort her.

On Wednesday, August 3, Jennie went out again with Jimmy, Walter, and Blanche. Walter's father had gone to Saratoga, so the two couples stayed all night at the mansion. Jennie returned home Thursday morning accompanied by Blanche, and had a terrible argument with her mother, who was upset over what the neighbors would think. Blanche said that Jennie had stayed in her hotel room and nothing improper had happened. Mrs. Cramer would have none of it and told Jennie if she were going to stay out all night, she should find a new place to live. Jennie left with Blanche. It was the last time her mother saw her alive.

Around dawn on Saturday, August 6, an oysterman named Asahel Curtis, while preparing his boat before heading out for his day's catch, saw a white object on a nearby sandbar swaying back and forth with the incoming tide. It was the body of a young woman, finely dressed, all in white; she had died recently enough that there had been no decomposition. It would not have been unusual for a young woman to be so dressed up at the beach; the popular Savin Rock Amusement Park was nearby and a woman fitting Jennie's description was seen there the night before. Other observers soon recognized her as Jennie Cramer, and though there were indications to the contrary, it was assumed that she had drowned. When the circumstances of her disappearance were learned, it was further assumed that she had drowned herself in despair.

While the body was still in a boathouse on the beach, Doctor Painter and Doctor Shepard performed an examination. They determined that there was no water in her lungs or stomach and it was unlikely that she had drowned. They also found that she had lost her virginity within twenty-four to forty-eight hours of her death. Damage to the fourchette, a tough tendon near the vaginal entrance, indicated that she had been violently raped. An inquest was scheduled for the following Monday.

Jimmy, Walter, and Blanche were questioned by reporters and Sheriff Peck, and after some initially contradictory statements, they all agreed that they had been with Jennie Wednesday night, but none of them had seen her after noon on Thursday. They had not been at Savin Rock Friday night.

Edward Malley returned from Saratoga to find his son and nephew implicated in the death of Jennie Cramer. He wasted no time hiring two powerful attorneys to represent the boys and Blanche Douglas and two private detectives to track down clues and witnesses. When confronted by reporters about Walter's relationship with Blanche, and the goings-on at the mansion on Wednesday night, he denied any knowledge of Walter ever being with a girl, then added, "Boys will be boys. And you'll find that's all there is to the matter." An autopsy that lasted seven hours produced no new information. It was almost certain that Jennie Cramer did not drown, but the cause of death remained unknown. Various organs were removed and preserved in jars, leading to rumors that the doctors would look for traces of drugs or poison. It was popularly thought that Jennie had been drugged with laudanum or chloroform before she was raped.

At the inquest, Blanche Douglas testified that the two couples had been at the Malley mansion on Wednesday night and that Blanche had been too sick to return to her hotel. Walter said she could sleep there and she persuaded Jennie to stay with her. They slept in the same room. The next morning they had breakfast together, then Jenny left her.

After her testimony, Blanche returned to New York. The prosecution realized that talking to Blanche away from the Malleys was their best hope of getting a conviction. When they went looking for her in New York, they found she had given a false address. She was soon tracked down to Lizzie Bundy's and her true identity was made known. She was arrested for perjury and extradited to New Haven. One of the autopsy doctors, Dr. Painter, had taken a special interest in the case and advised Blanche to sever her ties with the Malleys since they were likely to betray her. Blanche was afraid of jail and agreed to cooperate when Sheriff Peck offered to let her stay with his family rather than be locked in jail.

In several closed-door sessions, Blanche made a confession of sorts to the inquest jury. She revealed that she had been part of a scheme to assist Jimmy in seducing Jennie. The night Jennie had stayed out until 4:00 a.m., they had been in a private room over the Redcliffe Restaurant. She and Walter went to another room and she could hear Jennie crying loudly, "Don't, don't." On Wednesday night, August 3, they were at the mansion and got quite drunk on wine. Then Blanche feigned sickness to get Jennie to stay with her. But they did not stay together; Blanche went with Walter, and Jimmy carried Jennie, kicking and screaming, to another room. That night she heard loud, frightening screams from that room. She also testified that two men, one of whom was Edward Malley's brother, came to her in New York and asked how much money would convince her to take an ocean liner to Europe for a year or so.

But she still insisted that she did not see Jennie Cramer after Thursday at noon, saying, "If you was to hang a rope around my neck, I couldn't say different."

A chemical analysis of Jennie's organs had revealed eight-tenths of a grain of arsenic distributed among her stomach, esophagus, liver, kidneys, heart, lungs, intestines, and brain, indicating that two to four grains, a lethal dose of arsenic, had been ingested prior to death.

Jimmy and Walter Malley were arrested for murder on August 15. The inquest, which began on August 6, interviewed more than fifty witnesses and lasted until September 3.

Blanche had been held on perjury charges but when it was determined that she would give no more information, the charge was changed to murder. Before the murder trial itself, the case was put before the justice court to determine if there was probable cause to try the Malleys and Blanche for murder. Five counts of murder were listed in the indictment against the Malleys: arsenic poisoning, drowning, suffocation/asphyxiation, chloroform, and the use of liquor and drugs. For Blanche, the only charge was arsenic poisoning. The trial before Justice Steven Booth examined more than two hundred witnesses—mostly people claiming to have seen the defendants at various times and places—and lasted until the end of October. At the end, Justice Booth found probable cause to charge James Malley, Walter Malley, and Blanche Douglas with murder but limited to one count: arsenic poisoning.

Trial: April 25, 1882

The trial would not be held until April 25, 1882. It would take a week to empanel a jury because of the difficulty in finding anyone in New Haven who did not already have an opinion on the guilt of the Malleys.

The charge of arsenic poisoning presented a problem for both the prosecution and the defense. The prosecution could not accuse the defendants of suffocating Jennie on impulse; arsenic poisoning implied planning and deliberation. The defense would have trouble proving the Jennie fell or jumped deliberately into the water. Both sides agreed to exhume the body for a complete analysis, including the bones, to determine exactly how much arsenic was ingested. While the prosecution wanted an exact amount to present to the jury, the defense hoped to prove that Jennie was an "arsenic eater"—a woman who indulged in the popular Victorian practice of ingesting small amounts of arsenic to lighten the complexion. It was determined that Jennie had ingested at least three grains of arsenic, but there was none in her bones, indicating that she was not an habitual user.

In the end, however, there was only circumstantial evidence—sparse and vague—that the defendants had poisoned Jennie Cramer. After deliberating only an hour, the jury returned a verdict of not guilty.

Verdict: Not Guilty

Aftermath:

Jacob Cramer had been devastated by the death of his daughter and did not live to see the end of the trial. The official cause of death was listed as phthisis, another word for consumption, but it was more likely suicide. By 1883 Christia Cramer had become mentally unbalanced and was convinced that her daughter was not dead and would be coming back to her. In July 1891, Christia Cramer hanged herself.

In February 1882, Malley's Department Store burned to the ground. Arson was suspected, and the insurance company refused payment on a technicality. Walter Malley used his time in prison to draw landscapes on the cell wall and to compose a waltz, "Under the Elms," which was published and sold as sheet music.

Another piece of music, "Found Drifting with the Tide," was written about Jennie Cramer by A. C. Willis.

Following the verdict the Malley's held a lavish party at the Tontine Hotel, which was sharply criticized by the press. Blanche Douglas went back to jail that night because she had nowhere else to go.

Walter Malley kept in contact with Blanche Douglas and at one point was the target of a blackmail scheme involving letters stolen from Blanche. He married a woman named Anna Madden, who many believe was actually Blanche Douglas (Anna Kearns.)

The true circumstances surrounding the poisoning of Jennie Cramer have never been determined.

Alexander P. Crittenden

12.   THE WOMAN IN BLACK

A prominent California legislator was sitting with his wife and son on board the Oakland-San Francisco ferryboat *El Capitan* the evening of November 3, 1870. They did not notice the woman, dressed entirely in black, wearing a broad-brimmed black hat with a black veil covering her face, as she approached them. From the folds of her dress, the woman pulled a derringer and shot the man in the chest. The family recognized the woman in black then; it was Laura Fair, and she was finally ending her tumultuous affair with Alexander P. Crittenden.

LAURA D. FAIR

Date: November 3, 1870

Location: San Francisco, California

Victim: Alexander P. Crittenden

Cause of Death: Gunshot

Accused: Laura D. Fair

Synopsis:

She was born Laura Hunt in Holly Springs, Mississippi, and at age sixteen, she was married to a New Orleans liquor dealer named William Stone, twenty years her senior. Within a year Stone died of cirrhosis of the liver. Soon after she married Thomas J. Grayson, who was also a drunk—the violent kind. After less than six months with Grayson, Laura fled to California with her mother.

After a brief stay in San Francisco, she went to Shasta, where she met and married another older man, an attorney named William Fair. Laura and William had a daughter they named Lillian Loraine. The family moved back to San Francisco, but William was unable to establish himself there. Despondent over his finances, William Fair put a gun to his head and ended his troubles.

Laura and her mother moved to Sacramento and with her meager inheritance, they bought a boardinghouse. When this venture failed to pan out, she turned to acting, performing in a play in Sacramento and another in San Francisco. Her reviews were good, but acting was not for Laura. She took her pay and moved again, this time to Virginia City, Nevada, just as the Comstock silver lode was making everyone rich. She bought a hotel called the Tahoe House, and this time it paid off. Alexander Crittenden also traveled to Virginia City to get a piece of the silver bonanza. Crittenden had been in the California legislature and had a successful law practice in San Francisco. But in 1864, with a wife and seven children to support, he needed more money. While his family waited in San Francisco, Crittenden went to Virginia City to establish a practice there. He stayed at the Tahoe House.

Laura Fair was instantly attracted to the tall, handsome lawyer and before long, they spent all their nights together in Laura's bedroom. But this was no idle dalliance; soon they were declaring undying love for each other and when Laura suggested marriage, Crittenden agreed. Laura, of course, did not know that Crittenden was already married.

In early 1865, Laura learned the truth when Crittenden's wife, Clara, arrived in Virginia City with the children. Laura was upset, but took Crittenden at his word when he promised to divorce his wife and marry Laura at the earliest convenience. He rented a house for his family but kept a room at the Tahoe House "for business reasons." Crittenden would shuttle back and forth between the two, unwilling to give up his family or the lovely Laura Fair. Variations of this scheme would continue in Virginia City and San Francisco for the next five years.

Clara Crittenden was aware of Laura Fair but appeared to believe her husband when he said they were only friends. At one point she even agreed to his suggestion that Laura live in a room in their house. Laura, still anxiously waiting for Crittenden to divorce his wife, agreed to whatever he proposed. He sent her to Indiana, where divorce laws were more lenient than California and promised to marry her there. Crittenden never showed up.

In 1870, the Crittendens were back in San Francisco. Laura Fair had moved there as well and was living with her mother. Alexander Crittenden would still visit Laura Fair, but now the visits often ended in arguments.

Laura had purchased a Colt revolver and one night she fired at him as she chased him down her staircase. Another time she threatened suicide if he would not leave his wife.

In desperation Laura finally gave up on Alexander Crittenden and married a man named Jesse Snyder. Crittenden was livid; the thought of Laura with another man was driving him insane. He wrote her a letter describing his state of mind:

> No—I cannot—cannot be content. You are to me the sun—air—life—everything; and without you—as we are now—there can be no existence. I am wretched, insufferably, infinitely wretched. I have no heart or mind for anything—can think of nothing but you. Day and night I wander about like a ghost…

The letter moved Laura and she agreed to meet with Crittenden. They reconciled and once again pledged undying love to each other. Now each would need a divorce and each made a solemn vow to begin the proceedings. Laura made good on her promise; Crittenden did not.

Laura's divorce became final on October 5, 1871. Clara Crittenden had gone east, and Laura believed that she was finally going to become Alexander's wife. But when Laura learned that Crittenden had not divorced his wife, something inside of her snapped. She found out that Clara would be returning soon to San Francisco, and Crittenden had purchased new furniture in anticipation. Laura went to a gunsmith and traded in her Colt revolver for a four-barrel Sharps derringer.

On November 3rd, Laura, dressed all in black with a black veil covering her face, followed Crittenden to the train station in Oakland and witnessed the loving reunion of Alexander and Clara. She followed them as they boarded the ferryboat *El Capitan*. The family took a seat on deck and Laura sat nearby watching them. Then, as the boat was leaving the harbor, she stood up and approached the Crittendens. She pulled the derringer from the folds of her dress and shot Alexander Crittenden once in the chest.

Laura hurried away and was chased by Crittenden's son Parker. When he confronted her in the wheelhouse, she said:

> I did it, certainly. Yes. I did it. I was looking for the clerk on the boat to give myself up. He has ruined me and my child, and I meant to kill him.

Alexander Crittenden was taken to his home where he managed to live for forty-eight hours with a bullet in his heart.

Trials: March 27, 1871

September 22, 1872

The question of jurisdiction delayed the prosecution of the case for a time; the boat was traveling between Alameda County and San Francisco County and it was not immediately clear in which county the murder had occurred. It took an official survey of the harbor to determine that Alexander Crittenden had been shot in San Francisco County.

The sensational trial of Laura D. Fair lasted twenty-six days, with the courtroom filled to capacity every day. Among the celebrities attending the trial were women's rights leaders Susan B. Anthony and Elizabeth Cady Stanton, who sympathized with Laura's plight.

While there was no question that Laura Fair murdered Alexander Crittenden, her defense attorneys argued that she was not responsible for her actions, as she was suffering from "partial intellectual insanity and partial moral insanity." While her years of emotional abuse from Crittenden would alone be sufficient to drive her insane, Laura Fair also suffered from "retarded menstruation," a condition that made her raving mad for several days prior to each menstrual period. On the witness stand, Laura claimed to have no recollection of what happened on the boat.

The jury was not convinced by this argument. After deliberating less than an hour, they returned with a verdict of guilty to first-degree murder. She was sentenced to be hanged on July 28.

The trial was appealed and in February 1872, the verdict was overturned on technicalities. The following September the case was retried. It was noted that during this trial Ms. Fair dressed entirely in black and wore a black veil. This time Laura Fair was found not guilty by reason of temporary insanity.

Verdicts: Guilty of first-degree murder; overturned on appeal
              Not guilty

Aftermath:

The verdict was almost universally criticized, with newspapers complaining that the court had given a "license to kill" to spurned adulterers. Though acquitted of murder, Laura's notoriety made her life miserable in San Francisco. In December 1872, Laura gave a public lecture entitled "Wolves in the Fold" before an audience of 2,000 in Platt's Hall in San Francisco. It was a bitter tirade against the judge and jury of her first trial and against the San Francisco press and clergy. The lecture was well received by the crowd. Eventually sensation around the case died down and although the story resurfaced from time to time, Laura Fair lived peacefully until her death in 1913.

Dr. Patrick Henry Cronin

13. CLAN-NA-GAEL

Dr. Patrick Henry Cronin was a prominent Chicago physician and a member of Clan-na-Gael, an American political organization formed to promote Irish independence from British rule. Clan-na-Gael was very effective at raising large sums of money for the cause, but the money was administered in secret by three members of the executive board led by Chicago lawyer Alexander Sullivan. When Dr. Cronin criticized the board's secrecy and accused them of embezzling funds, he was denounced as a traitor and a British spy. When his accusations persisted, Sullivan marked him for death and on May 4, 1889, Dr. Cronin disappeared.

THE MURDER OF DR. CRONIN

Date: May 4, 1889

Location: Chicago, Illinois

Victim: Dr. Patrick Henry Cronin

Cause of Death: Stab wounds to the head

Accused: Members of Clan-na-Gael

Synopsis:

Clan-na-Gael was the public name of a secret organization for Irish independence known to its members as the United Brotherhood. It was formed to replace the Fenian Brotherhood, which was discredited in America after their ill-conceived attempt to invade Canada in 1866. Clan-na-Gael was modeled after other secret societies, such as the Freemasons, with secret codes and symbols, initiation rites, and other oaths and rituals.

The organization had chapters, known as camps, in every major city. Camp 20, in Chicago, was their headquarters.

In 1881, Clan-na-Gael held a convention in Chicago, at which they established a five-man executive board to govern the organization. It wasn't long before three members of the board realized that, acting together, they could control every vote. Alexander Sullivan of Chicago, Michael Boland of Louisville, Kentucky, and D. S. Freely of Rochester, New York—known informally as the "Triangle"—worked together to control Clan-na-Gael in secret.

Clan-na-Gael was accused of supplying money and men for the "Dynamite War," a terrorist campaign in England. If true, this accusation would have alienated the more moderate members of the group. The Triangle vehemently denied the charge but was unable or unwilling to account for Clan-na-Gael funds estimated to be between $100,000 and $250,000.

Dr. Cronin publicly denounced the Triangle and demanded an accounting. Patrick Henry Cronin was born in County Cork in Ireland in 1846 and when he was quite young, moved with his family to Canada. When he was twenty-three, he moved to St. Louis, Missouri. Cronin was a very charismatic and ambitious young man. He had a fine tenor voice, and though a devout Catholic, Cronin sang in the choir of the Second Baptist Church. He began working as a porter for a wholesale house, but his winning personality impressed several St. Louis businessmen, who provided him with better employment and assisted with his education. Cronin began studying pharmacy but changed to medicine and graduated from the Missouri Medical College. He set up a private practice in St. Louis and joined a number of benevolent groups and secret societies, such as Royal Arcanum, Chosen Friends, and Clan-na-Gael. When he moved to Chicago in 1882, he joined the Foresters and the Royal League.

In Chicago he met and joined the anti-Triangle faction of Clan-na-Gael and soon became their spokesman. The Triangle retaliated by accusing Cronin of being a British spy. In Camp 20, he was brought to trial before a committee of its members, including Dan Coughlin, a detective in the Chicago police department. Cronin was found guilty of treason and expelled from the order, but Cronin now had a large following within Clan-na-Gael, and thousands of members quit the organization in sympathy and formed their own camps.

Leaders of both factions realized the goal of Irish independence could not be met unless they all worked together and urged their members to "bury the hatchet." Dr. Cronin agreed, provided that the actions of the Triangle were fully investigated.

A committee of six, including Dr. Cronin, investigated the Triangle but voted four to two that the charges had not been proven. Cronin called it a whitewash and threatened to make his notes of the proceedings public so the world would know the treachery of the Triangle. Triangle leader Alexander Sullivan was reportedly heard to say he wished Cronin could be "removed."

In Chicago, Dr. Cronin was approached by Patrick O'Sullivan, owner of an icehouse in Lake View, Illinois, offering him a job as the company physician. For $8 a month, Cronin agreed to respond whenever one of O'Sullivan's employees needed medical attention. It was an odd arrangement, since Cronin did not live near the icehouse, plus O'Sullivan had only four employees and their work was not hazardous.

On May 4, 1889, a man came to Cronin's house in a carriage asking for assistance for an injured worker at O'Sullivan's icehouse. Several people saw Dr. Cronin leave in a carriage pulled by a white horse. He never returned home and Dr. Cronin's friends suspected that he had been murdered. When a bloodstained trunk was found north of the city containing what appeared to be strands of Dr. Cronin's hair, they were convinced. But he was reportedly seen on a streetcar by a friend late that night. The sighting was verified by the streetcar conductor. And on May 10, Chicago's newspapers received a dispatch from Toronto claiming that Dr. Cronin was in Canada, on his way to England. He had admitted to being a British spy and was on his way to testify against Clan-na-Gael.

The matter was settled on May 22 when the public works department in Lake View was investigating a jammed sewer. The workmen found the decomposing body of Dr. Cronin wedged into the catch basin. He was completely naked with a bloody towel wrapped around his neck. Beneath the towel, around his neck, he wore an Agnus Dei—a Catholic medal depicting the Lamb of God. When the body was examined, the coroner found five scalp wounds made by a sharp, narrow weapon such as an icepick.

The investigation began near O'Sullivan's icehouse, where neighbors told police about a strange man who had rented a cottage nearby and never moved in. Though the cottage was unoccupied, sometimes lights burned inside late at night. When police went into the cottage, they could tell at a glance that it was the scene of the murder. There was a considerable amount of blood on the front steps and in several of the rooms, and the floor had recently been painted yellow in a clumsy attempt to hide the blood.

They traced the furniture to Revel's Furniture Store; there they learned the furniture items, as well as the bloodstained trunk, had been rented by a man calling himself J. B. Simmonds. Police suspected that Simmonds was actually Pat Cooney, alias "The Fox," a companion of O'Sullivan and Detective Coughlin, and a bitter enemy of Cronin's.

Police identified the horse and carriage and found that it had been rented the day of the murder by Detective Dan Coughlin. John Kunze, a friend of Coughlin, was identified as the man who drove the carriage. On June 29, O'Sullivan, Coughlin, Cooney, and Kunze were indicted for the murder of Dr. Cronin, along with Frank Burke, Frank Woodruff, and John Beggs, members of Camp 20 and associates of Coughlin. Burke fled to Winnipeg but was captured there and after a long and bitter extradition hearing, was returned, under heavy guard, to Chicago.

Alexander Sullivan was also arrested at the recommendation of the coroner's jury. It was not the first time Sullivan was arrested for murder. In 1876 Frank Hanford, principal of the school where Sullivan's wife was teaching, accused Mrs. Sullivan of creating dissention on the school board. Sullivan and his wife paid a visit on Mr. Hanford, a squabble ensued, and Sullivan shot and killed Hanford. After two trials Alexander Sullivan was acquitted.

In the Cronin murder, Sullivan was released on $20,000 bail and charges were eventually dropped due to lack of evidence.

Trial: August 26, 1889 – Beggs, Caughlin, Burke,
              O'Sullivan, Kunze

The trial went on for three and a half months, with closing arguments lasting fourteen days. The prosecution charged that Dr. Cronin had been condemned to die "by a tribunal self-constituted; a tribunal that was accuser, witness, judge, and executioner at the same time; a tribunal which hides itself from the light of day."

Alternately, the defense tried to paint Dr. Cronin as a violent radical and a British spy.

The jury deliberated for seventy hours before returning a mixed verdict:

Verdicts: John F. Beggs – Not guilty
                 John Kunze – Guilty of manslaughter
                 Daniel Coughlin, Patrick O'Sullivan,
                    Martin Burke – Guilty of first-degree murder

There was not enough evidence against Frank Woodruff and his case was stricken from the docket. Kunze appealed his verdict and was granted a new trial, which resulted in his acquittal. Coughlin was granted a new trial on the grounds that two jurors were prejudiced against him. He was also acquitted on his second trial.

Aftermath:

The murder of Dr. Cronin was called, at the time, "The Crime of the Century" but as Edmund Pearson pointed out, "...anyone with the faintest knowledge of Chicago will remember that that city has a Crime of the Century every four or five years."

Dr. Cronin certainly had one of Chicago's most spectacular funerals. Nearly 8,000 men—Hibernians, Clan-na-Gaels, Foresters, and members of Catholic benevolent societies and other orders of which Cronin was member—marched in line. The procession included several drum corps and a marching band.

After his release from prison, Daniel Coughlin opened a saloon in Chicago, but he did not stay in business long. He was charged with attempting to bribe jurors in damage suit cases when he was an employee of the Illinois Railway Company. When the indictments were brought against him, Coughlin fled to Honduras.

Patrick O'Sullivan and Martin Burke died in the penitentiary.

A modern observer of the murder of Dr. Cronin is left with the feeling that the real conspirators were not charged and the true story has never been told. To quote Edmund Pearson once more, "It was one of those murders over which men nod their heads and look portentous and intimate that 'everything hasn't come out yet.'"

Katie Curran and Horace Millen

14. THE BOSTON BOY FIEND

On December 22, 1871, four-year-old Billy Paine was found hanging by his wrists, half-naked, from the roof beam of a tumbledown privy on Powder Horn Hill in Chelsea, Massachusetts. His back was covered with welts from a whipping. Over the next nine months, seven more children, none older than eight, were found tied and brutally tortured in Chelsea and South Boston. The assaults became increasingly vicious and in 1874 resulted in the deaths of a four-year-old boy and a ten-year-old girl. When the killer was proven to be fourteen-year-old Jesse Pomeroy, Massachusetts had to face two tough questions: Could someone so brutal be considered sane? And if so, did the commonwealth have the will to execute the "boy fiend?"

JESSE HARDING POMEROY

Dates:	March 18, 1874 and April 22, 1874
Location:	Boston, Massachusetts
Victims:	Katie Curran and Horace Millen
Cause of Death:	Stabbing
Accused:	Jesse Harding Pomeroy

Synopsis:

Jesse Pomeroy did not have an easy time as a young boy. From infancy his right eye had been covered over with a white film—some said due to cataracts, others blamed a virulent infection or reaction to a smallpox vaccination. It left him with an appearance that many people found revolting and made him the object of ridicule among older boys. Jesse's own father, Thomas Pomeroy, could barely stand to look at him. When angry at his son, Thomas would flog Jesse's bare back with his belt. After one such beating, Jesse's mother, Ruth Ann Pomeroy, drove her husband out of the house with a kitchen knife and he never returned.

Jesse was an intelligent boy, if somewhat antisocial. He would not join the other boys in baseball games or other athletic pursuits, but he was fond of playing "scouts and Indians," where he would invariably be an Indian and devise elaborate imaginary tortures for captive scouts. Jesse had always been a problem for his mother. She knew he stole money from her and was always playing hooky from school. And she knew he had a vicious streak; years earlier she had come home from work one day to find the heads twisted off her pet canaries.

The Pomeroys were living in Chelsea, a suburb of Boston, when young Billy Paine was found beaten in the Powder Horn Hill outhouse. Billy was unable to describe his attacker, and no one suspected that the assailant was a child himself. On February 21, 1872, seven-year-old Tracy Hayden had been lured to the same abandoned outhouse by "a big boy with brown hair." He was tied, stripped naked, and whipped across the back. The boy hit him in the face with a board, breaking his nose and knocking out two teeth. Then he threatened to cut off Tracy's penis. A third victim, Robert Maier, age eight, was taken to the same outhouse on May 20 and given similar treatment.

Over the next few weeks, Chelsea police questioned hundreds of boys but made no arrests. A rumor began to circulate that the attacker was a young man with fiery-red hair, pale skin, arched eyebrows, and a pointy chin with a wispy red beard. In their communal fear, the people of Chelsea had described the devil. After seven-year-old Johnny Balch was stripped and flogged on July 22, the press named the assailant "the boy torturer" and a $500 reward was offered for his capture.

While all of the parents in Chelsea were worried for the safety of their children, Ruth Ann Pomeroy worried for a different reason—she feared the attacker might be her own child. Ruth Ann decided it would be a good time to leave Chelsea. She moved her family to South Boston and opened a dress shop.

The assaults moved to South Boston as well, becoming increasingly frequent and increasingly brutal. On August 17, seven-year-old George Pratt was abducted. Pratt was not just flogged; this time the abductor stuck a needle in his arm and his groin and bit chunks of flesh from his face and buttocks. On September 5, the assailant began using a knife, stabbing six-year-old Harry Austin under the arms and between the shoulder blades, and he attempted, unsuccessfully, to cut off his penis. Less than a week later, he used a knife on six-year-old Joseph Kennedy, then threw salt water on the wounds. Six days after that, wielding two knives, he slashed five-year-old Robert Gould's scalp and threatened to kill him, but was interrupted by some approaching railroad workers.

Robert Gould, the eighth victim, was the first to give a useful description of his attacker. He said it was "a big bad boy with a funny eye." When asked about the eye, Robert said it was like a "milky," the children's name for a milk-white marble.

The police wanted Robert Gould to go to local schools and identify his attackers from the boys sitting in class, but Robert's scalp had required stitches and his parents would not let him leave the house. They took Joseph Kennedy instead, and though he was taken to Jesse Pomeroy's class, he was unable to identify his attacker.

That day, after school, for reasons Jesse was never able to explain, he went to the police station. Seeing Joseph Kennedy there, he quickly turned and left the station, but a policeman followed him out and brought him back. Now, looking closer, young Joseph saw the white eye and identified Jesse as his torturer. Jesse was held in a cell overnight and was persuaded to confess. The next day all of the victims identified him as their attacker. Jesse, then twelve years old, was sentenced to the reformatory, "for the term of his minority"—a period of six years.

At the Massachusetts House of Reformation in Westborough, Jesse quickly adapted. He stayed away from the older boys who taunted him, as they always had, and the younger boys, who knew why he was there, steered clear of Jesse. Knowing that good behavior was the only way to leave the reformatory early, he did his work, applied himself to studies, and even informed on his fellow inmates. Outside, Ruth Ann continually pressed for her son's release until on January 24, 1874, less than seventeen months after his arrest, Jesse Pomeroy was set free on probation.

The morning March 18, 1874, ten-year-old Katie Curran left her home to buy a notebook for school and never returned. She was last seen entering Mrs. Pomeroy's store. Everyone in the neighborhood knew Jesse's history, and the Currans feared the worst. At the police station, Captain Dyer assured Mrs. Curran that Jesse could not be involved—he had been completely rehabilitated. Besides, he was only known to attack little boys. Katie's father was a Catholic and, reflecting the attitudes of the time, local rumors said he sent her to a convent without telling her mother.

On April 22, 1874, four-year-old Horace Millen disappeared. Several people that day had seen a little boy accompanied by an older boy heading toward McCay's wharf. That afternoon, in a clambake pit on Savin Hill Beach, Horace Millen's half-naked corpse was found. He had been stabbed six times in the chest, his head was nearly severed, and he was partially castrated.

When Boston's chief of police, Edward Hartwell Savage, heard of the murder, his first thought was of Jesse Pomeroy, but he believed Pomeroy was still safely at the reformatory. When his men told him that Jesse was out on probation, Savage ordered his immediate arrest. On the beach the police found footprints left by the two boys and were able to make plaster casts of the larger ones. They matched Jesse's shoes perfectly. Jesse was questioned and confronted with the evidence, but refused to confess. Finally they took him to the funeral parlor to view the body and he broke down. He admitted he killed Horace—that something made him do it. He was sorry and wanted to leave. He told the policemen, "Put me somewhere, so I can't do such things."

The notoriety was terrible for Mrs. Pomeroy's dress business and she was forced to close her shop and work out of her house. The building was taken over by Nash's Grocery Store and while workmen were doing renovations, they experienced a terrible odor coming from the basement. The source was the decaying body of Katie Curran found under an ash heap. She was identified by her clothing, and though badly decomposed, police could tell she had been stabbed and mutilated.

Mrs. Pomeroy and her other son, Charles, were arrested for murder. Jesse was told this and questioned aggressively about Katie Curran until he finally confessed to the murder. Later he would claim he confessed only to save his mother but was not really guilty. He would also recant his confession to Horace Millen's murder.

Trial: December 8, 1874

The trial of Jesse Pomeroy for the murder of Horace Millen lasted four days. The prosecution introduced testimony of those who had found the body and those who saw Horace with a bigger boy that day. Some could identify Jesse in court as that boy. Their strongest evidence was the confession Jesse had made at the time of his arrest.

The defense argued that Jesse was innocent by reason of insanity. They called Jesse's victims, some still seriously disfigured from the attacks, to prove the insanity of his actions. They also introduced testimony from physicians and alienists who believed that Jesse was insane. The prosecution had its own experts, who concluded that Jesse knew right from wrong and acted anyway.

The jury deliberated less than five hours and returned a verdict of guilty of first-degree murder. Though Massachusetts law required mandatory execution for first-degree murder, the jury recommended the sentence be commuted to life in prison. That issue would not be resolved for another year and nine months.

Verdict: Guilty of first-degree murder

Aftermath:

The debate raged locally and nationally—in the press, in public opinion, and among lawyers and politicians—whether justice and public safety could only be accommodated by the hanging of Jesse Pomeroy, or whether it was immoral to hang a boy who was only fourteen at the time of his crime. The matter was settled in August 1876 when the Massachusetts Executive Council decided to commute the sentence to solitary confinement for the rest of Jesse Pomeroy's life.

Jesse Pomeroy was sixteen years old when he entered Charlestown State Prison. Except for a brief period in the 1880s when the prison was being renovated, he spent the next fifty-three years there, forty-one of those years in solitary confinement. Only one prisoner in American history was in solitary confinement longer—Robert Stroud, "the Birdman of Alcatraz"—and only by one year.

Though he had attempted to escape many times, Jesse would never leave prison. In 1929, old and infirm, he was transferred to the state prison farm at Bridgewater, where he could be better cared for. He died there on September 29, 1932, two months before his seventy-third birthday.

William Druse

15.   THE DRUSE BUTCHERY

December 1884, William Druse of Herkimer County, New York, was brutally murdered, dismembered, and burned, his ashes and bones dumped in a swamp. Evidence strongly pointed to his wife, Mrs. Roxalana Druse, who was convicted and sentenced to death. Women's rights activists took up Roxy's cause, calling the trial unfair because she did not have the same rights as her all-male jury. More to the point, though, there is a good chance Roxalana Druse was not guilty of murder.

ROXALANA DRUSE

Date:	December 18, 1884
Location:	Little Falls, New York
Victim:	William Druse
Cause of Death:	Shooting, blows from an axe
Accused:	Roxalana Druse

Synopsis:

On December 18, 1884 neighbors of William Druse, near the village of Little Falls, in Herkimer County New York, found his door locked and windows covered with newspaper. There was no response when they knocked on his door, but they knew someone was home because a dense, black, foul-smelling smoke was issuing from the chimney. Druse lived in the dingy yellow farmhouse with his wife, Roxalana (known as Roxy), his nineteen-year-old daughter, Mary, his ten-year-old son, George, and his fourteen-year-old nephew, Frank Gates. William Druse, aged sixty, was eighteen years older than his wife, and was considered by neighbors to be lazy, ill-tempered, and abusive. Their fear at first was that William had murdered his family and fled.

Soon after, Mrs. Druse and the children were seen alive but Mr. Druse was missing. When asked about her husband, Mrs. Druse said he had gone to New York City, but the unusual circumstances, especially the offensive smoke, prompted neighbors to suspect that William Druse had been the victim of foul play. Rumors began to spread, prompting an official inquiry. Herkimer district attorney A. B. Steele arrested Druse's nephew, Frank Gates. Under severe questioning Gates admitted the he had participated in the murder of William Druse and implicated the rest of the family as well.

Frank Gates told a horrifying story of his uncle's murder. Mr. and Mrs. Druse had been arguing during breakfast over a grocery bill. When the argument became heated, she sent the two boys out of the room then came up behind William Druse and fired a revolver into the back of his neck. Mary flung a rope around her father's neck and pulled him to the floor and her mother fired two more shots. Druse was still alive, but she was having trouble with the pistol. She called Frank back into the room and ordered him, under penalty of death, to finish the deed. Frank emptied the pistol into his uncle, but he still was not dead. Mrs. Druse then took an axe and struck her husband on the head while he exclaimed, "Oh, Roxy, don't!"

A second axe blow to the head killed William Druse. Roxy then used the axe to sever the head from the body and threw the head into the kitchen stove.

Mrs. Druse sent Frank and George out to get a sharper axe. They returned with an axe from the barn then went into another room to play checkers while Mrs. Druse, using the axe, a razor, a jack knife, a board, and a chopping block, dismembered the body and chopped it into little pieces, which she then burned in the stove. She had Frank saw the bloodstained handle off of the axe, and she burned that as well. The next day, she and Frank took the ashes to Ball's Swamp about half a mile from the house.

Using Frank Gates's confession, the coroner was able to find the axe head and the charred remains in the swamp. Being late December, the remains were frozen together into a solid mass. It consisted of eighteen to twenty small pieces of bone, one to two inches long, two kneecaps, and the upper end of the left tibia. It was enough for the coroner to determine the remains were human.

At the inquest, held on January 17, neighbors testified to the black smoke from the Druse's chimney on December 18, and some testified that Mr. and Mrs. Druse frequently quarreled. Frank Gates told the same story as he had when arrested. Ten-year-old George Druse told a similar story of the murder but claimed his uncle, Charley Gates, Frank's father, was there as well and had handed his mother the revolver.

Mrs. Druse was called to testify, but said she did not wish to make any statements. After the inquest she declared that her brother-in-law, Charles Gates, had been present when her husband died. She had also said this at the time of her arrest, claiming the Charles had fired several shots from his own revolver. She claimed they would find two different types of bullets in the body; however, any bullets in the body had been destroyed by the fire.

The coroner's jury charged Roxalana Druse with murdering her husband by shooting and striking him with an axe. Mary Druse, George Druse, and Frank Gates were charged with giving comfort, aid, and abet to Roxalana in committing felony and murder. They were taken to jail in the county seat of Herkimer in a close-covered sleigh.

William and Roxalana Druse had been married for twenty years, and during that time William had kept his wife isolated in the farmhouse, subjecting her to continuous verbal and physical abuse. It was common knowledge that they had not slept in the same room for ten years. William, George, and Frank—who worked on the farm in exchange for room and board—slept upstairs. Roxy and Mary slept downstairs in the parlor. Roxy said the only time her husband had been a decent man was on their wedding day. On her trip to prison, she declared that whether she was sentenced to life in prison or hanging, at least she would never live with William Druse again. Her first night in jail, she commented, "Well, I hope I may be able to procure tonight what I have not had before in two years: a good night's rest."

Trial: September 24, 1885

The trial of Roxalana Druse lasted two weeks and primarily consisted of the same testimony as at the inquest with the addition of some bloodstained floorboards extracted from the house entered as evidence. Mrs. Druse did not testify, but her attorneys tried to claim that she had acted in self-defense, citing years of threats and abuse. In the end, the prosecution's case, especially the testimony of Frank Gates, was too strong. Roxy Druse was found guilty of murder and sentenced to hang.

Verdict: Guilty of first-degree murder

Aftermath:

After a lengthy and unsuccessful appeal, Roxalana Druse was sentenced to hang on February 28, 1887. The case aroused much public opinion both for and against her execution. One man offered to go to the gallows himself, in place of Mrs. Druse, another offered $10 if he could act as executioner. Souvenir hunters tried to get items of her clothing—shoes, buttons, hairpins, shoestrings.

Women's rights groups were strongly opposed to her hanging, saying an all-male jury did not constitute a jury of her peers. Also, since she did not have the right to vote, her status in society was the same as a minor's and as such, she should not be put to death.

But in spite of many petitions for clemency, New York governor David Hill remained unmoved and would not change the sentence.

On February 28, Mrs. Druse was hanged in Herkimer in front of twenty-five witnesses, though hundreds stood in the cold outside the prison. The hanging used the "modern" method where, rather than falling through a trapdoor, the condemned person was jerked upward when a counterweight—in this case, 213 pounds—was dropped. Though she was jerked four feet into the air, her neck was not broken and it took her fifteen minutes to die of strangulation. Roxalana Druse was the last woman hanged in the state of New York, and her botched execution was instrumental in the state replacing the gallows with the "more humane" electric chair.

The day before her execution, Roxalana Druse made a confession to her spiritual advisor, Dr. Powell, in which she declared that her brother-in-law, Charles Gates, instigated her to commit the murder and provided her with the revolver. She said the she had fired the first shot, but Gates fired the next three from the window and that Gates took the body and burned it.

Mary Druse was sentenced to life in prison, but was pardoned after ten years. She claimed that her mother had never told the whole story.

A book entitled *An Innocent Woman Hanged* was published sometime after the execution—author and publication date uncertain—which quotes Mary as blaming the entire murder on her uncle, Charles Gates. Roxalana Druse, she said, had gone to the gallows innocent, to protect her brother-in-law.

James Fisk, Jr

16.   THE FISK ASSASSINATION

"Jubilee" Jim Fisk was the consummate Gilded Age robber baron Together with his partner Jay Gould, Fisk managed to wrest the Erie Railroad from Cornelius Vanderbilt, and by attempting to corner the gold market, triggered the 1869 financial panic known as "Black Friday." But unlike his dour partner, Jim Fisk lived a personal life as large and extravagant as his business dealings. Everything he had or did had to be the biggest and best, so when Fisk cheated on his wife, it was with the most beautiful woman in America. When that relationship turned scandalous,

THE MURDER OF JAMES FISK

it was an epic scandal filled with blackmail, courtroom drama, and finally murder.

Date: January 6, 1872

Location: New York, New York

Victim: James Fisk Jr.

Cause of Death: Gunshot

Accused: Edward S. Stokes

Synopsis:

The life of James Fisk Jr. is a true American success story. He was born in a small Vermont town in 1835 and quit school at twelve to assist his father as a travelling peddler, selling housewares and notions. At fifteen he left that occupation to join Van Amberg's Mammoth Circus and Menagerie. At eighteen he left the circus and applied the showmanship he had learned to the peddling business and by age twenty-one, he was running five wagons throughout New England. He made his first fortune working for Jordan Marsh, providing textiles to the army during the Civil War. Then he discovered the stock market.

He learned the tricks of the trade from Daniel Drew, who was a master at manipulating stock prices. Fisk teamed up with Drew and Jay Gould for the "Erie War"—a fight to keep Cornelius Vanderbilt from gaining control of the Erie Railroad. Fisk and his partners won by continually issuing fraudulent Erie stock, unbeknownst to Vanderbilt, until Vanderbilt finally conceded. The Erie Railroad became the center of Fisk's operations.

In 1867, while deeply involved in the "Erie War," Jim Fisk met the woman who would change his life. While on a visit to the notorious Manhattan bordello of Annie Wood, he was introduced to Helen Josephine "Josie" Mansfield. She was an unemployed actress, a friend of Miss Wood, and clearly not one of her prostitutes. At the time Josie only owned one passable dress and her rent was hopelessly overdue. Though Jim Fisk had a wife back in Vermont, he was smitten by the poor girl and was pleased to pay her rent and provide her with finery.

Josie Mansfield was considered extraordinarily beautiful, a fact that she discovered early in life and had always used to her advantage. As one historian put it, "Perhaps a colder disgrace to her sex has never helped to ruin man since the world began."

She was born in Boston, but when she was around ten years old, the family moved to Stockton, California. Soon after, her father was killed in a duel over a political matter and her mother remarried a man named Warren. As Josie was growing up, she earned the reputation as an incorrigible flirt. She caught the eye of a middle-aged attorney named D. W. Perley, and Warren had to chase him away twice, with a pistol to his head. The matter became something of a scandal, but Josie would later say she was being used by her parents in a blackmail plot.

She married a wandering actor named Frank Lawler. The marriage had been Josie's idea, Lawler said. "Finally I did marry her to save her from the evil influence of her own parents," he said.

The couple drifted east, but Josie began to stray. They divorced after two years.

After meeting Jim Fisk, Josie gave up any attempt at acting. By 1870 she was living in a four-story house on Twenty-Fourth Street that Jim had given her along with an extensive wardrobe, fine jewelry, and virtually anything else she wanted.

The summer of 1869, Fisk met Edward S. "Ned" Stokes. Stokes was a handsome, athletic young man from a good family, but it was his less attractive side that Fisk was drawn to. Stokes was a gambler and a horseman who divided his time between racetracks and saloons. He was a flashy dresser who liked be the center of attention, much like Jim Fisk himself, except that Stokes spent money at a faster rate than he could make it. Stokes's mother owned an oil refinery in Brooklyn that had been closed for several years. Fisk and Stokes formed a company to reopen in, with Fisk providing the capital and discounted freight rates on the Erie Railroad for transferring oil. Stokes treated the treasury as his personal account.

On New Year's Day, 1870, Josie Mansfield hosted an open house with an ample punch bowl and people were coming and going all day. Fisk invited Ned Stokes to join him at the party and there introduced him to Josie. As they chatted around the punchbowl, people commented on what a handsome couple Josie and Ned made. At the time it pleased Fisk to see them together—his sweetheart and his bosom friend.

Not long after that, Ned Stokes began paying call on Josie Mansfield and the relationship soon became a full-blown love affair. When Fisk found out, he sent a letter to Josie to find out where matters stood. She responded by accusing him of seeing actresses behind her back—a rumor that was circulating Manhattan at the time. This initiated a long series of letters between Jim and Josie that were, on both sides, sometimes accusatory, sometimes loving.

Fisk confronted Stokes, asking him to leave Josie alone.

"Ask me anything else, Jim," he replied. "Anything else in the world, I'll do; but I can't keep away from Josie. I love her—and she loves me!"

Fisk thought he could handle the matter as if it were a business deal. He proposed they ask Josie to settle things once and for all by deciding which of them she wanted. Josie's response was, "I don't see why we can't all three be friends."

To which Jim replied, "No, Josie, it won't do. You can't run two engines on the same track in contrary directions at the same time."

As far as Fisk was concerned, Josie had chosen Ned Stokes, but Josie continued to ask Fisk for money. She claimed that he had told her he was holding $25,000 in trust for her and she wanted it all. He refused this request, but agreed to pay any bills incurred up until five minutes to eleven o'clock three weeks prior—the time she had formally refused him. When he received her bills, some had been obviously backdated. He paid them anyway, and several after, but his relationship with Josie had taken a legalistic turn.

Fisk and Stokes began to fight over the refinery. Stokes demanded $200,000 or he would release Fisk's letters to Josie to the press. Fisk refused, though he desperately wanted the letters back. The refinery matter went to arbitration and Stokes surrendering his stock for $15,000 in addition to the money he had already stolen. As part of the settlement, Fisk's attorney took custody of the letters.

The $15,000 did not last Ned Stokes very long, and he sued Fisk for $200,000 in refinery profits he claimed he was owed. He also requested the letters back, declaring they would prove his claim. The Fisk-Mansfield letters were now the talk of the town. The press speculated that they were not merely love letters but contained evidence of Fisk's shady business practices. Fisk's friends, who knew the letters would do no more damage than had already been done, tried to persuade him to publish the letters himself and defuse Stokes's threats. Fisk came close to agreeing but refused, not wanting his soul splashed across the daily newspaper.

The judge dismissed Stokes's claim and stated that the status of the letters had already been decided. After the verdict Stokes was drowning his sorrows at Delmonico's when he heard the follow-up news—Fisk had filed a suit of his own charging Stokes and Mansfield with blackmail. It was more than Ned Stokes could stand, and he went looking for Fisk. He learned that Fisk was on his way to the Grand Central Hotel and he knew that Fisk always entered by the ladies entrance, so Stokes went in first and waited on the second-floor landing. When he heard Fisk climbing the stairs, Stokes started down, saying, "Now I've got you." Stokes fired two shots at Fisk with a Colt pistol, one to the abdomen and one to the left arm. Stokes tried to flee but was captured. Fisk lived long enough to identify his killer before dying from the abdominal wound. Jim Fisk was thirty-six years old.

Trials: June 19, 1872
December 18, 1872
October 6, 1873

Awaiting trial, Stokes was put on Murderer's Row in Manhattan's Tombs Prison. At the time, for men of means, prison meant confinement but not necessarily hardship. A prisoner could have whatever lifestyle he could afford. Stokes had a carpet on the floor, had his meals brought in from Delmonico's and had bottles of scented water for bathing. He met with reporters wearing a ruffled shirt with diamond studs.

At his trial, Stokes's defense was multipronged: he claimed, by turns, that he had shot out of self-defense, that he had been driven insane by Fisk's persecution, that the doctors' extensive probing had done more damage than his bullets, or that Fisk was killed by the morphine given to him by the doctors. The trial resulted in a hung jury—at least one juror was suspected of being bribed.

At his second trial, Stokes was convicted of first-degree murder and sentenced to be hanged, but the verdict was overturned on appeal. In his third trial, Stokes was found guilty of manslaughter and sentenced to six years at Sing Sing Prison.

"Had Stokes been an illiterate laborer," Edmund Stedman commented, "he would have dangled in a noose two months later."

Verdicts: Hung Jury
                      Guilty of first-degree murder; overturned on appeal
                      Guilty of manslaughter

Aftermath:

Jubilee Jim Fisk lay in state for a day at the Grand Opera House, a theatre that he had owned and managed. More than 20,000 people passed by to pay their respects and more than a 100,000 more stood in the street. The body was taken by train to Brattleboro, Vermont; at every station crowds gathered to watch the train go by. In Brattleboro he lay in state one more day before being lowered into the ground.

Jim Fisk's flamboyant personality was sadly missed in New York. Though in life his business practices and personal morals had been criticized from pulpit and podium, and his market manipulations had directly or indirectly harmed much of the population, Fisk was remembered at his death for his acts of charity—most notably sending a trainload of supplies to the victims of the Great Chicago Fire of 1871. In song and story, Jim Fisk became a lovable rogue and a friend to the workingman.

Thirty-nine letters from Jim Fisk to Josie Mansfield were published in the New York Herald one week after Jim Fisk's death. To the dismay of scandal mongers, they contained no insight into his business dealings, just evidence of his love for Josie and his jealousy of Ned Stokes.

Josie Mansfield left New York for Paris, France, where she married Robert L. Read, an expatriate American lawyer. When he died she moved to Boston, then in 1899, in failing health, to Philadelphia to live with her sister. In 1909, in dire poverty, she moved with a brother to Watertown, South Dakota. Somehow she returned to Paris, where she lived for many years. Josie died in 1931 at the American Hospital in Paris.

Ballad:

"Jim Fisk, or, He Never Went Back on the Poor" published in 1874 was written and composed by a Fisk supporter known only as J.S.

Jim Fisk, or, He Never Went Back on the Poor.

*1. If you'll listen awhile I'll sing you a song
About this glorious land of the free,
And the difference I'll show twixt the rich and the poor
In a trial by jury, you see.*

*If you've plenty of "stamps" you can hold up your head
And walk out from your own prison door.
But they'll hang you up high if you've no friends or gold,
Let the "rich" go but hang up the poor.*

*In the trials for murder we've had now-a-days
The rich ones get off swift and sure.
While they've thousands to pay to the jury and judge,
You can bet they'll go back on the poor.*

*2. Let me speak of a man who's now dead in his grave,
A good man as ever was born.
Jim Fisk he was called and his money he gave
To the outcast, the poor and forlorn.*

*We all know he loved both women and wine,
But his heart it was right, I am sure.
Though he lived like a "prince" in a palace so fine,
Yet he never went back on the poor.*

*If a man was in trouble, Fisk helped him along
To drive the "grim wolf" from the door.
He strove to do right, though he may have done wrong,
But he never went back on the poor.*

*3. Jim Fisk was a man who wore "his heart on his sleeve."
No matter what people would say,
And he did all his deeds, (both the good and the bad)
In the broad open light of the day.*

With his grand six-in-hand on the beach at Long Branch
He cut a "big dash," to be sure.
But "Chicago's great fire" showed the world that Jim Fisk
With his "wealth" still remembered the poor.

When the telegram came that the homeless that night
Were starving to death, slow but sure,
His "Lightning Express" manned by noble Jim Fisk
Flew to feed all her hungry and poor.

4. Now what do you think of this trial of Stokes,
Who murdered this friend of the poor?
When such men get free, is there anyone safe
If they step from outside their own door?

Is there one law for the poor and one for the rich?
It seems so ---at least so I say---
If they hang up the poor, why ---damn it--- the rich
Ought to hang up the very same way.

Don't show any favor to friend or to foe,
The beggar or prince at his door.
The big millionaire you must hang up also
But never go back on the poor.

Laura Foster

17.   HANG DOWN YOUR HEAD TOM DULA

The stories behind murder ballads are never as pretty as the songs. The story behind "Tom Dooley"—the 1866 murder of Laura Foster by Tom Dula in Elkville, North Carolina—is particularly ugly. Tom Dula was having an affair with Mrs. Ann Foster Melton and when her cousin Pauline Foster came to work at the Melton home, Tom Dula took her to bed as well. Another cousin, Laura Foster, came to

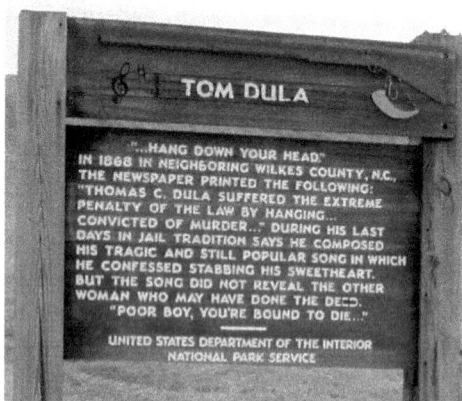

HISTORICAL MARKER, BLUE RIDGE PARKWAY, NC

town and Tom had her, too. One member of this group contracted syphilis and soon they were all infected. Tom Dula blamed Laura Foster and soon after, her body was found in a shallow grave and Tom Dula had left for Tennessee. Might have gotten away if it "hadn't been for Grayson."

Date: June 18, 1866

Location: Elkville, North Carolina

Victim: Laura Foster

Cause of Death: Stabbing

Accused: Tom Dula

Synopsis:

A good storyteller never lets the facts get in the way. When an event is preserved in song and story, the tale will change at the whim of the teller. The sordid tale of Laura Foster's murder in 1866 has changed through more than 140 years of telling to the point where those involved would hardly recognize it. Mythical villains have emerged, love triangles have sprung from thin air, and vengeance and cowardice have been recast as honor.

78

In the traditional story, Laura Foster was a beautiful young girl with blue eyes and chestnut hair who was being courted by Bob Cummings (some say Bob Grayson), a Yankee schoolteacher. When Laura met Tom Dula, a tall, handsome Confederate soldier returning from the war, she instantly fell in love. Ann Melton also fell in love with Tom Dula. She was a wealthy, married woman who was even more beautiful than Laura. Ann Melton stabbed Laura Foster to death out of jealousy and Tom Dula was blamed. Dula was hunted relentlessly, with Cummings in the lead. He was captured and brought to trial. A witness who could have provided an alibi for Dula was paid by Cummings not to testify. Tom Dula was found guilty and sentenced to hang. Before his execution he confessed to the murder and exonerated Ann Melton. Years later when Ann Melton died, people heard the sizzling of cooking meat and saw a black cat climb the wall as the devil came to take her to hell.

That's the storyteller's version, but newspapers and the transcripts of Tom Dula's trials tell a different tale.

The section of North Carolina known as Happy Valley was marked by sharp class distinctions in the 1860s. The town of Elkville and the fertile lands along the Yadkin River were home to merchants and gentleman farmers. But in the ridges of the mountains, a lower class of people lived in squalid cabins on subsistence farms. In an 1868 article, the *New York Herald* described conditions there: "A state of immorality unexemplified in the history of any country exists among these people, and such a general system of freeloveism prevails that it is 'a wise child that knows its father.'"

Tom Dula was born and raised in these mountains and became sexually active at a tender age. Ann Foster married James Melton, a successful cobbler, when she was fourteen or fifteen. Almost immediately she began an affair with Tom Dula, who was about the same age as she was. At age seventeen Tom joined the 42nd Regiment North Carolina Infantry (not 26th Regiment, as is sometimes reported) and fought for the Confederacy in the Civil War. When he returned from the war, he picked up his relationship with Ann Melton where it had left off. James Melton, who no longer slept with his wife, didn't seem to mind when Tom shared his wife's bed in their one-room cabin.

There were three beds in the Melton cabin. The third was occupied by Pauline Foster, a distant cousin of Ann's who was hired to do house and farm work. Tom would sometimes share her bed as well, and sometimes Ann, Pauline, and Tom would all sleep together. Unbeknownst to Tom and the Meltons, Pauline Foster had come to Elkville seeking treatment for syphilis.

In March of 1866, when Tom Dula was twenty-one, he began to visit Laura Foster, another cousin of Ann Melton, about the same age, who lived with her father, Wilson Foster. Laura was described by the newspaper as "frail but beautiful." She had large front teeth with a large gap between them. Laura had been with many men, but there is no record of a Bob Cummings or a schoolteacher of any name courting her.

Tom Dula frequently spent the night with Laura in her father's house and though Wilson Foster was well aware of this, it didn't seem to bother him. Not long after he started seeing Laura, Tom went to Dr. George N. Carter in Elkville and was diagnosed with syphilis. Tom blamed the disease on Laura Foster and told a friend that he intended to "put through" the woman who gave it to him.

The date of Laura Foster's disappearance is uncertain—three separate trials recorded three different dates—but from trial testimony, it can be deduced that the date was Friday, May 25, 1866. When Wilson Foster woke up that morning, his daughter was gone and so was the mare he kept tied to a tree. The following day the mare returned to Foster's cabin alone. It was assumed that Laura had died, and men in the community spent weeks looking for her body. On June 24, in a spot in the woods near Tom Dula's place, they found the rope used to tie the mare to a tree and a spot on the ground presumed to be blood.

As rumors began to spread that Tom Dula had killed Laura Foster, Tom left for Tennessee. Around the same time, Pauline Foster also went to Tennessee for some undisclosed reason. When she returned, a friend said she must have gone because she killed Laura Foster. Jokingly Pauline replied, "Yes, I and Dula killed her, and I ran away to Tennessee." Two or three weeks after the remark, Pauline was arrested as an accessory to murder and taken to Wilkesboro Jail. Pauline decided to tell all she knew. She said that Tom Dula and Ann Melton had killed Laura Foster and on September 1, she led a search party to a spot Ann Melton had pointed out as the place they buried Laura. At the spot, one of the horses snorted at a foul order coming out of the ground. The men dug there and found a woman's body, badly decomposed but identified as Laura Foster by the dress she wore and the gap in her teeth. She had been stabbed through the ribs under the left breast.

In Tennessee, Tom Dula had already been captured. He had changed his name to Hall and was working as a farmhand for Col. James Grayson when deputies from Wilkes County, North Carolina, came to arrest him. Dula had left Grayson's farm by the time deputies arrived. After hearing the story, Col. Grayson joined the deputies in the search for Tom Dula. They caught up with him in Pandora, Tennessee, and Col. Grayson persuaded him to surrender. He spent the night under guard at Grayson's farm before being taken back to Elkville.

Trials: October 1, 1866
            January 20, 1868

In a move that surprised everyone involved, Tom Dula's defense was handled, pro bono, by Zebulon B. Vance, former governor of North Carolina and colonel of the 26th North Carolina Regiment, who fought valiantly for the Confederacy. Tom Dula is often incorrectly identified as a member of the 26th Regiment—an attempt to explain why Governor Vance took the case.

The trial opened in Wilkesboro, North Carolina, on October 1, 1866. The defense requested a severance—that Tom Dula and Ann Melton be tried separately—and also requested a change of venue. Both were granted and Dula's trial was moved to Statesville, North Carolina.

The case against Tom Dula was circumstantial but compelling. All of the dirty laundry was aired, the promiscuity, the syphilis, and the threats made by Tom against Laura Foster. While there were many witnesses who testified on each of these aspects, the most damaging testimony came from Pauline Foster, who held nothing back.

Tom Dula was found guilty of murder, but the verdict was thrown out on appeal due to some irregularities in the admission of testimony.

The second trial was delayed twice as each side was granted a continuance when witnesses did not appear. To end the delay, a special court of Oyer and Terminer was convened in Statesville on January 20, 1868. Once again Tom Dula was found guilty of murder. This verdict was appealed as well, but the appeal was declined. Dula was sentenced to death.

Verdicts: Guilty of murder; overturned on appeal
            Guilty of murder

Aftermath:

On May 1, 1868, Tom Dula was taken to the old depot in Statesville to a makeshift gallows, with a cart as a scaffold. According to the *New York Herald*, he spoke for nearly an hour about his childhood, about politics, and about all the people who had perjured themselves at his trials, but he did not confess to the crime or exonerate Ann Melton. Allegedly, his last words were, "You have such a nice, clean rope, I ought to have washed my neck."

Gov. Mike Easley of North Carolina received a request, on January 9, 2009, his last day in office, from the Wilkes County newspaper, The Record, and the Wilkes Playmakers, a theatre group performing a play about the murder, to pardon Tom Dula posthumously. The group claimed that Laura Foster was pregnant when she died and Tom Dula was planning to marry her. Their request was denied.

Ballad:

The legend says that Tom Dula rode to his execution in a wagon, sitting atop his coffin, playing the banjo and writing a song about the murder. There is no evidence that Tom Dula ever played banjo, but several people testified that he made one trip to the Melton cabin specifically to retrieve his fiddle. It is unlikely that Tom Dula wrote the song we know as "Tom Dooley," but its true origins remain unknown. The song was recorded by several artists before the Kingston Trio, whose version of "Tom Dooley" reached number one on the *Billboard* charts on November 22, 1958.

Tom Dooley

Chorus:
Hang down your head, Tom Dooley
Hang down your head and cry
Killed poor Laura Foster
You know you're bound to die

You took her on the hillside, as God almighty knows
You took her on the hillside and there you hid her clothes

You took her by the roadside where you begged to be excused
You took her by the roadside where there you hid her shoes

Chorus

You took her on the hillside to make her your wife
You took her on the hillside where there you took her life

Chorus

Take down my old violin and play it as you please
At this time tomorrow, it'll be no use to me

Chorus

I dug a grave four foot long, I dug it three feet deep
And throwed the cold clay o'er her and tramped it with my feet

Chorus:

This world and one more then where do you reckon I'd be
If it hadn't been for Grayson, I'd a-been in Tennessee

Delia Green

18.   DELIA'S GONE, ONE MORE ROUND

On Christmas Eve 1900, Cooney Houston shot and killed Delia Green. If that isn't tragic enough, they were both just fourteen years old. Their sad story would have been long forgotten, even in Yamacraw—the African American neighborhood in the western end of Savannah, Georgia, where the killing took place—if it hadn't been for a song. The ballad of Delia's murder traveled from Georgia to the Bahamas, then back to the States during the folk boom of the 1950s. Though the facts have been altered along the way, Delia's story has been sung by generations of folk singers, and has been recorded by musical icons such as Bob Dylan and Johnny Cash.

SAVANNAH, GA

Date: December 24, 1900

Location: Savannah, Georgia

Victim: Delia Green

Cause of Death: Gunshot

Accused: Moses "Cooney" Houston

Synopsis:

The facts of Delia Green's murder, sketchy as they are, were uncovered by folklorist Robert Winslow Gordon—who collected twenty-eight versions of the murder song—and later by ballad expert John Garst. They traced the location to Yamacraw, a black section of Savannah, Georgia, and the date to December 24, 1900 (at the tail end of the nineteenth century). From newspaper accounts and trial transcripts, they reconstructed the events of that night.

Delia Green and Moses "Cooney" Houston were at a Christmas Eve party at the home of Willie West, where Delia worked as a scrub girl. Delia and Cooney had been going together for several months and, though they both were only fourteen years old, the relationship was probably sexual. That night they were fighting; Cooney was very drunk and started teasing Delia. According to trial transcripts, this is what transpired between them (as printed in *The Rose and the Briar*):

> Cooney: "My little wife is mad with me tonight. She does not hear me. She is not saying anything to me. (To Delia:) You don't know how I love you."
> This was followed by mutual cursing.
> Delia: "You son of a bitch. You have been going with me for four months. You know I am a lady."
> Cooney: "That is a damn lie. You know I have had you as many times as I have fingers and toes."
> Delia: "You lie!"

Delia, angry at being characterized as Cooney's wife, called him a son of a bitch, an epithet that carried much more weight in 1900 than it does today. At this point Willie West told Cooney to leave. As he was approaching the door, Cooney pulled out a pistol and shot Delia in the groin.

Cooney fled the scene, but Willie West chased after and caught him. West turned him over to police patrolman J. T. Williams, who later testified that Cooney confessed to shooting Delia because she called him a son of a bitch. He said he shot her and he would do it again.

Trial: Spring 1901

Cooney Houston appeared in court wearing short pants; no doubt attempting to emphasize his youth. Georgia had no juvenile justice system in 1901, so Houston was tried as an adult.

In court he told a different story than the one he told Officer Williams. He claimed that Willie West had sent him to retrieve a pistol from the repair shop. He brought the pistol to the house and put it on the table under a napkin. Later he and a friend, Eddie Cohen, got into a friendly tussle over the gun and it went off accidently, killing Delia. Cohen testified that he was not there at the time of the murder and that he never struggled with Houston over the gun.

No one believed Cooney Huston's story, and the jury found him guilty but recommended mercy. Judge Paul F. Seabrook sentenced him to life in prison instead of death.

Verdict: Guilty

Aftermath:

Moses "Cooney" Houston was paroled on October 15, 1913, by order of Governor John Slaton, after serving just over twelve years of his life sentence. He continued to have trouble with the law. Allegedly, he moved to New York City, where he died in 1927.

Ballad:

The song of Delia's murder—authorship unknown—took on a life of its own. Each singer had his own rendition of the song, but there are two major versions: "Delia" recorded by Georgia blues singer Blind Willie McTell in the 1920s, and "Delia's Gone" recorded by Alphonso "Blind Blake" Higgs (not to be confused with ragtime guitarist Blind Arthur Blake)

In McTell's version the singer laments that "she's all I've got, is gone" and blames Delia's demise on associating with gamblers. "Blind Blake" Higgs, who also introduced "Sloop John B" to the United States, claimed authorship of "Delia's Gone." More likely it was brought to the Bahamas by sailors coming from Georgia. In any case, the Higgs version, with the memorable line "Delia's gone, one more round, Delia's gone," captured the imagination of American folk singers and was recorded by Pete Seeger, Bob Dylan, and others.

In each version, the story deviates more from the facts. The killer is no longer Cooney, but Curly or Tony, and he shoots her more than once. The most extreme deviation from the facts occurs in Johnny Cash's version where the killer ties Delia to a chair and shoots her with his "sub-mo-chine."

This is the Alphonso Higgs version.

Delia's Gone

Now Delia cursed Tony
Twas on one Saturday night.
And she cursed him such a wicked curse,
That he swear to take her life.
Delia's Gone one more round, Delias gone.

86

First time Tony shot Delia
He show her right in her side.
The second time he shot her,
She gave up the ghost and died.
Delia's Gone one more round, Delias gone.

The reason why Tony shot Delia
Because she cursed him a wicked curse
And if Tony hadn't shot lil Delia,
She might have cursed him worse.
Delia's Gone one more round, Delias gone.

Now Delia's friend is in prison
Drinking out the silver cup
Whilest Delia she lying in the grave
Fighting her level best to get up
Delia's Gone one more round, Delias gone.

On Monday Tony was arrested
On Tuesday his case was tried
The juryman brought him down guilty
He began to rollin his goo-goo eyes
Delia's Gone one more round, Delias gone.

A rubber tire buggy
A double seated hack
Took little Delia to the graveyard
And they never brought her back
Delia's Gone one more round, Delias gone.

I went down to the graveyard
Just to look in my dDelia's face
I said "Delia girl, you know I love you"
But I just couldn't take your place."
Delia's Gone one more round, Delias gone.

Jailor, Oh Jailor!
Tony said, How can I sleep?
When all around my bed-side,
I can hear little Delia's feet?
Delia's Gone one more round, Delias gone.

The man that shot my Delia
He was riding on a wheel,
He rode that wheel so mighty fast
They think it was an automobile
Delia's Gone one more round, Delias gone.

Some give Delia a nickel
Some give Delia a dime,
I didn't give her one red cent
Because she wasn't a gal of mine
Delia's Gone one more round, Delias gone.

Sixty four years in prison
Tony told the judge that aint no time
He said my younger brother's in the penitentiary
Servin nine hundred ninety and nine.
Delia's Gone one more round, Delias gone.

Mary Ann Wyatt Green

19. THE ARSENIC TRAGEDY

GREEN ADMINISTERING POISON TO HIS BRIDE

A troupe of temperance players who visited the town of Berlin, New York, in December 1844 had a profound effect on Henry G. Green. It was not their message of sobriety that moved Henry, but the charm and beauty of their leading lady, Mary Ann Wyatt. When the troupe left Berlin, Henry followed and soon began a whirlwind courtship of Mary Ann and on February 10, they were married. Eight days after that, Mary Ann Wyatt Green was dead from arsenic poisoning. There is little doubt that Henry Green murdered his wife, but his motive in doing so is an enduring mystery.

Date: February 18, 1845

Location: Berlin, New York

Victim: Mary Ann Wyatt Green

Cause of Death: Poisoning

Accused: Henry G. Green

Synopsis:

Mary Ann Wyatt was born in Thornton, New Hampshire, in 1822. When she was eighteen, she left home with her brother David to work in the mills in Lowell, Massachusetts. They worked in Lowell for three years, then in 1843, they joined a travelling company of temperance players performing a play called *The Reformed Drunkard*—probably a pirated version of the popular play, *The Drunkard*, later produced by P. T. Barnum.

Henry Green saw them perform during a three-night engagement in Berlin, New York, that opened on December 30. He saw them again in early January in New Lebanon, New York, where Henry and another young man from Berlin decided to join the acting company.

Henry G. Green was the same age as Mary Ann Wyatt. He was from a prominent family that had lived in Rensselaer County for several generations. In 1842 he opened a store in Berlin and around the same time he had been publicly reprimanded and expelled from the Baptist Church for intoxication. His business faltered and in the fall of 1844, a suspicious fire destroyed the store and although Green collected insurance on the store, rumors of arson persisted. During this period he had been courting a woman named Alzina Godfrey who refused Green's proposal of marriage. He joined the temperance players soon after, looking for a new start.

At first Green just sang in the chorus, but soon he had an acting role. He was also making progress winning the affections of Mary Anne Wyatt and came to replace her brother David as Mary Ann's source of strength.

The performing company was not doing well financially and after an engagement in Kinderhook, New York, they disbanded. Henry and Mary Ann decided to marry and return to Berlin. Henry and David went to Berlin to prepare for the wedding while Mary Ann waited in Stephentown. The date was set for February 17, and Henry invited all of his friends, including Alzina Godfrey. On February 10, Henry went back to Stephentown to see Mary Ann, and there and then, despite the wedding plans, Henry Green and Mary Ann Wyatt were married.

The following Tuesday the bride and groom traveled to Berlin and took up residence at a rooming house run by Mr. and Mrs. Ferdinand Hull. On Wednesday Henry Green's mother and sister arrived from Troy, New York, and stayed at the Dennison and Streeter Tavern across the street from Hull's. She sent a message for her son to meet her in the parlor of the tavern and there she and her daughter had a long discussion with Henry. According to Polly Ann Boone, maid at the tavern, she overheard Henry's mother making derogatory remarks about Mary Ann's character, saying she had not been virtuous in Troy, where she had performed before coming to

Berlin. Mrs. Green did not think Mary Ann Wyatt was fit to be her son's wife, and she did not cross the street to meet her new daughter-in-law.

On Thursday Henry organized a sleigh ride for his friends to make up for the missed wedding. Alzina Godfrey was along on the ride and reportedly said to Henry, "Why did you marry Mary? I would have married you in the end."

Mary Ann caught cold on the sleigh ride and stayed in bed on Friday as Henry began to treat her. He first persuaded her to take six pills that had been prescribed for him by Dr. Rhodes. They allegedly contained opium to comfort her. On Saturday he was with some friends at Dennison and Streeter's, which was a grocery store as well as a tavern. Henry exclaimed that he had seen a mouse on one of the shelves and asked Dennison why he did not put out arsenic to kill the mice. A conversation ensued as to the danger of arsenic, and it was later alleged that Henry had stolen some arsenic from Dennison and Streeter.

Later that day Henry prepared a solution for Mary Ann and told her it was soda. Henry left again and Mrs. Hull found Mary Ann vomiting and apparently at the brink of death. She sent for Dr. Ferdinand Hull, who recommended that her stomach be rinsed with hot water. Henry objected to this and obstructed every treatment the doctor ordered. Mary Ann's condition continued to worsen and Henry was seen several times giving her powders not prescribed by the doctor. He gave her crust coffee—a drink made from toasted bread crust and water—which Mary Ann complained did not taste right. He gave her a white solution he claimed was cream of tartar. Mrs. Hull and other boarders caring for Mary Ann saw Henry taint wine and soup with white powder. They managed to secure some of the powder and it was later determined to be arsenic.

On Saturday night David Wyatt asked Dr. Hull about his sister's condition and he was told that she would soon die. David went to his sister and said, "Mary, the doctor thinks you can't live."

Mary Ann then called Henry to her bedside. She asked him if she had ever deceived him in any respect and if she had ever done anything to injure his feelings. He answered no to both questions. She told Dr. Hull she knew she was about to die and told him about everything Henry had administered to her. Dr. Hull had her repeat the information to the authorities. Her condition worsened to the point where she could no longer speak and at 10:00 a.m. Monday morning, she died.

A coroner's inquest was held and a postmortem examination proved that Mary Ann had died of arsenic poisoning. Henry Green was arrested for the murder of his wife.

Trial: July 7, 1845

Henry G. Green was tried before Judge A. J. Parker in the court of Oyer and Terminer of Rensselaer County. The testimony of Doctor Hull and all of those who cared for or observed Mary Ann Wyatt Green on her deathbed formed a very strong case of circumstantial evidence against Henry Green. The defense could offer little more than character witnesses for their client. The jury returned a verdict of guilty.

Henry Green was asked if he had anything to say why the judgment of law should not be pronounced. Green said faintly, "Not guilty." To which Judge Parker replied:

> *That is adding nothing to what has been said before. That plea was put in for you by your counsel, and the issue has been tried with every advantage on your part. You have had the advantage of very distinguished counsel whose endeavors have been unremitting to secure your acquittal. You have had the aid of rich and powerful friends—friends of high respectability and character, who have secured you every opportunity of presenting your whole case to the jury fully and fairly…Your case, in all its aspects, exceeds in enormity any of which I have ever heard. It will no doubt stand out on the page of history as the most criminal, awful case of murder that ever came before a court and jury.*

Henry Green was sentenced to hang on September 10, 1845.

Verdict: Guilty of murder

Aftermath:

Though an appeal was denied, Henry Green's "rich and powerful friends" worked very hard to pressure Governor Silas Wright for executive clemency. They called Green insane; they requested time for the legislature to change the murder laws; they requested time for Green to adequately prepare for death. Henry Green was so sure that he would be reprieved that in August, he helped his cellmate escape from the Troy jail but did not escape himself.

In the end, the governor refused all of the requests and on September 10, Green was hanged. It was a private hanging with only fifty spectators, but outside the jail yard, thousands of people had gathered for the event. Five days after the hanging, Henry Green's confession was published. In it he exonerated his mother and Alzina Godfrey but offered little to explain why he had murdered his wife.

The murder of Mary Anne Wyatt Green greatly affected the community of Berlin, New York. A monument was erected in her honor with this inscription:

> *This monument is erected by the Citizens of Berlin in memory of Mary Ann Wyatt, wife of Henry G. Green, who was married Feb. 9, 1845 and on the 14th day of the same month was poisoned by her husband with arsenic without any real or pretended cause.*
>
> *Beautiful, intelligent, and virtuous, she was wept over by the community, and the violated law justly exacted the life of her murderer as a penalty for his crime.*

One more bit of folklore: Around 1885 Mary Ann Wyatt's body was exhumed to make room for building lots. When her coffin was brought to the surface, it broke open revealing a white skeleton in rotted clothing. Over the head and shoulders was a cascade of beautiful auburn hair, visible only for a moment before a gust of wind "shattered it to nothingness."

Ballad:

The murder inspired a number of ballads. As Olive Woolley Burt said in *American Murder Ballads and Their Stories*:

> *This case had everything a balladeer could ask for: a rich young man, a beautiful bride, passion, jealousy, married bliss, and tragedy. Practically everyone who could make a rhyme, it seems, composed verses about the crime*

There are at least seven known version of this story in song, with titles such as "The Arsenic Tragedy, "The Berlin Murder Case," "The Murder of Miss Wyatt," and "The Murdered Wife or the Case of Henry G. Green."

The Arsenic Tragedy

> *Come listen to my tragedy, good people young and old,*
> *It's of a dreadful story to you I will unfold*
> *Concerning a fair damsel, Miss Wires was her name,*
> *She was murdered by her husband, and he hung for the same.*
>
> *Young Mary, she was beautiful, not of a high degree;*
> *Young Henry Green was wealthy, I'd have you plainly see*
> *And he says, "My dearest Mary, if you will be my wife,*

I'll guard, guide and protect you all through this gloomy life."

"Oh Henry, dearest Henry, I fear that never could be
For you have rich relations, I've none so rich as you,
And when your parents come to know, they'd scorn me from their door;
I'd rather you marry some other girl with wealth laid up in store.

"Oh Mary, dearest Mary, why doth torment me so?
"Oh Mary, dearest Mary, why doth torment me so?
For just as long as you deny, so quick I'll end my life,
For I no longer wish to live, unless you be my wife."

So there, believing all he said was true, she then became his wife
But little did she think or know he meant to take her life:
Little did she think or know, or little did she expect
He meant to give her arsenic, the just one to protect.

They hadn't been married scarce three weeks when she was taken ill
Great doctors, they were sent for, all for to try their skill
The doctors came from far and near, but her they could not save,
So then it was pronounced by all she must go to the grave.

Her brother, hearing of the news, straightway to her did go,
Saying, "Sister dear, you're dying, the doctors tell me so;
Now sister, since you're dying and on your bed of death,
Pray, haven't you been poisoned by him you thought your love?"

"Oh brother, I know I'm dying and on my bed of death;
"Oh brother, I know I'm dying and on my bed of death;
Young Henry Green has poisoned me, dear brother, for him send,
For I do love him just as well as when he was my friend."

When Henry got these tidings, he went his wife to see;
She says, "Dearest Henry, was you ever deceived by me?"
Three times she cried, "Dear Henry!" and sank into a tomb;
He gazed on her indifferent ways and silent left the room.

Now he is took to the bloody hills and led upon the stand
To answer for the blackest crime committed in our land,
But he says, "I am not guilty, her friends I do deny;
I am not guilty of the crime for that which I die."

Helen Jewett

20.   THE GIRL IN GREEN

The New York City newspapers referred to her as "the girl in green"—green was her color and it caught reporters' eyes. Twenty-three-year-old Helen Jewett was a beautiful, intelligent, sophisticated prostitute at Rosina Townsend's upscale brothel not far from New York's city hall. Her clients included politicians, lawyers, journalists, and wealthy merchants. One cold April night in 1836, one of them smashed her skull with an axe and set her bed on fire. It was the story that shocked New York and gave birth to a new genre of sensational journalism.

HELEN JEWETT

Date: April 9, 1836

Location: New York, New York

Victim: Helen Jewett

Cause of Death: Blows from an axe

Accused: Richard P. Robinson

Synopsis:

For women in the nineteenth century, prostitution was a last resort when poverty, shame, or abandonment left them with nowhere to turn. But for Helen Jewett, it was a true calling, and she embraced it with enthusiasm.

She was born Dorcas Doyen in 1814 in Temple, Maine, daughter of a poor shoemaker. Her mother died when Dorcas was a young girl and when her father remarried; he put his daughter out to service as a maid. At age thirteen, she secured a position in the Augusta, Maine, home of Nathan

Weston, chief justice of the Maine Supreme Judicial Court. By arrangement, she was to work there as a servant until her eighteenth birthday, and the Westons agreed to raise her almost as if she were their own child. The work was hard, but it was a tremendous opportunity for a bright young girl to learn culture and civility. She was also given access to Judge Weston's library, where she became a voracious reader, especially fond of novels.

When she was sixteen or seventeen, Dorcas became sexually active. The details of her seduction are not clear, but the act appears to have been consensual and among the men suggested as her possible seducer, was Judge Weston himself. When the story became public, the judge had to do something. Though Dorcas was only seventeen, she and the Westons agreed to say she was eighteen and end her service, freeing the judge from having to take action against her seducer, and allowed Dorcas to go her own way.

Dorcas Doyen may have been kept by a lover briefly after she left the Westons, but three months later, she was living in an Augusta brothel kept by Maria Stanley. Soon after, she changed her name to Helen Mar and moved to Boston. She worked there as prostitute for five or six months then changed her name again and moved to New York City. Now known as Helen Jewett, she went to work in an upscale Manhattan brothel run by Rosina Townsend.

In New York, Helen Jewett was more a courtesan than a common prostitute. Her clients included successful lawyers, merchants, and politicians who viewed their relationships with her almost as romances, with rendezvous and exchanges of gifts and letters.

Her favorite client was a young man who went by the name of Frank Rivers. He was handsome and dashing—the girls at Mrs. Townsend's house referred to him as "Pretty Frank." His real name was Richard P. Robinson, an eighteen-year-old clerk with a promising career at a Maiden Lane dry goods store. They began spending time together and corresponding when they were apart. They were very fond of each other, but Robinson hated her profession and began to see other, more respectable women. Helen wanted him to herself and threatened to publicly humiliate him.

Three days before the murder, Helen sent him a letter trying to reconcile and renew their relationship, but closed by saying, "You have known how I have loved, do not—oh, do not—provoke the experiment of seeing how I can hate." In his response Richard Robinson said, "You are never so foolish as when you threaten me. Keep quiet until I come on Saturday night and then we will see if we cannot be better friends hereafter."

The following Sunday, April 10, 1836, Mrs. Townsend was awakened by a noise at around three in the morning. She found the back door ajar and a lamp that belonged in a second-floor bedroom burning in the hall. When she opened the door to Helen's room, black smoke billowed out. She yelled "fire," and the girls and their male companions hurried into the street. Three watchmen came and helped her put the fire out. As the smoke cleared, they saw Helen's charred body on the floor. Her head had been smashed by someone wielding an axe.

Mrs. Townsend recalled seeing Robinson with Helen that night wearing a long dark cloak. Outside they found a bloody hatchet and the cloak she had seen Robinson wearing. Richard Robinson was arrested and the police, trying to elicit a confession, brought him to the scene of the crime. But he showed no emotion, and just calmly denied killing Helen Jewett.

Trial: June 2, 1836

The 1830s marked the beginning of the "penny press"—cheap tabloids appealing to a lower-class audience—and the Helen Jewett murder was made-to-order for sensational journalism. Competing New York newspapers were in a frenzy to print all the information they could find on Helen Jewett and Richard Robinson, and the public could not get enough. By the time of the trial, the murder had become national news, and for the first time, reporters from other cities came to cover a New York City murder trial.

A movement had begun to grow among young men who sympathized with Robinson, asserting that men should not be subject to threats from prostitutes. They expressed their support by wearing black cloaks similar to the one worn by Robinson. In opposition, women who wanted to see Helen's killer punished wore white beaver caps trimmed with black crepe.

The evidence against Robinson was largely circumstantial, easily countered by the defense. The prosecution was not allowed to enter Robinson's diary into evidence and was only allowed one letter from the volume of incriminating correspondence between Richard and Helen. Most of the testimony against Robinson came from Mrs. Townsend and other prostitutes from her house. In his instructions to the jury, the judge told them that prostitutes were not to be believed.

The jury deliberated for half an hour. There were cheers from Robinson's supporters when they returned a verdict of not guilty. After leaving the courtroom, a companion of Robinson's was reportedly seen giving an envelope to one of the jurors.

Verdict: Not guilty

Aftermath:

Soon after the trial, Richard Robinson left New York for Texas. He died two years later of a fever. Reportedly, on his deathbed, he repeated the name Helen Jewett.

Phillip Barton Key

21.   TEMPORARY INSANITY

THE MURDER OF PHILLIP BARTON KEY

Dan Sickles, congressman from New York, was married to the most beautiful woman in Washington but his other interests, including his mistresses, often kept him away from home. Feeling lonely and abandoned, his lonely young wife, Teresa, found comfort in the arms of Philip Barton Key. When Sickles learned of their affair, he armed himself and confronted Key on the street. Blinded by rage he shot and killed his wife's lover. Was it premeditated murder or temporary insanity?

Date: February 27, 1859

Location: Washington, DC

Victim: Phillip Barton Key

Cause of Death: Gunshot

Accused: Daniel Edgar Sickles

Synopsis:

When Daniel Sickles married Teresa Bagioli in 1852, she was fifteen years old and he was thirty-three. She was the daughter of his music teacher and had known Sickles all her life. Her family refused to give their consent to the marriage, but, undeterred, the couple was married in a civil ceremony. Seven months later, their only child, Laura Buchanan Sickles, was born.

At the time of their marriage, Dan Sickles was an attorney and a New York assemblyman, a rising star in Tammany Hall's Democratic political machine. Sickles also had a reputation as a ladies' man. Though he loved his beautiful young wife, he continued his extramarital affairs, including a long-term relationship with Fanny White, owner of a well-known New York brothel. If Teresa knew of these affairs, she chose to endure them in silence.

In 1856, Dan Sickles was elected to the US Congress and moved his wife and young daughter to Washington, D C. The Sickles were very popular in Washington social circles. Teresa, beautiful, charming, and well educated, was a perfect Washington hostess, winning the admiration of men and women alike. But when they weren't entertaining, Dan's work and other interests kept him away and Teresa spent much of her time alone.

To ease her loneliness, Teresa began spending time in the company of Philip Barton Key, the Washington, DC, district attorney and son of Francis Scott Key, author of "The Star Spangled Banner." It began as innocent meetings on the street, but soon it became a torrid romance. When Dan was away, their trysts would end in the parlor of the Sickles's home. At other times they met at a house in a poor section of Washington that Key had rented specifically for their rendezvous.

In spite of Key's precautions, their affair became common knowledge in Washington's social circle. Dan Sickle seemed to be the only one in the city unaware of his wife's romance with Philip Barton Key. That situation changed when Sickles received an anonymous letter giving the details of Teresa's affair with Key stating "...I do assure you, he has as much use of your wife as you do." Sickles made some inquiries and when he was convinced the story was true, he confronted Teresa on February 26, 1859 and forced her to sign a complete confession.

The following day, Key, unaware that they had been discovered, stood in Lafayette Park, across the street from the Sickles's home, waving a handkerchief to get Teresa's attention. Dan Sickles saw the signal and went into a rage. He armed himself with several pistols and rushed into the square, saying, "Key, you scoundrel, you have dishonored my home; you must die."

Sickles fired a pistol at close range, but it only caused a glancing blow to Key's hand. Key grabbed Sickles's lapels. Sickles dropped the derringer he was holding and the two men grappled. Sickles pulled away and drew another pistol. In defense, Key threw the only weapon he had, a pair of opera glasses, at his opponent. Sickles fired again, hitting Key near the groin. Key fell to the ground, and Sickles fired a third shot that struck Key in the chest. Sickles backed off then, and onlookers took Key to a nearby house. He died soon after.

Trial: April 4, 1859

Dan Sickles had a team of high-powered attorneys handling his case, including Edwin M. Stanton, who would later become secretary of war. Sickles had the sympathy of Washington society, and if adultery could have been used as defense to murder, he would have been easily acquitted. Instead, his attorneys argued that Teresa's infidelity had driven him temporarily insane. The jury agreed and for the first time in American history, temporary insanity was successfully used as a defense to the charge of murder.

Verdict: Not guilty

Aftermath:

Dan Sickles had the support of the public, who felt his action against Philip Barton Key was justified. Opinion changed dramatically that summer when Sickles took Teresa back and the two lived together again as husband and wife. This was considered a greater social transgression than killing Key.

Teresa never regained her position in society. She died of tuberculosis in 1867. Sickles went on to be a Union major general in Civil War and lost a leg at the Battle of Gettysburg. He died in 1914 at the age of ninety-four.

Blanche Lamont and Minnie Williams

22.   THE DEMON OF THE BELFRY

Theo Durrant, superintendent of Sunday school at San Francisco' Emanuel Baptist Church, was seen entering the church with Blanche Lamont on April 3, 1895, the day she disappeared. Though several people had seen them together that day, Durant was not considered as a suspect in her disappearance. But when Minnie Williams, another girl he had courted, was found murdered and mutilated in the church library and the corpse of Blanche Lamont was found in the bell tower, the innocent Sunday school teacher was recast as "The Demon of the Belfrey."

THEODORE DURRANT

Dates: April 3, 1895 and April 12, 1895

Location: San Francisco, California

Victims: Blanche Lamont and Minnie Williams

Cause of Death: Strangulation

Accused: Theodore Durrant

Synopsis:

Twenty-one-year-old Blanche Lamont moved to San Francisco from Montana in the fall of 1894 to study teaching. She moved in with her aunt in San Francisco's Mission District and began taking classes as a special student at the boys' high school. Blanche attended the Emmanuel Baptist Church near her home and she belonged to the Young People's Christian Endeavor Society, which held weekly meetings and held a social every month.

The leader of Christian Endeavor was twenty-three-year-old Theodore "Theo" Durrant. He was also the superintendent of Sunday school at the Emmanuel Baptist Church and did maintenance work in the building. Theo lived with his parents and attended Cooper Medical College, studying to be a doctor. Intelligent, hardworking, and generous, Theo was highly regarded by everyone who knew him.

Though at times he seemed romantically clumsy, Theo was never lacking in female company. He met Blanche Lamont at church, and they began spending time together. Theo was smitten, and less than three months after they met, he gave Blanche a ring and asked her to marry him. Blanche liked Theo but thought he was joking and would not give him an answer. Later, when he dimmed the gaslight and tried to kiss her, she pushed him away. Blanche finally ended their relationship when she learned that Theo had been unofficially engaged to Flo Upton, another member of Emmanuel Baptist Church, when he proposed to her.

At the same time, he had been going out with twenty-one-year-old Minnie Williams, a domestic servant who was also a member of the church. She had told her friends that Theo made improper advances when the two had been on a picnic, alone in an isolated spot. Though Minnie rebuffed him at the time, the incident was not serious enough to end their relationship. It was Theo who broke it off after he started seeing Blanche.

On April 3, 1895, Theo and Blanche Lamont appeared to have reconciled. He met her at her school and the two rode together on a cable car laughing and talking intimately. They were seen by Blanche's schoolmates and by friends of Theo. Mrs. Caroline Leak, who lived near Emmanuel Baptist, saw Theo open the church door for Blanche to enter. It was the last time Blanche Lamont was seen alive.

When Blanche did not return home that night, her aunt reported her missing and a frantic search began throughout San Francisco. Theo Durrant joined in the search and suggested that she might have been lured away to a Barbary Coast brothel. No one suspected that Theo, himself, might be involved in Blanche's disappearance.

On Saturday April 13, 1895, the day before Easter, members of Emmanuel Baptist were preparing the church for Sunday's service. Someone entered the library and discovered the mutilated body of a young woman lying across the threshold of the library closet. She had been strangled and stabbed, cut on the head and face, and her wrists slashed so deeply the hands were almost separated from the body. Cloth torn from her undergarments had been shoved down her throat with a sharp stick. When police examined the body, they determined she had also been raped.

At first she was assumed to be Blanche Lamont, but a church member identified her as Minnie Williams. When the police learned of Minnie's connection to Theo Durrant, he became their prime suspect in Minnie's murder and Blanche's disappearance. A thorough search of the building revealed another corpse in the church belfry. In contrast to Minnie's clothed but mangled body, this one was stark naked with hands folded across her chest, so white and serene she looked like a marble statue. It was Blanche Lamont; she had been strangled and probably raped, then posed by her killer. The same day, Blanche's aunt received a strange package by mail. Inside, wrapped in newspaper, were three rings that she recognized as belonging to Blanche. Police showed the rings to pawn shop dealers, one of whom had seen them before. A man fitting Theo Durrant's description had tried to pawn them.

At the time, Theo was on maneuvers with the Signal Corps of the California National Guard. Police arrested him and brought him back to San Francisco. He went peacefully, but strongly declared his innocence.

Trial: July 22, 1895

Theo Durrant was charged with both murders, but Blanche Lamont's case was tried first. She was the first to be murdered and was closely linked to Theo on the day of her disappearance. Like many sensational murders in the 1890s, the Durrant case was dubbed "The Crime of the Century," and the people of San Francisco took it to heart. The courtroom was filled to capacity throughout the trial. Women especially flocked to the courtroom for a glimpse of the handsome young killer. One young woman was nicknamed the "Sweet Pea Girl" because every morning she brought Theo a bouquet of sweet peas. He sometimes wore one on his lapel.

The prosecution included police and medical testimony as well as a parade of eyewitnesses who had seen Theo and Blanche together that day. For the duration of the trial, Blanche's torn dress was displayed on a dressmaker's dummy—an eerie presence, as if the dead girl herself were listening to the testimony. The defense was haphazard, pointing out the circumstantial nature of the evidence and implying that the murder could have just as easily been done by someone else at the church, even pastor. Rev. J. George Gibson. But it was Theo's testimony that probably clinched the verdict. He parsed his sentences carefully and complained often of being misquoted, but ultimately his testimony was contradictory and misleading.

The jury began their deliberation by taking two votes, both were unanimous: guilty of murder, to be punished by hanging. They reached their decision in five minutes but thought it was too soon to return so they finished their cigars first.

Verdict: Guilty of murder

Aftermath:

Theo Durrant was to be hung on February 1896, but the appeals process kept him alive for nearly two more years. On January 7, 1898, he climbed the scaffold. Theo was given the opportunity to speak and began a longwinded ramble declaring his innocence. He showed no sign of stopping, but when he paused in his speech, the executioner took the opportunity to spring the trap. The Demon of the Belfry was dead.

John Love

23.   THE THREE THAYERS

The year 1825 was a momentous one for Buffalo, New York. The Erie Canal opened, connecting Lake Erie to the Hudson River, a celebration honoring the Marquis de Lafayette, hero of the American Revolution was held in Buffalo, and the city held its first and only public hanging. At least 20,000 witnesses gathered in Niagara Square to watch three brothers—Nelson, Israel, and Isaac Thayer—hang from the same gallows.

FROM AN 1825 MURDER PAMPHLET

Date: December 15, 1824

Location: Boston, New York

Victim: John Love

Cause of Death: Gunshot

Accused: Nelson, Israel, and Isaac Thayer

Synopsis:

The Thayer brothers had a bad reputation in Buffalo even before they were accused of murder. They would haul lumber from their farms in Boston, New York—south of Buffalo—in a wagon pulled by two oxen, one named God Almighty and the other, Jesus Christ. The Thayers were profane and violent, and headed straight for the tavern once their business was transacted.

In Boston they owned a large amount of farm land. Nelson and Israel Jr. lived in separate houses with their wives. Isaac lived with his father, Israel Sr. The land was good and they raised enough crops to support themselves, but they were known to be "indolent and dissipated," neglecting farm work for shooting matches and visits to the tavern. They soon found themselves in debt to their neighbors to the extent that they were being threatened with lawsuits and imprisonment.

In October 1824, a man named John Love came to Boston and rented a room from Nelson Thayer. Love was a moneylender who would buy grain futures from the local farmers. He would loan them money using the promise of bushels of wheat as collateral; after the harvest the farmer would repay the debt or Love would take delivery of the wheat. Before long the Thayers were so deeply in debt to Love that they were in danger of losing their property to him.

The Thayer brothers decided that their only hope was to murder John Love and they planned the crime for weeks. On December 15, 1824, Israel Jr. was preparing to butcher his hogs. He sent his wife and a boy who was living at his house to visit a neighbor and on some pretext invited John Love to spend the night. Love was sitting by the fire talking with Nelson when Isaac came to the window and from outside shot Love in the head with a rifle. The shot did not kill him, so Nelson finished him off with several blows from a meat axe.

Nelson and Israel dragged the body outside and hid it by the house while they finished cutting up the hogs. They brought some meat from the butchered hogs into the house and laid it on the chair where Love had been sitting—this would explain blood stains on the chair. Isaac left, and Nelson and Israel took the body to a brook in a ravine about thirty rods form Israel's house. They had intended to dig a deep grave but struck rock very soon, so they just covered the body over with dirt.

The brothers immediately took possession of Love's cash and disposed of the notes Love had on them. Then they tried to collect the debts Love had on others. Finding that they would need power of attorney to collect the debts, they forged this document and claimed that Love had gone to Canada, leaving them in charge of his business.

By February the people had become suspicious of the Thayers's story and began a search for John Love's body. It was not hard to find; Love's grave had been so shallow that his toes were sticking out of the ground and visible from a footpath nearby. On February 23, 1825, the body was spotted by F. T. Jones; it was dug up and taken to the schoolhouse where a coroner's inquest was held. The body was positively identified as John Love, and two doctors determined that he had been shot in the head and struck several times with an axe. The three Thayer brothers and their father, Israel Thayer Sr., were arrested for murder and taken to jail in Buffalo.

Trials: April 21, 1825 – Isaac Thayer and Israel Thayer Jr.
                 April 23, 1825 – Nelson Thayer

Charges were dropped against Israel Sr. and two trials were held for the brothers. Isaac and Israel Jr. were tried together first, then Nelson was tried.

The case against Isaac and Israel was circumstantial but compelling. Witnesses saw Love with the Thayers on December 15, the day the hogs were slaughtered, but did not see him any time after. Several neighbors recalled hearing a gunshot on the night of December 15. The body was buried near Israel's house and the brothers had attempted to profit by Love's absence.

Israel and Isaac's defense team, led by Thomas C. Love (no relation to the deceased) attempted to challenge the facts and the conclusions drawn by them, cautioning the jury against convicting innocent men on circumstantial evidence. But the jury was not swayed by Love and after deliberating half an hour, returned a verdict of guilty.

Nelson's trial was held on April 23 and was essentially the same as his brothers'. At 11:00 that night, after deliberating for only a few minutes, the jury returned a guilty verdict.

All three Thayer brothers were sentenced to hang.

Verdicts: Isaac Thayer and Israel Thayer Jr. – Guilty
                    Nelson Thayer – Guilty

Aftermath:

Before their hanging the Thayers together made a full confession, confirming the presumptions made by the prosecution. When asked why they did it, Nelson explained that through small loans at high interest, Love had obtained nearly all of their property. With the threat of debtors' prison hanging over them, they decided murder was the only solution. Nelson added, "I thought I might as well run the risk of being hung as to lose my property and go to prison, too."

The Eire Canal would soon make Buffalo a large industrial and shipping center, but in 1825 Buffalo was a frontier village with a population of just 2,000 people. Though Buffalo itself was small, the execution of the Thayer brothers in Niagara Square in the center of town drew a crowd of 20,000–30,000 witnesses. The Thayers were led into the square wearing white caps and shrouds, preceded by a cart carrying three coffins. As they walked, surrounded by soldiers, a band played a slow and plaintive air. At 2:00 p.m. on June 17, 1825, Israel, Isaac, and Nelson Thayer were launched into eternity together, hanging from the same gallows.

Poem:

"The Mournful and Pathetic Ballad on the Murder of John Love" published anonymously in 1825, is presented here with its original spelling.

The Mournful and Pathetic Ballad on the Murder of John Love

In England some years ago
the sun was pleasant fair and gay
John Love on board of a ship he entered
And sald in to america

Love Was a man very perceverlng
in making trades with all he see
he soon ingaged to be a sailor
to sail up and down Lake Eri

he then went Into the Southern countries,
to trade for furs and other skins
but the cruel French and saveg Indians
came very near to killing him.

but God did spare him a little longer
he got his loging and come down the lake
he went into the town of lockport
Where he made the grate mistake

with Nelson Thayer he made his station
thrue the summer for to stay
Nelson had two brothers Isaac and Israel
Love lent them money for thare debts to pay

Love lent them quite a sum of money
he did befriend them every way
but the cruel cretres tha couldent be quiet
till they had taken his sweet life away

one day as tha ware all three to gether
this dreadful murder tha did contrive
tha agreed to kill Love and keep it secret
and then to live and spend thare lives

109

on the fifteenth evening of last december
in eighteen hundred and twenty four
tha invited Love to go home with them
and tha killed and murdered him on the floor

first Isaac with his gun he shot him
he left his gun and went away
then Nelson with his ax chopt him
tell he had no life that could perceve

after tha had killed and most mortly bras's him
tha drawd him out where tha killed thare hogs
tha then carried him of a pease from the house
and deposited him down by a log

the next day tha were so very bold
tha had Loves horses riding round
some asked the reason of Loves being absent
tha sed he had clered and left the town

tha sed he had forged in the town of Erie
the sheriff was in pursuit of him
he left the place and run awa
and left his debts to collect by them

tha went and forgd a power of turney
to collect Loves note when tha was due
tha tore and stormed to git thare pay
and several nabors tha did sue

after tha had run to high degree
In killing Love and in forgery
Tha soon were taken and put in prison
Where tha remained for thare cruelty

Tha were bound in irons in the dark dunjon
For to remain for a little time
Tha were condemd by the grand jury
For this most foul and dreadful crime

Then the judge pronounced thare dredful sentence

110

Whith grate candidness to behold
You must all be hanged untell your ded
And lord mursey on your souls

Louise Luetgert

24.   THE SAUSAGE VAT MURDER

Adolph Luetgert was known as the "Sausage King" of Chicago. H owned the A. L. Luetgert Sausage & Packing Company and when business was booming, he was a successful, highly regarded family man. But when the business turned bad and money was scarce, he and his wife Louise were constantly fighting. On May 1, 1897, Louise was reported missing. Adolph claimed she had walked out on him, but the police had other ideas. They accused him of killing his wife and dissolving her body in a vat of boiling potash.

LOUISE LUETGERT

Date: May 1, 1897

Location: Chicago, Illinois

Victim: Louise Luetgert

Cause of Death: Unknown

Accused: Adolph Luetgert

Synopsis:

Adolph Luetgert emigrated from Germany to the United States around 1865, a young man of twenty with thirty dollars in his pocket. By age forty-five, he owned a successful meatpacking firm and was one of the largest producers on sausages in Chicago. He had devised a way to manufacture sausages in summer as well as winter—something other sausage makers were not able to do—and became known as the "Sausage King."

He married his first wife, Caroline Roepke, in 1872 before he started in the sausage business. They had two children, one of whom died before his second birthday. Caroline died in 1877 and two months after her death, Adolph married Louise Bricknese. Louise worked as a domestic servant and like Adolph, had come from Germany. She was pretty and petite—five feet tall, weighing 115 pounds. He was thirty-two; she was twenty-three. They had four children together but only two lived past the age of two.

The sausage business grew rapidly, reaching a high point in 1893 when the A. L. Luetgert Sausage & Packing Company supplied frankfurters for The Columbian Exhibition in Chicago. But when the world's fair ended, Chicago's economy was hit hard by the depression that had already engulfed the rest of the county. Sausage orders fell drastically and many of Luetgert's customers could not pay in full for orders already received. He tried to sell the business but was defrauded by a potential buyer. Between the swindle and Chicago bank failures, Luetgert was left with nothing.

Adolph kept the news from Louise for as long as he could. She had been quite happy with her husband's success and had grown used to their high standard of living and when she learned of their true financial condition, Louise began fighting with Adolph about money. According to the neighbors, the arguments were loud and sometimes violent. Several people recalled Louise saying that she was planning to leave him.

Rumors began circulating that Adolph had been faithful to his wife. He kept a private office, with a bed, at the factory and would often sleep there. The family housekeeper, Mary Siemering, made the bed at Adolph's office and the two had been seen kissing by one of the factory workers. Christine Fields, a wealthy widow, had also allegedly been courted by Adolph Luetgert.

On May 1, 1897, Louise Luetgart left her home and never came back. Her brother reported her disappearance to the police, suspecting foul play, but Adolph claimed she had just made good on her promise to leave him. She had probably gone back to Germany, he said, probably with another man.

The night before she left, Adolph had been working late in the basement of the factory. He had the night watchman help him turn on the steam then sent him to a drug store to buy some patent medicine. The next day he had some workers clean in and around a large vat in the basement. It contained some thick, foul-smelling, reddish scum and the same substance was spattered on the floor of the basement. The watchman was suspicious and went to the police, who had the vat drained and inside they found what appeared to be pieces of bone. They also found some metal corset stays and two rings, one engraved with the initials "L. L." The police discovered that Luetgert had recently purchased large amounts of arsenic and potash, a powerful alkali used in making soap. The following morning Adolph Luetgert was arrested for the murder of his wife Louise. Police believed he had killed her and dissolved the corpse in a vat of boiling potash.

Trials: August 1897
              January 1898

Adolph Luetgert's trial in August 1897 was a spectacle from the beginning. Over a thousand spectators filled the courtroom every day. Women especially flocked in to get even a glimpse of the killer. Reporters came from newspapers all across America, including Julian Hawthorne, son of author Nathanial Hawthorne, writing for the New York Journal.

The prosecution faced a number of challenges in their case against Luetgert. First was the absence of a corpse. They claimed Adolph had completely and permanently disposed of the body, but the defense claimed that Louise was not dead; she had just left her husband. They were confident she would turn up and save Adolph. In fact, there had been dozens of sightings of Mrs. Luetgert throughout America. Most were proven to be hoaxes, and the rest were found to be insane or alcoholic women seen wandering alone.

The second challenge was proving that the debris in the bottom of the vat actually constituted the remains Louise Luetgert. The prosecution had bone experts testifying that the fragments found were from the bones of a small woman. The defense had experts who testified that it was impossible to say they were even human. Each side did its own experiments, dissolving cadavers in vats of potash; each side proved its own assertion.

In the end the prosecution was not able to convince twelve men of Luetgert's guilt. The trial ended in a hung jury.

The second trial began in January 1897. This time the expert testimony of George Dorsey, anthropologist at Chicago's Field Columbian Museum was convincing. Though Adolph Luetgert, through direct and cross-examination, testified on his own behalf for eighteen and a half hours, the jury returned a verdict of guilty.

Verdicts: Hung jury
               Guilty of murder

Aftermath:

Adolph Luetgert was given a life sentence at Joliet Prison. He died of heart problems on July 27, 1899.

Though it was proven that Louise Luetgert's murder had nothing to do with the manufacture of sausages, sausage sales in Chicago, by all makers, suffered during Adolph's arrest and trial.

William Lyons

25.   THAT BAD MAN STAGOLEE

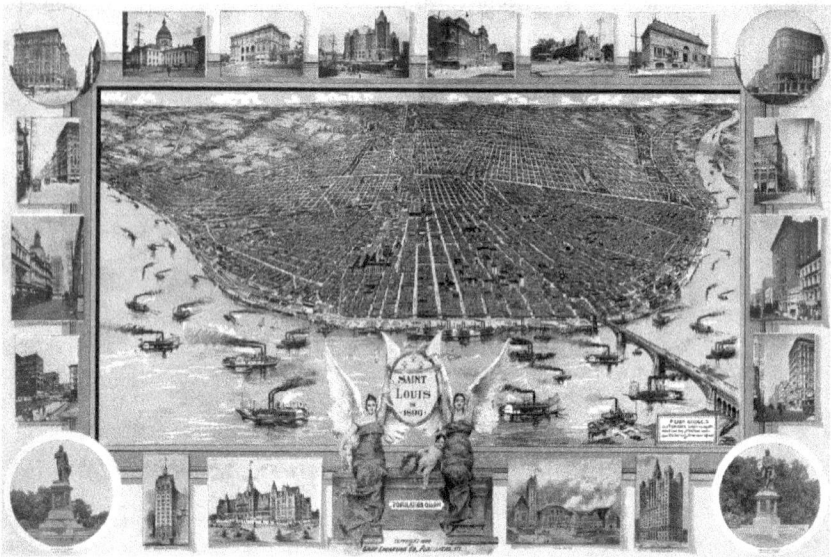

ST. LOUIS, MISSOURI

The story of Stagolee has been sung by troubadours for more than a hundred years. Each singer seems to know a different version and tell a different story of its origin. Under a variety of names—"Stagolee," "Staggerlee," "Stack O' Lee," "Stack O' Dollars"—this outlaw has become an American legend and an archetype of African American folklore. But his story is true: when Stack Lee Shelton shot Billy Lyons, in a fight over a Stetson hat, in Bill Curtis's Saloon, on Christmas night 1895, the legend was born.

Date: December 25, 1895

Location: St. Louis, Missouri

Victim: William "Billy" Lyons

Cause of Death: Gunshot

Accused: "Stack" Lee Shelton

Synopsis:

Stack Lee Shelton was the owner of a St. Louis saloon/brothel called the Modern Horseshoe Club, and he was a well-known figure in the black neighborhood of Deep Morgan. He belonged to a class of St. Louis pimps known as the "macks," who were famous for sporting a mode of dress that demanded attention. This is how Cecil Brown, in his book *Stagolee Shot Billy*, described Stack Lee's entrance to Bill Curtis's Saloon the night of the murder:

> *Shelton was dressed in a pair of tailored shoes known as 'St. Louis flats,' with almost no heels and long toes pointing upward. On the top of the toes were tiny mirrors that caught the electric light hanging overhead and sent sparkles upward. A pair of dove-colored spats covered Shelton's shoe tops. Gray-striped pants hung over his spats. The flaps of his black box-back coat fell open to reveal an elaborately patterned red velvet vest and a yellow embroidered shirt with a celluloid standing collar that kept his chin high in the air. Knuckle-length sleeve's almost covered the gold rings on his manicured fingers; his left hand clutched the gold head of an ebony walking cane, the other hand took a long cigar out of his mouth. On his head was a high-roller, milk-white Stetson. Along the hatband was an embroidered picture of his favorite girl, Lillie Shelton.*

Shelton saw his friend Billy Lyons standing at the bar and joined him for a drink. Lyons worked as a levee hand and did not dress with the flash of the macks. He was not a wealthy man, but he was well connected. His sister was married to Henry Bridgewater, one of the richest black men in St. Louis, and a leader in the Republican Party.

Stack Lee Shelton and Billy Lyons drank and talked amiably most of the evening, but when the discussion turned to politics, the exchange became heated. Billy was a Republican, like his brother-in-law, while Stack Lee was aligned with a growing faction of black St. Louis Democrats. Shelton grabbed Lyons's derby hat and broke the form. Lyons demanded six bits from Shelton to replace it. When Shelton refused, Lyons grabbed Shelton's Stetson hat. Shelton drew his .44 Smith and Wesson and the saloon patrons scattered. He threatened to blow out Lyons's brains if he did not return the hat.

Lyons called his bluff, pulled out his knife saying, "You cockeyed son of a bitch, I'm going to make you kill me."

But Shelton wasn't bluffing. He shot Billy Lyons, snatched back his hat, and coolly left the saloon. Billy Lyons was taken to an infirmary, then moved to a hospital where he died at around four in the morning. Stack Lee Shelton was home sleeping when police came to arrest him. He was released on $4,000 bail.

Trial: July 15, 1896

Shelton hired Col. Nat C. Dryden, one of the finest criminal lawyers in St. Louis. The trial opened on July 15, 1896 and lasted two days. Dryden argued that Shelton had killed Lyons in self-defense. The jury deliberated for twenty-two hours but could not agree on a verdict. Their final polling had seven jurors for second-degree murder, two for manslaughter, and three for acquittal.

Verdict: Hung jury

Aftermath:

Nat Dryden died on August 26, 1897, before Shelton could be retried. Though there is no surviving record of the second trial, it must have happened soon after because on October 7 Stack Lee Shelton began serving a twenty-five year sentence at the Missouri State Penitentiary in Jefferson City.

Shelton was paroled on Thanksgiving Day 1909, possibly helped by petitions from influential St. Louis Democrats. But two years later he was back in prison for robbery and assault. He died in prison of tuberculosis on March 11, 1912.

Ballad:

Even before his death, the killer of Billy Lyons, in song and story, had morphed into Stagolee, that mythic bad man who would not be refused. Since the murder, the song of Stagolee in all its versions and titles has been recorded at least 285 times.

This is Mississippi John Hurt's version.

Stack O'Lee Blues

Police Officer, how can it be?
You can arrest everybody but cruel Staggerlee
That bad man, oh cruel Staggerlee

Billy DeLyons told Staggerlee please don't take my life
I got two little babies and a darlin lovin wife
That bad man, oh cruel Staggerlee

What do I care about your two little babies or your darlin lovin wife

118

You done took my Stetson hat and I'm bound to take your life
That bad man, oh cruel Staggerlee

Boom boom boom boom went a forty-four
And when I spied Billy DeLyons he was lyin down on the floor
That bad man, oh cruel Staggerlee

Gentlemen of the jury, what do you think about that
Staggerlee killed Billy DeLyons about a five dollar Stetson hat
That bad man, oh cruel Staggerlee

Standin up on the gallows, Staggerlee began to cuss
The judge said, "Let's kill him boys, before he kills some of us."
That bad man, oh cruel Staggerlee

Statndin up on the gallows his head was held up high
At twelve o'clock they killed him, they was all glad to see him die
That bad man, oh cruel Staggerlee

Bertha M. Manchester

26.   STARTLING PARALLELISMS

Just five days before the start of Lizzie Borden's trial for the murder of her father and stepmother in Fall River, Massachusetts, the town was shocked by another brutal axe murder. The mutilated body of Bertha Manchester was found in the kitchen of her home. The "startling parallelism" between this case and the Borden murders—the excessive number of wounds in each case, the fact that both incidents occurred in broad daylight, the lack of any apparent motive—threatened to open a new line of defense in Lizzie's trial. It would, at very least, challenge many of the prosecution's stated assumptions.

STARTLING PARALLELISMS.

Many Points of Resemblance Found Between the Manchester and Borden Murders.

INTERIOR OF THE MANCHESTER KITCHEN, THE BODY OF THE GIRL LAY CLOSE BY THE STOVE AT CROSS.

BOSTON DAILY GLOBE, JUNE 1, 1893

Date: May 31, 1893

Location: Fall River, Massachusetts

Victim: Bertha M. Manchester

Cause of Death: Blows from an axe

Accused: Jose Correa De Mello

Synopsis:

Twenty-two-year-old Bertha M. Manchester lived with her father Stephen and brother Frederick on a dairy farm on New Boston Road in Fall River, Massachusetts. On the morning of May 31, 1893, Stephen and Freddie left to make their regular milk deliveries. When they returned that afternoon, they found Bertha's mangled body lying in a pool of blood, next to the stove in the kitchen. She had been hacked to death with an axe—the murder weapon was found lying by the woodpile outside. Bertha's watch and a purse containing a small amount of money had been taken; nothing else was missing from the house.

An autopsy revealed "twenty-three distinct and separate axe wounds on the back of the skull and its base." Defensive wounds and ripped clothing indicated that she had put up a fierce struggle with her assailant before being overpowered.

Stephen Manchester was a widower whose second wife had left him because he was mean and extremely cheap. Early in the investigation, he was considered a suspect because of his apparent indifference to his daughter death; he continued his daily routine as if nothing had happened. But soon suspicion fell on Manchester's hired hands, many of whom were disgruntled over the low pay they received from him.

He preferred to hire French and Portuguese immigrants, and paid them as little as possible. He told reporters:

> I can't remember the names of these Frenchmen and Portuguese I have had. Half of the time I don't know them. I have had Antoines and Joes and Georges. The police have been pestering me all day to remember some of the names, but I cannot break my jaw over their names. I always pay a man what I think he is worth, and if he don't like it, it don't make any difference. He won't get any more.

Suspicion soon fell on a man named Jose Correa De Mello who had recently left the farm on bad terms with his employer. De Mello was Portuguese, an immigrant from the Azores, and as such, would have been on the lowest rung of Fall River society. The police feared that if they began investigating, the Portuguese community would rally to De Mello's defense and they would get no information. Instead they used subterfuge to get De Mello to turn himself in.

The police contacted Jose De Mello's uncle, Jacintho Muniz Machado, and Frank Machado Silva, a leader in the Portuguese American community, and persuaded them to tell De Mello that they needed him as a witness to a horse theft and would pay a hefty witness fee. De Mello went to the police station with no idea that he was a murder suspect. There he was strenuously interrogated for four hours.

The main piece of evidence against Jose De Mello came from the owner of a shoe store who claimed that De Mello bought a new pair of shoes from him after the murder and tried to pay with a "trade dollar" and a "plugged half-dollar." These distinctive coins were known to have been in the purse stolen from Bertha Manchester.

Trial: January 8, 1894

De Mello could not afford a lawyer and an attorney was appointed by the court in September 1893. He first pled not guilty, but on September 18, he changed his plea to guilty of second-degree murder. On January 8, 1894, he was convicted and sentenced to life in state prison: "solitary one day, hard labor for his natural life, less one day."

Verdict: Guilty of second-degree murder

Aftermath:

De Mello's uncle, Jacintho Muniz Machado, became an outcast in the Portuguese community, where it was believed that he had sold out his nephew for $500. Jose De Mello refused to see his uncle when he came to visit him in prison. Less than eight weeks after De Mello's arrest, Jacintho Muniz Machado died in his home. The official cause of death was pneumonia, but friends said he "died of a broken heart."

When reporters asked Lizzie Borden's attorney, Andrew J. Jennings, about Bertha Manchester's murder, he said, "Well, are they going to say that Lizzie Borden did this also?"

Lizzie, of course, was in jail at the time, awaiting the start of her trial. But this shocking murder, so similar to the Borden murders, did change attitudes in the opposite direction—increasing the possibility that Lizzie didn't do it. The arrest of Jose De Mello occurred on the day Lizzie Borden's trial opened. De Mello had not arrived in the United States until April 1893, so could not have murdered the Bordens in August 1892, but this was not learned until after the jury was selected in Lizzie's trial.

The facts surrounding the murder of Bertha Manchester cast doubts on a number of assertions made by the prosecution in the Borden case. The Bordens each died of multiple blows from an axe—Abbey nineteen, Andrew twenty—this, said the prosecution, indicated a woman murderer; a man would use only one blow. Yet Bertha Manchester was murdered by a man using twenty-three blows. The fact that the Borden's were killed in broad daylight indicated that a member of the household did the murders, yet Bertha Manchester was killed around the same time of day, with neighbors at home just across the road, and no member of the Manchester household was involved.

While the murder of Bertha Manchester did not play a direct role in Lizzie's trial, the two cases were playing out side-by-side in the daily newspapers. It was not lost on anyone, in or out of court, how easy it was for a man to enter the Manchester house, commit a brutal axe murder in broad daylight, and leave without being noticed.

Jose Correa De Mello served nearly twenty years of his life sentence, then, through the persistence of John C. Santos, a prominent Portuguese resident of Taunton, Massachusetts, he was pardoned on December 31, 1913, with the following stipulation:

> *...on condition that if before the expiration of said sentence he commit any crime punishable by imprisonment, and he convicted thereof, either before or after the expiration of said sentence, he shall serve the remainder thereof.*

He was also required to return to his native Azores and never come back to the United States.

Gus, Delora, Hattie and Mary Meeks

27.   THE MEEKS FAMILY MURDER

The morning of May 11, 1894, six-year-old Nellie Meeks knocked on the door of Mrs. John Carter in Linn County, Missouri. Mrs. Carter was shocked by the little girl's appearance; her clothes were torn, her face was covered with dirt and blood, and she had a deep gash in her forehead. Her speech was barely coherent as she told Mrs. Carter that her parents and younger sisters had been murdered the night before. Nellie had managed to escape because the killers thought she was dead. Her story was verified, and the Meeks family murder became one of Missouri's most infamous crimes.

NELLIE MEEKS

Date: May 10, 1894

Location: Linn County, Missouri

Victims: Gus, Delora, Hattie, and Mary Meeks

Cause of Death: Shooting, Beating

Accused: George and William Taylor

Synopsis:

Mrs. Carter did not have a man in the house so she sent her nine-year-old son Jimmy to investigate Nellie's story. Jimmy could not find the bodies, so Nellie led him back to a haystack, under which was a shallow grave containing the bodies of Nellie's father, Gus Meeks, her mother, Delora, her four-year-old sister Hattie, and her eighteen-month-old sister

Mary. Mrs. Meeks had been pregnant and miscarried at the time of her death and the fetus was also in the grave. Though some later accounts say the Meeks had been murdered with an axe, the adults and Hattie had been shot to death; Mary and Nellie were beaten with a rock.

When they returned home, Mrs. Carter sent Jimmy out to notify the neighbors of the murder. On the way he ran into George Taylor harrowing his cornfield and told him about the bodies under the haystack. Taylor took Jimmy to his house and told him to wait outside while he hitched his horses and they would go and take a look. Jimmy waited but George Taylor never returned. What Jimmy did not know at the time was that George Taylor and his brother William would be the prime suspects in the murder.

While Nellie was being examined by a doctor, she explained what happened:

> *When we were going up the hill, the man without whiskers said his feet were cold and got out and walked along the side of the wagon and shot Papa, and Papa jumped out and started to run. Then Mama screamed and started to jump when they shot Mama and Sister. Then they hit me in the head, and I went to sleep.*

When she was thrown out of the wagon, she regained consciousness and heard the men trying to set the haystack on fire.

> *When the man put me in the straw, the one with the whiskers kicked me on the back and said, 'They are all dead now, the damn villain sons of bitches.' They covered me up and I could not breathe good. I heard them say it would not burn, as it would not catch.*

George and William Taylor were among the most wealthy and prominent citizens in northeastern Missouri. William was a graduate of the Missouri University School of Law, had served in the Missouri General Assembly, and also worked for the People's Exchange Bank in Browning, Missouri. But by the early 1890s, it became clear that the Taylors had not acquired their wealth through honest labor. They had been charged with forgery and larceny for writing false bank drafts and had also been indicted for arson and cattle rustling.

Gus Meeks, a tenant farmer on land owned by the Taylors, was implicated in one of their cattle rustling cases. Meeks was indicted, pled guilty, and was sent to the penitentiary. About a month before the murder, Meeks was pardoned by the governor in exchange for his promise to testify against the Taylor brothers.

The Taylors were anxious to get rid of Meeks and offered him $1,000 if he would leave the area. But when they came to pick him up, the night of May 10, 1894, Mrs. Meeks would not allow him to leave alone. Fearing for her husband's life, she insisted that the whole family leave with the Taylors. She did not believe the Taylors capable of murdering them all.

Nellie Meeks told her story at the coroner's inquest and indictments were issued for William P. Taylor and George E. Taylor for the murder of the Meeks family.

In June 1894, the Taylors were arrested in Batesville, Arkansas, and taken back to Missouri. Though they offered a bond of $50,000 each, bail was refused.

Trials: March 18, 1895
              July 24, 1895

The case was tried in Carrollton, Missouri. As the prisoners were being transported there, the train had to be diverted to St. Joe because the sheriff got word of a lynch mob—250 heavily armed men, faces covered with handkerchiefs—waiting for them in Brookfield.

At the trial a number of witnesses testified to hearing the Taylors threaten Gus Meeks, and Meeks's mother, who lived with the family, told of her fears that the Taylors would murder her son. Others testified to hearing gunshots and seeing the Taylors' wagon that night. The evidence was circumstantial, but was little doubt as to the defendants' guilt. After two days of deliberation, the jury reported that they were hopelessly deadlocked at seven to five for conviction. One juror and an alternate later reported that they had been offered $750 to vote for acquittal.

The second trial began in July 1895. This time the prosecution decided to charge the Taylor brothers with just one count of first-degree murder. While it was clear that the murder of Gus Meeks was premeditated, it would be more difficult to prove premeditation in the murders of Mrs. Meeks and the children.

During the trials, Nellie Meeks was the ward of Prosecuting Attorney Pierce and his wife. Though she did not testify in either trial, Nellie did attend the trials and during the proceedings would occasionally climb onto Prosecutor Pierce's lap.

The case was given to the jury on August 2, 1895. This time they reached a verdict of guilty in an hour and a half.

Verdicts: Hung jury
               Guilty of first-degree murder

Aftermath:

The Taylors appealed to the Missouri Supreme Court, but the verdict was upheld. George and William Taylor were sentenced to hang on April 30, 1896.

On April 11, 1896, the Taylor brothers broke out of the Carrollton jail. They knocked a bar out of their cell, went to the roof of the jail, and used a fifty-foot hose to climb down. William was quickly captured and taken to Kansas City for safekeeping until the hanging. George Taylor was never captured.

William Taylor was hanged at 11:00 a.m. on Thursday, April 30, 1896 before a crowd of hundreds. He left behind this written statement:

> *To the public: I have only this additional statement to make. I ought not to suffer as I am compelled to do. Prejudice and perjury convicted me. By this conviction, my wife is left a lonely widow, my babies are made orphans in a cruel world, my brothers mourn, and friends weep. You hasten my gray-haired mother and father to the grave. The mobs and that element have haunted me to the grave. I had hoped to live at least till the good people realize the injustice done me, but it cannot be so. I feel prepared to meet my God and now wing my way to the great unknown, where I believe everyone is properly judged. I hope my friends will meet me all in heaven. I believe I am going there. Good-bye, all.*

The Meeks family members are buried in a single grave in the Bute Cemetery five miles southeast of Owasco. There are separate markers for Hattie and Mamie.

Between the two trials, according the Quincy Daily Herald, little Nellie Meeks appeared for a week, telling her story at the Eden Museum in St. Joe. She was well received, drawing large crowds.

Nellie was raised by her maternal grandmother. She married Albert Spray and in 1910, died due to complications in the birth of her daughter, Hattie. All her life she had a deep scar—a "dint" she called it—in her forehead.

Ballads:

This is one of several annonymous folk songs about the Meeks murder.

Meeks Family Murder

About one mile from Browning, upon the Jenkins Hill

Gus Meeks and family were murdered by the Taylors, George and Bill.

The first they killed was Mr. Meeks; And the woman began to cry
And beg them to spare her little ones, but they told her all must die.

In vain they looked around for their mischief to conceal;
So loaded them into a wagon and drove to George's field.

Next morning George was seen with his team out in the field
Harrowing around the old straw stack where the bodies were concealed.

But the hand of Providence was there, as you all know very well,
To spare the life of the little one on the murderers to tell.

And when she rose from her strawy grave to Carter's house she went
And told them of the tragedy and the terrible night she had spent.

And when George Taylor heard of this he went to his brother Bill
And told him of the mistake they had made: "There is one we did not kill."

So they hustled around, as you all know, and soon they left the town;
And ever since been hunted for, but still they can't be found.

Now they are at large, and the officers seem to think that they are gone
And if ever they catch those desperate men I shall complete my song.

Fred A. Merrick

28.   THE MAN OF TWO LIVES

Edward   H.   Rulloff   was considered by many to be a genius, a man of great intellect, ahead of his time, ready to revolutionize the study of philology—and just as many thought him a fraud and a conman. He was well versed in medicine, law, and language and was an educator respected by his students. He was also a thief and a swindler who had trouble leaving any city without a run-in with the law. When an 1870 burglary in Binghamton, New York, went bad, leaving three men dead, the public would face the paradox of the "Man of Two Lives."

EDWARD H. RULLOFF

Date: August 17, 1870

Location: Binghamton, New York

Victim: Fred A. Merrick

Cause of Death: Gunshot

Accused: Edward H. Rulloff

Synopsis:

The early morning of August 17, 1870, Gilbert Burrows, a clerk at Halbert's dry goods store in Binghamton, New York, rushed from the store into the street to sound the alarm—Fred Merrick, another clerk, had been shot dead during a burglary. The store had been robbed before and Burrows and Merrick were serving as night watchmen to prevent it from happening again. About two thirty in the morning, the clerks were awakened by three men who had broken into the store. A fight ensued and one of the burglars started shooting. Merrick had a pistol and tried to shoot back, but the gun jammed. He was shot in the head at close range. Burrows ran out of the store and the burglars escaped.

Later that morning, two corpses were found floating in the Chenango River not far from Halbert's store. Three men had been seen fleeing the store and heading into the river. Apparently two of the burglars had drowned trying to get away.

Police began to round up suspicious individuals and before noon had three suspects in custody. One was a mysterious man, respectably dressed, carrying a satchel and an umbrella. He refused to stop when approached by the police and escaped them by running across a railroad track just before a train passed, blocking the road. They eventually found him crouching in the outhouse of a nearby farm.

The man first told the police his name was Charles Augustus, then later said he was George Williams. He was taken to see the two drowned men but did not recognize either of them. The bodies had been on public display all morning and hundreds of curiosity-seekers had passed by. Among them was Judge Ransom Balcom, who instantly recognized the suspect and said to him, "You are Edward H. Rulloff; you murdered your wife and child in Lansing in 1845."

Then he turned to the coroner's jury assembled near the corpses and said, "This man understands his rights better than you do, and will defend them to the last."

An 1871 biography of Edward Rulloff was entitled *The Man of Two Lives*. This was an understatement. Rulloff—also known as James Nelson, E. C. Howard, James Dalton, Edward Lieurio, etc.—had been a doctor, a lawyer, a schoolmaster, a photographer, a carpet designer, an inventor, and a phrenologist. Most notably, Rulloff was a philologist, who could speak Latin, Greek, and six modern languages and was working on a manuscript, *Method in the Formation of Language*, which he believed would revolutionize the field. The dichotomy of Edward Rulloff's life was the fact that he financed his research by theft and did much of his philological work in prison.

Rulloff started both sides of his life early, working in a law firm and spending two years in the penitentiary for theft, both before age twenty. In 1842 he moved to the town of Lansing in New York's Finger Lakes region, where he taught school and began studying botanical medicine with Dr. Henry W. Bull. A year later he married Harriet Schutt, but the marriage was in trouble from the start. Rulloff was extremely jealous and accused her of having an affair with Dr. Bull. The birth of their daughter, Priscilla, kept them together for a time, but Rulloff wanted to move west and Harriet did not.

Then, on June 23, 1844, Harriet and Priscilla disappeared. Rulloff said she had left him, but the people of Lansing were suspicious. By the time an investigation was launched, Rulloff had left town. Police searched his house and found Harriet's clothing and no evidence that she had moved out. When Rulloff returned to Lansing, he said that he had moved the family to Ohio. When this story was not believed, Rulloff slipped away again; he was pursued, captured, and charged with murder.

The problem with the charge of murder was the lack of corpses. The police believed that Rulloff had sunk the bodies in Lake Cayuga, but repeated dredging had turned up nothing. In 1846 he was brought to trial anyway. Rulloff directed his own defense, and tried to focus on the lack of evidence, but the jury was predisposed to convict him of something. He was found guilty of abduction and sentenced to ten years in Auburn Prison.

On the day of his release in 1856, a warrant was issued against Rulloff for the murder of his wife. Rulloff protested that it was double jeopardy, and rather than argue this point, the district attorney charged him instead with the murder of his daughter. Rulloff was tried again and convicted again. This time he appealed, but the verdict was upheld.

While awaiting sentencing in the Ithaca jail, Rulloff began tutoring Albert Jarvis, the son of the undersheriff, in Latin and Greek. He also became close with his mother, Jane Jarvis, who did not believe that Rulloff was a murderer. In 1857 Rulloff escaped from jail. It was fairly obvious that he had inside help, since in addition to a chain around his ankle, there were eight locks between his cell and the outside. Al Jarvis remained a friend and associate of Rulloff for the rest of his life, and Jane Jarvis would later secretly visit when Rulloff was living in Brooklyn.

Rulloff was recaptured and sentenced to hang. He appealed again and this time succeeded and a new trial was ordered. Tired of waiting for justice, the people of Ithaca formed a lynch mob, ready to storm the jail, but Rulloff was transferred to Auburn before any damage could be done.

Prosecutors decided there was little hope of success in trying him again for murder without corpses, and there was no interest in prosecuting him for escaping jail, so Rulloff was extradited to Erie, Pennsylvania, where he was wanted for jewel theft. Rulloff was not prosecuted there either. Though nearly everyone in western New York believed Rulloff was guilty of abduction, theft, assault, fraud, jailbreaking, and murder, he was now a free man.

Rulloff moved to New York City and was soon joined there by Al Jarvis. He spent his time working on his book and robbing stores with Al and other accomplices. They specialized in stealing "sewing silk," an expensive item that was easy to conceal and hard to identify. In 1861 Rulloff was arrested in Poughkeepsie and sentenced to two years in Sing Sing. In prison Rulloff met Billy Dexter and on his release, Billy joined the gang.

Though Al and Billy preferred to work without Rulloff—he had an unfortunate knack for getting caught—he was with them in Binghamton that night in 1870, robbing Halbert's dry goods store. Through the contents of their pockets, the drowned men were identified as Al Jarvis and Billy Dexter, and traced to the Brooklyn apartment where Rulloff had been living under the name Edward C. Howard. Rulloff was charged with the murder of Fred Merrick.

Trial: January 4, 1871

Edward Rulloff's murder trial received extensive press coverage and more than 2,000 people a day came to watch in a courtroom built for half that many. The prosecution introduced witnesses from Brooklyn, as well as the eyewitness Gilbert Burrows. Rulloff once again directed his own defense, claiming that he was not in Binghamton the night of the murder and that whoever committed the murder acted in self-defense and not premeditation. The jury deliberated for four and a half hours; the issue of debate was not guilt but the degree of the crime. Most wanted first-degree murder, but some were pressing for second-degree or manslaughter. In the end Edward Rulloff was convicted of first-degree murder and he was sentenced to hang on March 3, 1871.

Verdict: Guilty of first-degree murder

Aftermath:

Appeals moved the hanging date back two and a half months. While awaiting execution, the case became a subject of national debate. Some said it was wrong to take the life of such a learned man who may be on the verge of a great intellectual breakthrough. Horace Greely, owner of the *New York Tribune*, wrote, "In the prison in Binghamton, there is a man awaiting death who is too curious an intellectual problem to be wasted on the gallows."

Others, however, believed that Rulloff was an intellectual fraud; among them was Mark Twain, who satirized Greely's position, saying:

> *If a life be offered up to the gallows to atone for the murder Rulloff did, will that suffice? If so...I will bring forward a man who, in the interest of*

learning and science, will take Rulloff's crime upon himself and submit to be hanged in Rulloff's place.

Outside of court, the people of New York ascribed multiple murders to Rulloff. He had claimed that Al Jarvis and Billy Dexter drowned because they thought the river was shallow enough to walk across and neither man could swim, but the public saw their deaths as murder by Rulloff to prevent identification. He was also still accused of the murder of his wife and daughter, and now accused of killing his sister-in-law and her child who died while under Rulloff's medical care shortly before Harriet disappeared.

Before his execution, Rulloff confessed to killing his wife by smashing her skull with a pestle he used to grind medicine. He did not confess to killing his daughter, Priscilla, or anyone else. It was reported that Priscilla did not die but was raised by Rulloff's brother.

Edward Rulloff was hanged on May 18, 1871. He had requested that his body be put in a vault so it would not be desecrated, but his request was not honored. Before his lawyer could claim the body, it was placed on public display and the owner of a local art gallery made a plaster death mask. His lawyer gave the body to Dr. George Burr of the Geneva Medical College, who promised to bury the body in a private cemetery if he could keep the head for study. After the body was buried, it was dug up and stolen by medical students. Edward Rulloff's brain still exists as part of the Wilder Brain Collection at Cornell University.

Sarah Meservey

29.   THE HART-MESERVEY MURDER

The winter of 1877, Captain Luther Meservey went to sea leaving hi wife Sarah alone in their home in the village of Tenant's Harbor, Maine. When Sarah was found strangled in her own home, the people of this small but close-knit community were terrified at the thought of a killer in their midst. Nathan Hart, a neighbor of the Meserveys, was tried and convicted on evidence so circumstantial that many in town refused to accept the verdict. The controversy persisted for generations and to this day, the murder of Sarah Meservey is considered one of Maine's great unsolved crimes.

NATHAN HART

Date: December 22, 1877

Location: Tenant's Harbor, Maine

Victim: Mrs. Sarah Meservey

Cause of Death: Strangulation

Accused: Nathan Hart

Synopsis:

In 1877, Tenant's Harbor, Maine, was a tiny seacoast village consisting of around forty families of fishermen, lobstermen, and sailors. They were a sociable group with plenty of community activity to brighten the bitter winter months, but Sarah Meservey kept to herself and did not join them. In fact, some said she preferred it when her husband was away at sea and she lived alone. That is probably why no one seemed to notice when she

134

disappeared from public view for five weeks during that December and January.

Sarah was last seen on December 22, 1877, returning from the post office. A neighbor girl, Clara Wall, walked a few steps with her before Sarah entered her house. It was not until January 29, with the Meservey mail piling up at the post office, that community leaders decided to check on Sarah.

Captain Albion Meservey, Luther Meservey's cousin, went with two other men to Sarah's house. When they got no answer, they checked the windows and, finding one that was unlatched, they entered the house that way. They found the rooms in disarray—furniture overturned, drawers ransacked, mirrors broken. In a spare room on the first floor, they found the body of Sarah Meservey wrapped in a blanket. She had been strangled by her own scarf—a white woolen scarf commonly called a "cloud"— wound tightly around her neck and knotted. Her wrists had been bound behind her head with fisherman's cod line. She was fully clothed and still wearing her overcoat and rubbers, indicating that the killer attacked her soon after she entered the house.

The men found a message written on piece of brown paper. One side read:

Monday ev'n'g 24.

The other side read:

i came as a Womn She was out and I
(illegible) till she Came back, not
For Money but I killed her

The illegible word was believed to be "waited."

At first the people of Tenant's Harbor did not believe that one of their community members was a murderer. They thought the killer had come from the sea, as had happened five years earlier on Smuttynose Island, farther down the Maine coast, where two women were brutally murdered by a man who came to the island by rowboat. But those who entered the house could tell that this killer knew the layout and was searching for something. Spent matches on the floor indicated that he was searching by match light. Though he did not find all of her money, motive was surely robbery and the killer was someone from the village.

On February 19, Mrs. Levi Hart received the following letter:

> *Feb. 10, 1878*
> *To Mrs Livi Hart*
> *i thought i would drop you A line to tell you to tell your husband to be careful how he conducted things about Tenants Harbor cause if he dont he and a good many others of the men will get An ounce ball put threw him for tell them that it is no use trying to catch this chap for he will not be caught—so be careful who you take up in at st George you shall hear from me again in three months*
> *L M*

The letter to Mrs. Hart was dated February 10, but postmarked from Philadelphia on February 16. That, together with the condition of the envelope, led to the belief that the letter had been sent to Philadelphia in another envelope and mailed again from there.

Levi Hart and Nathan F. Hart were early suspects in the murder because both men were neighbors of the Meserveys and both were seen at the house after the body was discovered. Captain Albion Meservey was married to Nathan Hart's sister, Irene, and suspicion against Nathan Hart began with a simple statement by Meservey to Deacon Long, "I have been talking with Irene this morning; what if it was Nathan who done it?"

The authorities began to compile circumstantial evidence against Nathan Hart. His stepson Simeon was suddenly flush with cash; he claimed he had won it in a poker game with Nathan. The matches found in the house were an unusual English brand, used in the Hart household. Most importantly, the handwriting on both notes matched a sample of Nathan Hart's handwriting taken from a ship's log provided by Captain Albion Meservey.

Living in Tenant's Harbor at the time was a professor of penmanship and a handwriting expert named Alvin R. Dunton. Using as a benchmark, the ship's log, whose entries had been made by Nathan Hart when serving on Captain Albion Meservey's ship, Dunton ascertained that the hand that wrote the ship's log had also written both of the notes. Nathan Hart was arrested for the murder of Sarah Meservey.

In May 1878, with Nathan Hart still in prison, another letter came to Tenant's Harbor. This one was postmarked "Providence, Rhode Island," and was addressed to Mrs. Mahala Sweetland. The letter was long and rambling; in several thousand words, the killer explained that, a long time ago, he had gone with Sarah Merservey, had gotten fresh with her, and received a slap in the face. He returned the night of the murder to see if she had told anybody. He had planned to rob her and burn the house down. The letter told in detail how he fought with Sarah then strangled her with the scarf. He left the house with $1,100.

The sheriff first believed that this letter had been written by someone else, but Alvin Dunton concluded that it had been written in the same hand as the other two. It was then believed that Hart had written the letter in jail and given it to his wife to mail. He was allowed no more visits with his wife and the fact that no more letters arrived was considered proof that he had been the writer.

Trial: October 1, 1878

Nathan Hart was indicted by the Grand Jury on the strength of the circumstantial evidence—particularly Dunton's handwriting analysis. At the time of the indictment, neither Hart nor his wife could say for certain where Nathan Hart was the evening of December 22, when the murder was committed, or December 24, when the first note was left in the murder house.

At trial in October, however, Hart, his wife, and his stepdaughter all testified that they were positive Nathan Hart had been home the night of December 22, and that on December 24, he was visiting his granddaughter. But the most important witness to change his testimony was Alvin Dunton. He now believed that he had been deliberately deceived when Albion Meservey gave him the ship's log. The log had been written by two different people and, although the first part of the log matched the notes and letter, the second did not. He now believed the sample he was given was not written by Hart. Moreover, neither the notes nor the log matched more recent samples of Nathan Hart's handwriting. Dunton became convinced that Hart did not write the notes and at the trial testified for the defense.

In his closing arguments, County Attorney Lindley M. Staples stressed the discrepancies in the Harts' testimony. He maintained that Nathan Hart was the only man in the county with the character, disposition, opportunity, courage, and requisite knowledge to have done the deed.

The trial lasted six days. The jury deliberated for ninety minutes before returning a verdict of guilty.

Verdict: Guilty of first-degree murder

Aftermath:

Nathan Hart was sentenced to life in prison. (Maine had abolished capital punishment after the hanging of Louis Wagner for the Smuttynose murders. It would later be reinstated and abolished once more.)

Hart's attorney, J. H. Montgomery, had said in his closing arguments that, should Hart be sentenced to prison, he would make it his life's work to free him. However, no attempt was made to appeal the case.

Alvin Dunton was so distressed over his role in convicting a man that he now believed innocent that in 1882, he wrote a book, *The True Story of the Hart-Meservey Murder Trial*, describing how Nathan Hart had been railroaded. The book's subtitle is a good summary of its nature: *In Which Light is Thrown Upon Dark Deeds, Incompetency, and Perfidy; and Crime Fastened Upon Those Whose Position, If Not Manhood, Should have Commanded Honest Dealing*. In the book he not only attempted to prove Hart's innocence but in no uncertain terms, accused Captain Albion Meservey of murdering Sarah Meservey, writing the notes, and deceiving Dunton.

The book also indicted nearly everyone involved in the trial: Sheriff Low, County Attorney Staples, Hart's attorney, J. H. Montgomery, and even fourteen-year-old Cara Wall, who had testified to seeing Sarah Meservey the day she was murdered. Cara could not be trusted, he said, because she had later been accused of trying to poison a rival for her boyfriend's affections. Those mentioned in the book bought as many copies as they could, attempting to keep it out of circulation in Tenant's Harbor. Captain Albion Meservey sued Dunton for libel, seeking $20,000 damages. He was awarded $1,855, but could not collect because Professor Dunton had moved to Boston. Dunton continued to accuse Meservey of murder. Meservey sued again and was awarded $1,686.78, but he never collected that amount either.

Nathan Hart died in prison of "malignant jaundice," five years after being sentenced. Legend in Tenant's Harbor says that Hart actually died from eating a poisoned cake that a woman had brought to him in prison.

More than fifty years later, Hart's attorney, J. H. Montgomery decided to reveal the "facts" in the case. He said that Nathan Hart had actually murdered Mrs. Meservey. He never intended to kill her, just to choke her into submission. Hardly anyone in Tenant's Harbor believed this story.

Most commentators today believe that Nathan Hart was guilty, but the belief is not universal. It will never be known exactly what happened on that day in 1877, and the Hart-Meservey murder remains "Maine's most unusual unsolved murder case."

Benjamin Nathan

30.   WHO KILLED BENJAMIN NATHAN?

THE SCENE OF BENJAMIN NATHAN'S MURDER

Benjamin Nathan, a wealthy stockbroker and philanthropist, was found brutally beaten to death in his Manhattan home the morning of July 29, 1870. Some jewelry and a small amount of cash were stolen and the police were quick to rule the incident a burglary gone bad. But if so, how and when did the burglars enter? And how could four others staying in the house sleep through the violent attack? In fact, the Nathan murder looked more like a classic "locked-room" mystery—a mystery that remains unsolved.

Date: July 29, 1870

Location: New York, New York

Victim: Benjamin Nathan

Cause of Death: Blows to the head

Accused: Washington Nathan, William Kelly,
                     Billy Forester, Daniel Kelly

Synopsis:

July 1870 was oppressively hot in New York City, and the Nathan family was staying at their country home in Morristown, New Jersey. Benjamin Nathan, aged fifty-six, came from a prominent Sephardic Jewish family and was a respected member of the New York Stock Exchange. He regularly commuted that summer from New Jersey to his Broad Street office and on occasion would spend the night at his townhouse on West Twenty-Third Street. Nathan and his two sons, Frederick, age twenty-six, and Washington, age twenty-two, surprised Mrs. Kelly, the housekeeper, when they arrived to spend the night on July 28. The house was in the process of being redecorated and the furniture was in disarray. The bedstead in Mr. Nathan's room had been taken down so he had Mrs. Kelly make a temporary bed of mattresses on the floor of the small reception room leading to his office on the second floor. He had some work he wanted to do before bed. Nathan's sons slept in their rooms on the third floor. Mrs. Kelly slept in the rear of the second floor, and her son William slept on the fourth floor.

Frederick and Washington went out separately that night. Around 11:15 Frederick returned and spoke briefly with his father before retiring. A violent thunderstorm kept Washington out later than he had anticipated. He returned between midnight and one o'clock and, passing the open door of his father's room, saw the old man sleeping.

The two sons awoke early the next morning, as they planned to accompany their father to the synagogue to offer prayers commemorating the anniversary of his mother's death a year earlier. Around six in the morning, Washington came downstairs in his nightshirt to awaken his father. He was shocked to find his father lying in a pool of blood with numerous gaping wounds in his skull. Blood was spattered on the walls and furniture and an overturned chair was smeared with blood. Washington screamed for his brother, who hurried downstairs and, seeing the carnage, ran to the body and cradled his father's head in his arms. They ran out to the street, both in their nightshirts, Frederick's covered with blood, and called for a policeman.

It appeared that Benjamin Nathan had been hit from behind while sitting at his writing desk. The first blow had not been sufficient and there was evidence of a struggle. Two fingers of his left hand had been fractured while warding off a blow. He had at least fifteen wounds on his head, with bone splinters and brain matter exuding in a dozen places. In Nathan's office, the door of his safe was wide open. Missing from the safe were two to three hundred dollars in cash and a gold medal commemorating Mr. Nathan's charitable work. Missing from his clothing were a gold watch and three diamond studs, valued at $700. The police made a thorough search of

140

the house, including floorboards and drainpipes, but the stolen goods were not found.

Some of the injuries to Nathan's head had been made by a blunt object, others by something sharp, so it was first thought that there were two assailants using two different weapons. This view changed when, during the search, Frederick Nathan found an iron tool, known as a carpenter's "dog," covered with blood and hair, lying on the floor near the front door. It was an eighteen-inch iron bar with the ends turned down and sharpened, in the shape of a staple. The "dog" could have inflicted both types of wounds and was clearly the murder weapon.

The announcement of the murder caused a great sensation in New York, and traffic on Twenty-Third Street was blocked all day by sightseers trying to get a look at Nathan's townhouse. The mayor of New York, together with Mr. Nathan's widow, offered a $30,000 reward for information leading to the arrest and conviction of the murderer and a total of $7,000 for the recovery of the various stolen objects. The New York Stock Exchange opened that day with the flag flying at half-mast and the Stock Exchange added $10,000 to the reward.

Police chief John Jordan and Chief Detective James J. Kelso took command of the investigation.

Officer John Mangam was put in charge of the crime scene. Officer Mangam, who had been walking the beat on Twenty-Third Street that night, said he had tried the front door of Nathan's house, once at 1:30 and again at 4:30, as was his custom, and found it locked both times. There were no marks on the lock of the front door to indicate that it had been picked. Mangam later found that the basement door was unlocked—though there was no evidence that anyone entered through the basement, and it was suggested that the killer had unlocked it from the inside for misdirection. John Nies, a newsboy delivering papers that morning, found the front door open at 5:10 a.m. He also witnessed a man, "dressed as a mason," pick up a scrap of paper that looked "like a check" from the steps of the Nathan's house and walk away with it.

Beyond the fact that the murder must have taken place sometime between Washington Nathan's arrival home and 5:10 when the newsboy saw the front door open, none of the evidence was helpful in identifying the killer. What was baffling everyone was how four people staying in the house that night were able to sleep through what had clearly been a violent struggle.

For the press and the public, the prime suspect in the Nathan murder became Washington Nathan. He was an intemperate man who frequently fought with his father over his "habits of life"—drinking, whoring, and reckless spending. His character made him the likely killer, and the press noted that he did not exhibit the same level of emotion as his brother Frederick.

But Washington would not benefit from his father's death. Benjamin Nathan bequeathed $75,000 to each of his eight children, but in Washington's case, the will stipulated that the money would be held in trust until "he married a lady born in and professing the Hebrew faith" or turned twenty-five; even then his mother would have to sign a declaration stating that he was "living a life of regularity and sobriety" before he would get the money. And in spite of their disagreement over lifestyle, Washington and his father were not bitter enemies; Nathan had recently loaned his son $5,000 to capitalize his business.

The inquest on the murder, which lasted nearly a month, appeared to be as much about exonerating Washington Nathan as determining the true killer. He provided a detailed, unabashed account of his whereabouts the night of July 28; he had drinks at the St. James Hotel on Fifth Avenue, read the paper at Delmonico's, went back to the St. James for more drinks, then to a house on East Fourteenth Street, where he remained until nearly midnight with a prostitute named Clara Dale. Miss Dale corroborated his testimony in court. While the murder surely took place after Washington returned home, his doings prior to that time did not indicate a man intent on murder.

Frederick Nathan was never seriously considered as a suspect. He was devoted to his father and was devastated by his death. As a successful broker in his own right, Frederick did not need the money and would not be tempted to kill for his inheritance.

Mrs. Anne Kelly, the housekeeper, was not a suspect either. She was not physically capable of delivering the kind of beating Benjamin Nathan received and she had nothing to gain by his death. The murder left her unemployed and homeless.

However, William Kelly, Mrs. Kelly's adult son, was considered a suspect. Kelly was living on a small army pension and whatever he could earn as a handyman. At the inquest he was thoroughly brow-beaten by the district attorney; he was forced to admit that he was of illegitimate birth, and he was accused on the stand of being a bounty-jumper and deserter in the army, a drunk, and, most importantly, he was accused of consorting with men on the fringes of the criminal world. But no charges were filed against William Kelly; in the end the inquest found that Benjamin Nathan was murdered by a person or persons unknown.

From the start the police believed the murder had been committed by professional burglars. They canvassed all of the pawn shops in the city looking for the stolen goods and brought in at least thirty known burglars for questioning. But it brought them no closer to solving the crime. For a number of reasons, the murder did not look like the work of professionals. The monetary value of the goods taken was quite small for burglars used to stealing thousands, even hundreds of thousands of dollars. The attack on Mr. Nathan was extraordinarily violent for a professional burglar—a profession that sought to avoid violence. And with Nathan away from the house most nights that summer, why would they choose a night when he was there? The weapon, the carpenter's "dog," was baffling as well. The police learned that it was used in professions as diverse as a boat-builder, post-trimmer, ladder-maker, slater, sawyer, sceneshifter in theatres, and iron-molder; but it was not commonly used by burglars.

In spite of its unlikely nature, the burglar theory received a boost in March 1871 when George Ellis, a prisoner in Sing Sing Prison, claimed he knew who killed Nathan and asked for a deal. When brought back to New York City, he claimed that he had done some burglaries together with a professional thief named Billy Forester that summer. Forrester knew that the Nathans had gone to the country and had talked about robbing their house.

Forester became a wanted man but he was not found until more than a year later in September 1872. He immediately called in the law firm of Howe & Hummel, the city's most effective criminal lawyers. Howe & Hummel specialized in murder cases and recently had defended Jacob Rosenzweig for the murder of Alice Bowlsby. Forester's case was not that difficult; he had been in prison in New Orleans most of 1870 and prosecutors could not even prove he was in New York at the time of the murder. The charges against him were dropped.

The burglar theory was revived again in 1873 when professional criminal John T. Irving, serving time in prison in California, confessed to the Nathan robbery. He was brought to New York, where he gave a written confession that he, along with Caleb Gunnion, Nick Jones, Daniel Kelly (no relation to Anne and William Kelly) and a man named McNally, broke into Nathan's house that night. It was Daniel Kelly, Irving said, who committed the murder. He promised to provide corroborating evidence if charges were dropped on two burglaries he had committed in New York—with stolen property valued at over $200,000. Irving's story was not believed and the deal fell through; he was returned to prison.

Speculations:

The lack of any real evidence in the Nathan case inspired a flood of speculation that continued for years:

• From the beginning, the police received hundreds of letters from people who claimed to have evidence in the case or had hunches that they knew were correct. None of these proved to be of any value.

• During the investigation of Billy Forester, George Ellis was questioned by Superintendent Jourdan. Afterward he said this to one of the detectives: "I'm not in this case, but I'll tell you the man that killed Benjamin Nathan is killing Superintendent Jourdan. The chief knows who the murderer is, and the secret is taking him to the grave." In fact Jourdan's health had begun to fail shortly after the crime and he died of pleurisy on October 1, 1872. Any secrets he carried died with him.

• New York police inspector Thomas Byrnes (who did not work the Nathan case), writing in 1886, put much emphasis on John Irving's confession.

• Former New York police chief George W. Walling (who also did not work the case) stated in his1887 autobiography that he believed the killer was William Kelly, the son of the housekeeper. He believed that Kelly admitted his confederates into the house with a view of robbing the safe; in doing so, they aroused Mr. Nathan, who engaged in a struggle that resulted in his death.

• Suspicion would continue to dog Washington Nathan throughout his life, though he was exonerated by the police. He continued his wayward lifestyle after his father's death and in 1879, while paying a call on an actress at the Coleman House, he was shot in the neck by another woman; the bullet lodged in his jaw. A plan was conceived to learn the truth by interrogating Washington Nathan while under anesthesia during the operation to remove the bullet, but the operation never took place. In 1884 Nathan married a Mrs. Arnett, a widowed opera singer (and a gentile) and took his bride to Europe. He died in Boulogne at age forty-four and never received his inheritance.

• Years later attorney Abraham Hummel implied that the killer was his client, Billy Forester, saying, "I cannot speak fully without violating professional honor, for the man is a client of my office, but I can say this, that from what I learned from him, Washington Nathan had no more to do with the killing of his father than I."

• In 1905, Will M. Clemens, a nephew of Mark Twain, wrote a magazine article summarizing the crime and giving his thoughts on the murderer. He believed the killer was an intruder, someone known to Nathan and familiar with the house, who had hidden himself inside until early morning. He was not seeking money or jewelry, but documents from Nathan's safe. When the old man caught him in the act, the thief killed him to avoid identification. The thief then staged the scene to look like a burglary and left through the front door with the documents he sought. Clemens further stated that he knew who the murderer was, "The murderer still lives. Thirty-four years have doubtless changed neither his face, his manner, nor his habit. His name? This is not the time nor place." Clemens never found the proper time and place and never revealed his suspect's name in print.

• Writing in 1924, Edmund Pearson dismissed the notion that the case involved a document ("dear to the hearts of writers of melodrama") and, finding no logical suspects, was content to leave the murder unsolved.

The Nathan murder continues to baffle. Given the evidence available to the police, it would be difficult to prove that a murder had been committed at all, but for the mutilated body in Benjamin Nathan's office. Questions remain: Was the killer an intruder, or a member of the household? Had the motive been money, revenge, information, or something else entirely? What was the origin of the peculiar murder weapon? How did four people manage to sleep through the violent struggle? We are no closer to answers today than in 1870. The Nathan case is, as Inspector Byrnes observed, "The most celebrated and certainly the most mysterious murder that has ever been perpetrated in New York City."

Dr. George Parkman

31.   THE PEDESTRIAN

Called "The Pedestrian" by one Boston newspaper, Dr. George Parkman was famous for his regular daily walks through town to collect rent and loan payments. He did not even own a horse, though he could have easily afforded one, coming from one of the richest families in Boston. His habits were so regular that when he failed to meet his wife for lunch November 23, 1849, it was impossible for her to imagine anything but foul play. Equally impossible to imagine was that the perpetrator was someone from his own social class. When his killer was found to be a former Harvard classmate and current Harvard professor, it became a society crime with a public following to rival America's greatest celebrity murders.

GEORGE PARKMAN

Date: November 23, 1849

Location: Cambridge, Massachusetts

Victim: Dr. George Parkman

Cause of Death: Stabbing

Accused: Dr. John White Webster

Synopsis:

Dr. George Parkman was a man of regular habits. Every day he could be seen walking through Beacon Hill and Boston's West End, where he owned a number of rental properties. His daily routine was so predictable that his neighbors said they could set their watches by the sight of his gaunt figure rushing past. Every afternoon at 2:00 p.m. he met his wife for lunch. When he failed to keep this appointment on Friday, November 23, 1849 and did not return home that evening, his family suspected foul play.

That afternoon he had planned to see Dr. John Webster, a professor of chemistry at the Harvard Medical College, to discuss repayment of a loan. Dr. Webster had been borrowing money, putting up his possessions as collateral. He had borrowed money from Robert Gould Shaw, Parkman's brother-in-law and business partner, using his mineral collection as collateral. Parkman was livid when he learned this because he had already loaned Webster money against the same mineral collection.

George Parkman and John Webster were both members of Boston's privileged class—the class that would later be called "Boston Brahmans"—and had known each other since childhood. They had been classmates at Harvard, graduating two years apart, and Parkman had helped Webster get his position teaching there. But in appearance and attitude the two could not have been more different. Parkman was tall and slender, while Webster was short and stout. Parkman was energetic, but austere and frugal to the extreme; Webster, though, was somewhat dull as a professor, but amiable and fond of food, drink, and good company. Terrible at managing money, Webster was constantly in debt; a growing concern with three daughters approaching marrying age. He owed more than $2,400 and his annual salary was $1,200.

Parkman had studied medicine in Europe with a particular interest in mental illness. He returned to Boston anxious to implement his ideas on treatment of the mentally ill. Though he helped organize and finance the McLean Hospital, he was passed over for the office of director. Devastated by the rejection, Parkman gave up medicine and took over the family business in real estate and lending.

Dr. Parkman was last seen at the Harvard Medical College that Friday. On Saturday his family printed flyers offering a $3,000 reward for information leading to his discovery. Dr. Webster came forward and confirmed that he had met with Dr. Parkman on Friday and had, in fact, paid off one of his loans.

After meeting with Parkman, Dr. Webster had supper at a restaurant and went home. That evening he went with his family to a party, where he enjoyed himself with his neighbors, playing whist and discussing the affairs of the day, including the disappearance of Dr. Parkman. In the days following Parkman's disappearance, there was nothing unusual in Dr. Webster's behavior, with one exception. Webster had a long discussion with Ephraim Littlefield, the janitor at the medical college, concerning Dr.

Parkman's visit to the college on November 23. It was more than the two men had spoken in the twenty years of working at the same college. He also gave Littlefield a turkey for Thanksgiving, something he had never done before.

Littlefield and his wife lived in an apartment next to Dr. Webster's laboratory. He made a small salary cleaning the professors' labs and offices, which he augmented by supplying professors and students with corpses for dissection. It was not clear whether he purchased the corpses from "resurrectionists" or dug them up himself.

What Littlefield remembered about November 23 was that Dr. Webster had kept his laboratory door locked all afternoon and that the fire in his furnace was so hot it could be felt through the wall. Littlefield was in the laboratory when the police came to question Dr. Webster and noticed that the door to his privy was locked. When the police asked what was behind the door, Webster directed their attention elsewhere.

Access to the privy was shared by the dissecting room next door. It had an opening to a brick vault below the basement of the building and was used to dispose of body parts when the students were finished dissecting. Littlefield was convinced that Dr. Webster had murdered Dr. Parkman in his laboratory, chopped him up, and disposed of the pieces in the privy. Working on Thanksgiving Day and the day after, while his wife kept lookout, Littlefield took borrowed tools into the crawlspace under the basement and chipped through several layers of brick on the privy vault. When he finally broke through the wall and shone a lantern through the hole, he saw a man's pelvis with genitals still attached and part of a leg. He knew the students had not been dissecting that week; it had to be Dr. Parkman.

Marshal Turkey of the Boston police was notified of the find and the marshal brought a contingent of policemen to the college. They extracted the body parts from the vault and searched Dr. Webster's laboratory, finding charred bones in the doctor's furnace and more body parts in a tea chest in a room adjoining the laboratory. The body parts were shown to Dr. Parkman's wife who identified them as her husband's remains from some markings on the skin and the extreme hairiness of the body.

The police went to Dr. Webster's home and he agreed to accompany them to the Harvard Medical School to answer some more questions. They took him instead to the Boston jail, where he was arrested for the murder of Dr. Parkman.

Trial: March 19, 1850

The trial of Dr. Webster received national and even international coverage, taking on the characteristics of the celebrity trials of the twentieth century. Sixty thousand Bostonians came to the courthouse to view the trial, and they were admitted to the courtroom in ten-minute shifts.

The prosecution had the daunting task of proving that the remains found at the medical college were, in fact, those of Dr. Parkman. A number of doctors testified that the remains were consistent with a man of Dr. Parkman's age, height, and build, and that they were not the remains of a dissected corpse. Dr. Nathan Keep, Parkman's dentist, testified that a piece of dental work in the jawbone found in Webster's furnace was, without a doubt, made by him for Dr. Parkman, marking the first time human remains were identified in court by dental work.

The defense countered with doctors and dentists of their own who testified that the body could not be conclusively identified and that there was nothing unique in Dr. Parkman's dental work.

The most damaging witness for the prosecution was Ephraim Littlefield, who told of overhearing Dr. Parkman angrily demand payment from Dr. Webster. He testified that Webster had later asked about the privy vault, whether it was possible to shine a light on what was in it. Littlefield responded that it was not, because the gasses put out the flame. And Littlefield related all of the events and suspicions that led him to investigate the vault.

At 8:00 p.m. on March 30, 1850, the jury began deliberation; shortly after 10:00 p.m., they returned with a verdict. Dr. Webster was found guilty and sentenced to hang.

Verdict: Guilty

Aftermath:

The defense filed a writ of error, claiming the judge's instructions to the jury were biased. The writ was denied. Webster asked for a full pardon and that was denied as well.

As the date of Dr. Webster's execution approached, the community—in Boston and beyond—was still divided as to his guilt. Boston authorities received letters from around the country from people opposed to hanging a man on circumstantial evidence and those generally opposed to capital punishment.

In a bid for clemency, Dr. Webster admitted to killing Dr. Parkman but in self-defense, not premeditation. Parkman, he said, had become violently angry over the loan on the mineral collection and Webster picked up a stick and fought him off. Had he intended to commit murder, Wagner said, he certainly would not have done it at the college.

Though petitions were circulated to commute his sentence, the request was refused. On August 30, 1850, Dr. Webster was publically hanged. The fall broke his neck and he was dead within four minutes. He was buried in Copp's Hill Burying Ground, in an unmarked grave to discourage grave robbers.

The case had such notoriety that when Charles Dickens came to America, one of his requests was to visit the room where George Parkman was murdered.

Benjamin Pitezel, et. al

32. "I WAS BORN WITH THE DEVIL IN ME"

Visitors enjoying the color and light of the 1893 World's Columbian Exhibition in Chicago had no idea that not far away Dr. Henry Howard Holmes had set up his own dark, private exhibition of death and torture on a scale comparable to that of the fair itself. Though sometimes mistakenly called America's first serial killer, he could very well be its most prodigious. He was convicted of only one murder, but Holmes confessed to twenty-seven, and the actual total could have been as high as 230.

H. H. HOLMES

Dates: 1879?–1894

Locations: Chicago, IL; Irvington, IN; Toronto, Ontario, Philadelphia, PA

Victims: Benjamin Pitezel and an estimated 230 others.

Cause of Death: Burning, Asphyxiation, Torture

Accused: Herman Webster Mudgett
                      (Dr. Henry Howard Holmes)

Synopsis:

Dr. Henry Howard Holmes was born Herman Webster Mudgett on May 16, 1861 in Galmanton, New Hampshire. While a student at the University of Michigan Medical School, Holmes began to hone his skills as a con artist, stealing cadavers from the university and using the bodies to collect on fraudulent insurance policies. Following his graduation in 1884, he took the name H. H. Holmes and moved to Chicago, ostensibly to practice pharmacy, but actually continuing his lucrative career in fraud.

Holmes took a job at the drugstore of Dr. E. S. Holton on the corner of Wallace and Sixty-Third Street in Englewood, Illinois, south of Chicago. Holton was dying of cancer and Holmes convinced Holton's wife to sell him the store, assuring her she could continue living upstairs after the doctor died. She did not live there very long; after Dr. Holton died, Holmes murdered Mrs. Holton, disposed of her body, and told her friends and relative she had moved to California.

In the lot across from the drugstore, Holmes designed and supervised construction of an enormous three-story building known locally as "the Castle." He made sure that none of the workers stayed on the job long enough to know the full layout of the building, which was a maze of more than 100 rooms, including trapdoors, sliding walls, false floors, airtight doors, and stairways to nowhere.

He operated the Castle as a hotel for visitors to the fair. In the privacy of his soundproof rooms, Holmes would torture and kill hotel guests. Some were locked in rooms fitted with gas lines, which he controlled; he would turn on the gas when they slept. Others were locked in a bank vault near his office where he could listen to their screams as they suffocated. The bodies were dropped down a greased chute to the basement, which was outfitted with a dissecting table, a lime pit, and an enormous furnace. After removing the flesh and cleaning the bones, he would reassemble the skeletons and sell them to medical schools.

When the fair ended, Holmes left Chicago to flee his creditors. He traveled around the United States and Canada, continuing with insurance fraud and other swindles. In Philadelphia he and his longtime associate, Benjamin Pitezel, conspired to fake Pitezel's death for the insurance. Holmes was to procure a charred corpse and claim it was Pitezel, burned in a laboratory explosion. Instead of following their plan, he got Pitezel drunk, and then set him on fire after he passed out.

Though Holmes collected the insurance money, police had been alerted to the plot and Philadelphia detective Frank Geyer began following Holmes in his travels across America. Geyer arrested Holmes in Boston on November 17, 1894 and took him back to Philadelphia to stand trial. In the course of his investigation, Geyer had uncovered the remains of three of Pitezel's children.

Trial: October 28, 1895

Holmes had dismissed his attorneys, choosing to handle his own defense at the trial. The *Philadelphia Inquirer* described his performance as "vigorous and remarkable." But he had failed to establish his case and by the end of the first day, he realized he was failing and brought back his two attorneys. The prosecution's presentation was thorough and methodical and in the end, they prevailed.

Verdict: Guilty of first-degree murder

Aftermath:

H. H. Holmes was sentenced to hang. After his conviction, the Hearst newspapers paid Holmes $7,500 to tell his story. In a series of articles, he confessed to killing twenty-seven people in Chicago. Chicago police investigated the Castle and, using missing persons lists and testimony of neighbors, placed the estimated body count closer to 230.

On May 7, 1896, H. H. Holmes was hanged at Moyamensing Prison in Philadelphia. In accordance with his last wishes, Holmes's coffin was filled with cement before being nailed shut and buried in a grave ten-feet deep with two feet of sand and concrete poured in before it was covered with dirt. He wanted to guarantee that no one would dissect his corpse as he had done to so many others.

Charles Arthur Preller

33.   THE ST LOUIS TRUNK TRAGEDY

On Sunday, April 12, 1885, the manager of the Southern Hotel in St. Louis, Missouri, entered room 144 responding to guests' complaints of a foul odor emanating from inside. The manager found nothing amiss on Sunday but by Tuesday, the stench was unbearable. He checked room 144 again and it appeared that the occupants had moved out, leaving behind several trunks. Inside one was the decomposing body of a man wearing only a pair of white drawers. Apparently one of the two young Englishmen sharing the room had murdered the other. Though the death had been made to look like a political assassination, it was in fact the tragic ending of a "peculiar relationship."

NO. 253.

The Trunk, When Opened, Showing Position of Body, Sketched by Post-Dispatch Artist.

So perish all traitors to the great cause.

Fac-Simile of the Inscription in Trunk, from Tracing Made by Post-Dispatch Artist.

ST. LOUIS POST-DISPATCH, APRIL 14, 1885

Date:	April 5, 1885
Location:	St. Louis, Missouri
Victim:	Charles Arthur Preller
Cause of Death:	Poisoning
Accused:	Hugh Mottram Brooks (Walter H. Lennox Maxwell, MD)

Synopsis:

Charles Arthur Preller and Hugh Mottram Brooks met in Liverpool, England, in January 1885 and travelled together to Boston on the steamship *Cephalonia*. Preller was a successful thirty-two-year-old international travelling salesman for J. H. Dixon, a London textile company. Brooks, twenty-four, was an attorney who had also studied medicine. He was travelling under the name Walter H. Lennox Maxwell, MD.

The two men became fast friends as they crossed the Atlantic; in fact, correspondence found later—described as "not fit for publication"— indicated that they had begun a homosexual relationship. They had planned to travel together to Auckland, New Zealand, but Preller had calls to make in North America first. Maxwell stayed in Boston while Preller went to Montreal; they agreed to meet in St. Louis a few weeks later.

Maxwell arrived in St. Louis on March 30, checked into the Southern Hotel, and was assigned to room 144. Preller arrived on April 3, and though he checked into a room of his own, it was well known that both men were sleeping in room 144. Hotel employees observed that Preller displayed a considerable amount of money, mostly in $100 bills. Maxwell appeared to be broke.

On April 5, Easter Sunday, Maxwell told several people around the hotel that Preller would be traveling in the country but would return to the hotel in a few days. At 10:15 that night, Maxwell was drunk in the hotel bar where, according to Henry Arlington, the headwaiter, he displayed a pistol and a roll of $100 bills. He asked Arlington, "If a man committed murder in this country and had $600, could he beat the case?"

The next day Maxwell went to Hickman's barber shop and had his beard shaved off. He then went to a trunk dealer, Frederick Beiger, and purchased a canvas trunk and two trunk straps. Later that day he paid his hotel bill and disappeared, leaving behind several trunks. It was presumed that Preller would return for them, so the trunks were left undisturbed.

Six days later a peculiar odor was noticed in the room and on April 14, the stench became unbearable. The odor was emanating from a zinc trunk that was bound by ropes and straps that had been purchased at Beiger's. The trunk was opened and inside was the body of a man, naked but for a pair of white drawers with "H. M. Brooks" on the waistband. His mustache had been cut off with scissors and a cross was cut, skin deep, in his breast. Also in the trunk was a paper placard with the inscription: "So perish all traitors to the great cause."

The writing style matched Maxwell's signature on the hotel register. St. Louis police believed the placard was a deliberate attempt to give the misleading impression that the murder was a political assassination.

Among the belongings that Maxwell left behind, the police found several prescription blanks from Fernon's drug store in St. Louis. Mr. Fernon told detectives that he knew Maxwell and that at 2:00 p.m. on April 5, he sold him four ounces of chloroform and at 4:00 p.m. another two ounces. An autopsy was performed on the body and it was determined that Preller had died from chloroform poisoning.

155

A letter among Preller's belongings confirmed what others at the hotel had heard; that the two men had planned to travel together to New Zealand. Police suspected that Maxwell would now be making the journey alone and checking at the train depot, they ascertained that a man fitting Maxwell's description had purchased a ticket to San Francisco, giving the name of "H. M. Brooks."

St. Louis police telegraphed San Francisco's captain of detectives, I. W. Lees, who began a search for Maxwell. A man fitting his description had checked into the Palace Hotel under the name T. C. D'Auguier of Paris. The clerk said that he had a strong French accent. A man named Robbins, who checked in around the same time, recalled talking to D'Auguier on the train. Speaking with a strong French accent, D'Auguier told him he was a French brigadier. As it happened, Robbins spoke fluent French and began addressing D'Auguier in his native language. D'Auguier was forced to admit that he did not speak French, but continued to use the accent for the rest of the trip.

This and other evidence convinced Lees that D'Auguier was the man that was wanted in St. Louis. He also determined that D'Auguier had booked passage on the City of Sydney, a steamer bound for Auckland, New Zealand.

St. Louis police chief Harrigan sent a cablegram to the US consul in Auckland. The cost for a cablegram to New Zealand was $3.34 a word and the message was 155 words, for a total cost of $517.70—an enormous sum in 1885. The St. Louis Globe-Democrat reported at the time that the message was "the most expensive police message ever sent from a telegraph office in the United States." Maxwell was taken into custody when the City of Sydney arrived in Auckland.

Missouri governor Marmaduke obtained extradition papers signed by President Grover Cleveland and sent St. Louis detectives James Tracey and George Badger to New Zealand to pick up the prisoner. After a delay of seventy-seven days, the prisoner was turned over to the detectives, who arrived in San Francisco on August 11. A crowd of more than 2,000 people met them at the train depot when they arrived in St. Louis five days later.

Trial: May 1886

The trial of Walter Maxwell—now known to the court to be Hugh Brooks—was held in St. Louis's Four Courts building and lasted three weeks. Hotel employees, Hickman the barber, Beiger the trunk dealer, Fernon the druggist, and others who had known or seen the two men in St. Louis testified for the prosecution. Their most effective witness, however, was John McCollough, a detective for the Missouri Pacific Railroad.

McCollough had been planted in jail under false charges and for forty-seven days was Hugh Brooks's cellmate. McCollough testified that Brooks had told him he was enraged that Preller refused to pay his passage to Auckland and decided, "on account of his meanness, to fix him."

Brooks told McCollough that Preller had complained of a "private disease" that Brooks said he could cure. He injected Preller with a large amount of morphine to render him unconscious, then he tied a cloth about his face and kept it saturated with chloroform until Preller was dead.

The defense challenged the admissibility of this evidence, but their objection was overruled.

On May 26, Brooks took the stand and testified in his own defense. He claimed that the Sunday after he arrived in St. Louis, Preller complained that he was unwell. From the symptoms, Brooks concluded that he was suffering from a stricture that he could cure by inserting a catheter in the urethra. Preller agreed to the operation and Brooks administered chloroform as an anesthetic. Though unconscious, Preller began to wince as though in pain during the procedure. Brooks administered more chloroform and Preller's breathing became labored and despite Brooks's efforts at resuscitation, Preller died. Brooks fled out of fear that his story would not be believed.

Preller's body was exhumed and examined again to determine if there was any truth to Brooks's story. An autopsy determined that Preller did not have a stricture and had not been treated with a catheter.

On the night of June 4, the case was submitted to the jury and on the following morning, they returned a verdict of guilty.

Verdict: Guilty of murder

Aftermath:

Appeals and requests for new trials were denied, but Brooks was given extra time before his execution so that his parents could arrive from England. On August 10, 1888, as fifty police officers held back the crowd, Hugh Mottram Brooks, alias Walter H. Lennox Maxwell, was hanged in the yard behind Four Courts. It was a double hanging; Brooks was hanged along with Henry Landgraff who, in an unrelated case, was convicted of murdering his girlfriend in 1885.

In jail Brooks had converted to Catholicism and was buried at Calvary Cemetery, St. Louis's main Catholic cemetery, in a plot purchased by his father. Preller was buried in an unmarked grave in the neighboring Bellefontaine Cemetery.

Ballad:

This song about the Preller murder in an adaptation of "Charles Guiteau" a song about the assassination of President Garfield.

Ewing Brooks

My name is Ewin' Brooks,
My name I did deny,
An' left my aged parents
In sorrow for to die.
But little did they think
While in my youth an' bloom,
That on the fifth of August
I'll meet my fatal doom.

I come to old America,
Old Engiand I forsook,
I took the name of Maxwell,
Denied of Ewin' Brooks.
I bein' a very reckless man,
A spendthrift too was I,
I murdered Arthur Fralow
My wants to satisfy.

I went down to the old depot
An' boarded a Frisco train,
I knew that after such a crime
I could not there remain.
The speedin' of the train was fast
An' I thought that I was free,
I did not know a telegram
Was on ahead of me.

I stepped aboard the old steamship
Sayin', "Now I'm free, I know."
The officers arrested me
Down on old Yeland Shore.
They took me back to old Saint Louis
An' placed me in a cell
For the crime that I committed
In the Southern Old Hotel.

158

I bid my friends farewell,
My mother an ' sister so young,
Who pled with Governor Marhouse
That I might not be hung.
He would not even grant them time
To send my father word,
To cross the brinery water
To say,"Farewell, my son."

I place my treasures all in heaven,
My earthly hopes are fled,
I know my friends will grieve for me
Long after I am dead.
An' when I'm dead an' laid away
Within my grave to rest,
I know we'll meet in heaven there
To be forever blest.

Albert Deane Richardson

34.   THE RICHARDSON-MCFARLAND TRAGEDY

On the afternoon of November 25, 1869, Daniel McFarland walked into the office of the *New York Tribune* and shot and killed Albert Richardson, a *Tribune* editor. Richardson had planned to marry Daniel McFarland's ex-wife, Abby Sage McFarland. The facts of the murder were irrefutable, but the trial that followed focused instead on the behavior of Abby McFarland. Was her adultery an attack on the sanctity of marriage that drove Daniel McFarland to murderous insanity? Or had she been justified in leaving a drunken, abusive husband, running to the safety of another man's arms?

THE MURDER OF ALBERT RICHARDSON

Date: November 25, 1869

Location: New York, New York

Victim: Albert Deane Richardson

Cause of Death: Gunshot

Accused: Daniel McFarland

Synopsis:

In a long article published after Daniel McFarland's trial for the murder of Albert Richardson, Daniel McFarland's ex-wife Abby told of their years together as husband and wife. Abby Sage was nineteen years old in 1857 when she married thirty-eight-year-old Daniel McFarland. She was well educated and came from a respectable New England family. At the time she was working as a teacher and had begun writing for publication. McFarland represented himself as a prominent member of the bar in Madison, Wisconsin, with brilliant political prospects. He professed to be a man with

160

temperate habits, holding property worth $20,000 to $30,000. He seemed to be a well-established man who would make Abby a fine husband.

After the wedding they moved to Madison, where Abby learned that Daniel did not have a law practice in Wisconsin; he had only been there for land speculation. He owned several thousand acres, deeply leveraged, and planned to go next to New York where there were opportunities to trade them. At this time he had only enough money to pay their fares to New York. When they reached New York, Abby had to pawn her jewelry to pay for their lodging.

They had not been married long before Abby learned that her husband had a fondness for alcohol and a violent temper. When he was drunk, Daniel would become terribly profane and fly into a rage over some perceived insult. Other times he would become morose and not speak for days. Sometimes Abby would hide knives and scissors out of fear that Daniel would do her or himself harm. After at his violent fits of rage, he would always be remorseful, promising to stop drinking and never frighten her again. But the cycle would always repeat.

Daniel made some profit from his Wisconsin land deals but his drinking made it difficult to hold a steady job. In spite of their poverty, Daniel and Abby had two sons, Percy born in 1860 and Daniel in 1864. During this time the family would move from boardinghouse to boardinghouse, always deeply in debt.

Abby tried her hand at dramatic reading and found she had a flair for it, and at Daniel's urging she began to augment their income by giving public readings. She soon became an actress as well, taking roles at Edwin Booth's Winter Garden theatre. She also began publishing her writings. Her new career allowed Abby to broaden her social circle. She became close friends with Horace Greely, owner of the *New York Tribune*, his sister, Mrs. John Cleveland, and Tribune editor Samuel Sinclair and his wife.

Daniel McFarland used Abby's new connections to secure a political appointment, but he was jealous of her new friends. He would open her mail and read her letters before giving them to her. And his temper had gotten worse. He was now threatening to kill Abby or himself and would sometimes physically strike her. He kept the money she earned from performing and spent much of it on drink.

In January 1867 the McFarlands moved to a boardinghouse at 86 Amity Street in New York. Not long after, Albert Deane Richardson also moved into the boardinghouse. Richardson was a writer and editor at the *New York Tribune*. He had been a war correspondent during the Civil War and in 1863, while trying to run the Confederate batteries at Vicksburg, was captured and spent a year and a half in Confederate prisons. In December he and another correspondent escaped from prison in Salisbury, North Carolina.

161

Richardson was married with five children but during his imprisonment Richardson's wife and infant daughter had died.

Abby knew Richardson socially through Horace Greely and his sister. During the day Richardson used his room as an office, with a stenographer, an artist, and a messenger boy to assist in his literary work. On February 19, 1867, Daniel McFarland came home to find his wife standing at Richardson's door, discussing a manuscript with him. The sight infuriated McFarland, who went into a three-day drunken rage during which he made the usual threats of murder and suicide. At one point he suggested they separate and Abby assented. He later changed his mind, but she did not. She left him for good on February 21.

After Abby left Daniel McFarland, Albert Richardson offered his sympathy and helped in any way he could and gradually they fell in love. On the evening of March 13, Richardson met her to walk her home from the theatre where she was performing. As they walked from the theatre, Daniel McFarland came up behind them and fired a pistol at Richardson, wounding him in the thigh. He fired two more times but did not hit either of them. McFarland was arrested but somehow managed to avoid prison.

As the love between Abby McFarland and Albert Richardson continued to blossom, Daniel McFarland began legal proceedings to get custody of the children. He agreed to a compromise where Percy would stay with him and Daniel with Abby. But to Daniel this meant that Abby would never see Percy again. In the spring of 1868, she attempted to see Percy but was barred by McFarland in another fit of rage. She decided then to take her friends' advice and file for divorce.

In New York, the only legal ground for divorce was adultery, and though Abby believed she could prove that Daniel was adulterous, she decided to go to Indiana where divorce was allowed for drunkenness, extreme cruelty, and failure to support a wife. She took up residency in Indiana for sixteen months, filed for divorce, then returned to her mother's house in October 1869, legally free from the bonds of marriage.

Abby and Albert had been guarded in their relationship and stayed apart while she was in Indiana. Now that her marriage was over, they felt free to be openly together and Albert spent Thanksgiving in Massachusetts with Abby and her family. The day after Thanksgiving, he returned to New York. Just a week later, Abby received word that Albert had been mortally wounded, shot by her ex-husband in the office of the New York Tribune. She hurried to New York to nurse him.

When she arrived in New York, Albert Richardson was on his deathbed, lying in a room at the Astor House. His dying wish was for them to marry. On November 30, 1869, Albert Richardson and Abby Sage McFarland were married by Reverend Henry Ward Beecher. Among the witnesses was Horace Greely. Two days later Albert Richardson was dead.

At first, New York journalists came to the defense of their fallen comrade and began digging up dirt on Daniel McFarland, including "the habit of opium eating for the purpose of drowning his sorrows." But very soon the mood changed. On December 2, the *New York Sun* published a lengthy editorial entitled "A Public Outrage on Religion and Decency" that condemned Albert Richardson for luring Abby away from her husband. When that edition sold out, the *Sun* dredged up everything they could find to portray Abby and Albert as sinful adulterers, including this allegation from Daniel McFarland's brother: "Abby went reading just to get a chance to paint her face, pass for beauty, and get in with that free-love tribe at Sam Sinclair's."

The rest of the New York papers followed the *Sun's* lead, but opposing views were also printed, sometimes in the same editions as the condemnations. The *Herald* printed this quote from Mrs. S. F. Norton, speaking in front of the Feminist Reform Club: "The recent shooting of Mr. Richardson is an unfortunate occurrence that illustrates the fundamental problem of marriage, inequality of rights between husband and wife."

The newspapers were forcing people to choose sides, and New Yorkers were overwhelmingly choosing McFarland's fight for the sanctity of marriage over Abby Richardson's immorality.

Trial: April 4, 1870

That mood held at the trial, where the courtroom was filled to capacity with spectators hoping to get a glimpse of the evil Abby Richardson. She never appeared at the trial, but McFarland's attorneys took full advantage of the audience and arranged to have ten-year-old Percy McFarland sit by his father's side. Percy, happy to be with his father, appeared oblivious to the trial's import.

Abby's supporters distrusted the ability of the district attorney and brought in former judge and current congressman Noah Davis to assist the prosecution. McFarland also brought in the big guns. He would be defended by John Graham, who had been associate council in the Sickles case, in which Daniel Sickles was acquitted of the murder of his wife's lover on the grounds of temporary insanity. He would take the same defense in the McFarland case.

The prosecution focused on the misery of the McFarland marriage, with Abby's relatives and friends, including Horace Greeley, giving testimony. The defense changed the focus to the adulterous relationship between Abby and Albert Richardson. An intercepted letter from Albert to Abby, coupled with Daniel McFarland's family history of mental instability, allegedly triggered the insanity in McFarland that led to the shooting.

The trial lasted five weeks. The jury deliberated for an hour and fifty-five minutes and found Daniel McFarland not guilty.

Verdict: Not guilty

Aftermath:

Abby published her version of the events leading to her ex-husband's death in the *Tribune* on May 11, 1870 and though it brought more of the public to her side, it was too late to affect the outcome of the trial. Abby Richardson kept the promise she made to her dying husband and raised the Richardson children as her own—not an easy task with the Richardson children in or near adolescence and resentful of this new mother. She was also raising her own youngest son, now renamed Willie. Eventually Percy returned to her and adopted the surname Sage, Abby's maiden name.

Abby continued her literary and dramatic pursuits, composing verse and writing and producing plays. Abby also edited a volume of Albert Richardson's unpublished work. She died of pneumonia in Rome, Italy, on December 5, 1900.

Daniel McFarland went west and was last heard from in Colorado in 1880.

Albert Richardson was buried in his hometown of Franklin, Massachusetts. There, still standing, is a monument commemorating his service during the Civil War. It bears the inscription: "Many give thee thanks who never new thy face, so, then, farewell, kind heart and true."

William Robinson, et al.

35. THE MASSACHUSETTS BORGIA

The Order of Pilgrim Fathers was a Massachusetts social group whose chief purpose was to provide cheap life insurance for working-class men and women. In the summer of 1886, the Order became suspicious of one of their members, Mrs. Sarah Jane Robinson, whose son William was on his deathbed just six months after the death of her daughter Lizzie. When officers of the Order of Pilgrim Fathers expressed their concerns to the chief of police, they learned that Mrs. Robinson was already under investigation for the death of her nephew just a few weeks earlier. In each case the

SARAH JANE ROBINSON

cause of death was arsenic poisoning and when the full tally of Mrs. Robinson's poison murders was revealed, the press would dub her "The Massachusetts Borgia."

Dates: 1881–1886

Location: Cambridge, Massachusetts

Victims: Oliver Sleeper, Moses Robinson, Lizzie Robinson, Annie Freeman, Prince Freeman, Emma Robinson, Tommy Freeman, William Robinson

Cause of Death: Poisoning

Accused: Sarah Jane Robinson

Synopsis:

Mrs. Robinson was born Sarah Jane Tennant in Northern Ireland and came to America when she was fourteen, along with her nine-year-old sister Annie. They lived in Cambridge, Massachusetts, with their older brother. Sarah Jane worked as a dressmaker and at nineteen, she married Moses Robinson, a machinist. They had eight children—three of which died in infancy or early childhood—and the family was too poor for Sarah Jane to stop working. They moved often, trying to evade debt collectors.

In 1881, the Robinson's landlord, Oliver Sleeper, took sick and after Sarah Jane's nursing, he was pronounced dead of heart disease. She submitted a bill of $50 to the estate to pay for her nursing services. Sleeper's relatives gave her a remission on her rent instead, but were more concerned about $3,000 in cash missing from Sleeper's apartment. Though it was never proven, it was assumed that Mrs. Robinson took the money and used it to pay her creditors.

Mrs. Robinson augmented the family's meager income by mortgaging their furniture and other belongings, and she would fraudulently mortgage the same property multiple times. To keep from getting caught, she periodically needed a large influx of cash to pay off her debts and start over. In 1882, her forty-five-year-old husband Moses died suddenly. He was insured by the Pilgrim Fathers for $2,000.

After Moses died, Sarah Jane's sister Annie and her husband, Prince Arthur Freeman (Prince was his name, not his title), came to live with her. Within a year, Annie and her husband were both dead, bringing Sarah Jane another $4,000 in insurance money.

But the household was still too large to maintain. Sarah Jane had four children of her own to take care of and was also caring for her sister's son, Tommy. In 1884, her ten-year-old daughter Emma died and two years later Tommy Freeman died as well. She persuaded her daughter Lizzie to enroll with the Pilgrim Fathers and Lizzie made her brother William the beneficiary. When Lizzie started talking about marrying and moving away, she suddenly took sick and three weeks later, Lizzie was dead. Mrs. Robinson told her friends that she had a dream in which Lizzie returned for her brother. Soon after, William was dead as well.

As William Robinson lay on his deathbed, the Pilgrim Fathers sent Dr. Emory White to the Robinson house to attend to him. White was aware of the other deaths at the Robinson's house and resolved to watch William closely. As William grew worse, Dr. White sent a specimen of his vomit to a Harvard chemist for analysis. When Dr. White discussed his suspicions with Boston police chief Parkhurst, he learned that they were already investigating the death of Tommy Freeman on the advice of another suspicious doctor. The chemical analysis proved that William Robinson's stomach was full of arsenic, but the knowledge came too late to save his life. Sarah Jane Robinson was arrested for the murder of her son.

At the suggestion of the Order of Pilgrim Fathers, the police exhumed the bodies of other insured relatives of Mrs. Robinson. Lizzie Robinson, Prince and Annie Freeman, and their son Tommy had all died of arsenic poisoning. The success of this investigation prompted police to go back even further. The bodies of Moses Robinson and Oliver Sleeper were exhumed; both had died of arsenic poisoning.

Trials: December 12, 1887
                February 6, 1888

Sarah Jane Robinson was tried for the murder of her son William. Also indicted were Dr. Charles C. Beers, a maker of patent medicine who was a longtime suitor of Mrs. Robinson; and Thomas Smith, chaplain for the Pilgrim Fathers who was calling on Mrs. Robinson almost daily around the time of her son's death. Beers and Smith were not prosecuted.

The prosecutors in Mrs. Robinson's case were hamstrung by the fact that they were prohibited from mentioning any of the arsenic deaths but William's. They were further hampered by a lackluster prosecuting attorney whose questions were described as "slow, rambling, and...pointless." The trial lasted six days and ended in a hung jury; the jury deliberated for forty-eight hours, but they could not reach an agreement.

On March 5, 1888, Mrs. Robinson was arraigned on four more indictments charging her with the murders of Prince and Annie Freeman, Tommy Freeman, Oliver Sleeper, and Moses Robinson. The murders of Mrs. Robinson's sister and brother-in-law, Annie and Prince Freeman, were considered part of the same plot to commit insurance fraud and would be tried together.

Testimony showed that Annie Freeman was stricken with pneumonia in her home in South Boston. She was gradually improving, but took a turn for the worse after Mrs. Robinson fired her nurse and took sole charge of her sister's health. Mrs. Robinson had a premonition that her sister would never recover, and, sure enough, Annie died soon after. She convinced Prince Freeman to move his family to her home in Cambridge and a few weeks later, one-year-old Elisabeth Freeman died. Mrs. Robinson had another premonition; her dead husband appeared and told her that Prince would soon die. This premonition came true as well.

The defense argued that Prince Freeman had died of natural causes, possibly from breathing fumes of sulfuric acid at his job for Norway Iron Works. Or he could have been murdered by someone else, such as Dr. Beers or Thomas Smith, who had both been indicted for William's murder.

167

But the Commonwealth's case was much stronger, and this time the jury took less than an hour to return a verdict of guilty.

Verdicts: Hung jury
                 Guilty of the first-degree murder

Aftermath:

Mrs. Robinson's attorneys appealed the case to the supreme judicial court on the grounds that the prosecution had not proven that she had plotted the insurance fraud so it was not valid to use the death of Annie Freeman in the prosecution of Prince Freeman's murder. The appeal was denied.

Sarah Jane Robinson was sentenced to hang on November 16, 1888. By the end of October, public sentiment had turned in Mrs. Robinson's favor and a petition to commute her sentence to life in prison was submitted to Governor Ames. Among the five hundred signers were seventy-six ministers and seven members of the jury that convicted her. On November 15, the governor commuted Mrs. Robinson's sentence to life in solitary confinement.

Sarah Jane Robinson died in prison January 3, 1906 at the age of sixty-seven from complications following a prolonged illness.

Horatio Sherman and nine others.

36. THE POISON FIEND

When Horatio Sherman took sick after returning home from a weeklong drunken spree, he said it was just one of his "old spells." His wife Lydia agreed, and dosed him with brandy as usual. But Horatio's doctor, who had treated his alcohol-induced "spells" before, was suspicious this time and when Horatio died two days later, the doctor ordered a postmortem examination that revealed the cause of death to be arsenic poisoning. When it was further learned that Lydia Sherman's first two husbands and seven of her children had died of arsenic poisoning as well, she was called "The Arch Murderess of Connecticut," "The Modern Borgia," and "The Poison Fiend."

MURDER PAMPHLET, 1873

Dates:	May 1864–May 1871
Locations:	Danbury, Connecticut; New York, New York
Victims:	Edward Struck, Martha Ann Struck, Edward Struck Jr., William Struck, George Whitfield Struck, Ann Eliza Struck, Dennis Hurlburt, Frank Sherman, Ada Sherman, Horatio Sherman
Cause of Death:	Poisoning
Accused:	Lydia Sherman

169

Synopsis:

Born Lydia Danbury in Burlington, New Jersey, in 1824, Lydia Sherman was orphaned at the age of nine months and raised by an uncle. At sixteen she was working as a tailor in New Brunswick, New Jersey, and had joined the Methodist Church. At church she met Edward Struck, a widower with four children, and when Lydia was around twenty, she and Edward were married.

They lived happily in New York City, raising six children, but their lives changed when Edward Struck took a job on the newly formed New York Metropolitan Police Force. Struck was called to a disturbance in a New York hotel and arrived too late to prevent a murder. A rumor began to circulate that Struck had stayed away out of fear for his own life. An inquest was held, and Struck was dismissed from the force.

Edward Struck became severely despondent after his dismissal and was unable to hold a job. Eventually he stopped trying to work and was ashamed to even leave the house. He began talking about suicide, and his former boss, a police captain, advised Lydia to send him to a lunatic asylum. Another policeman, a sergeant who lived in the same building, concluded that Struck was out of his mind and would never recover. He advised Lydia to "get him out of the way," and told her use arsenic, giving her instructions on where to buy it and how much to use.

After giving it some thought, Lydia bought some arsenic from a druggist and added a thimbleful to a portion of oatmeal gruel, which she gave to her husband. That night Struck became violently ill. A doctor was called, who told Lydia that her husband had "softening of the brain" and would never recover. Struck died at eight o'clock the next morning.

While Struck's death eased some of the tension on Lydia, she still had financial problems. She did not believe she could adequately support her two youngest children, six-year-old Martha Ann and four-year-old Edward, and decided "it would be better for them if they were out of the way." Lydia began giving them each small amounts of arsenic. When they became sick, the doctor said they had gastric fever. After severe vomiting, both children died. "He was a beautiful boy," Lydia said later about Edward, "and did not complain during his illness."

Lydia now had four children in the house and was working as a nurse and seamstress. Her fourteen-year-old son George was earning $2.50 a week as a painter. When George took sick with "painter's colic" and could no longer work, Lydia feared he would become a burden. She mixed a little arsenic with his tea. The doctor said George died of painter's colic.

The older children had moved out and now only Ann Eliza was living with Lydia. "Downhearted and much discouraged," Lydia thought that if she could get rid of Ann Eliza, then she and her oldest daughter Lydia could make a living together. When Ann Eliza came down with a fever that winter, Lydia added a little arsenic to her medicine. Ann Eliza died four days later.

That same winter, her oldest daughter died of natural causes, leaving Lydia all alone. After trying several other occupations, Lydia took a job as a housekeeper for an old woman in Stratford, Connecticut. Eight months later, she left this job for another housekeeping position with an old man named Dennis Hurlburt. Within a few days of her employment, Hurlburt proposed marriage and Lydia accepted.

Lydia was happy as Mrs. Hurlburt for about fourteen months, then Dennis Hurlburt took sick. Though it was later proven that Hurlburt died of arsenic poisoning, Lydia claimed in her confession that she was not responsible:

> *I wish to say that I never gave Mr. Hurlburt anything to my knowledge that would cause any sickness whatever. There may have been arsenic in one of the papers I put together, but if there was, I did not know it.*

In his will Dennis Hurlburt left Lydia the house and $10,000.

She was then approached by Horatio N. Sherman, a widower who was looking for someone to take care of his baby. He soon proposed to her, and although she did not agree right away, she was quite taken with Sherman and agreed to help him out of debt. They eventually were married, but things did not work out as she planned. Sherman turned out to be a hopeless alcoholic who could not be trusted with money.

Sherman's mother-in-law was still living with them and taking care of the baby, Frank. One day Sherman remarked to Lydia that he wished Frank would die so the old woman would have no reason to stay. This made sense to Lydia, who put some arsenic in little Frankie's milk. She also poisoned Sherman's fourteen-year-old daughter Ada.

Horatio Sherman's drinking increased. He did nothing to help his family and spent every cent Lydia gave him on liquor. Lydia finally convinced him to join a temperance society, and Sherman took a sobriety pledge. He kept the pledge for several weeks, then sold the piano for $300 and went on a binge.

Sherman was sick when he returned home a week later. Lydia put arsenic in a bottle of brandy, and the more Sherman drank, the sicker he got. When a doctor examined him, Sherman said, "It may be one of my old spells." But Dr. Beardsley did not think the symptoms were consistent with alcohol-related sickness and suspected foul play.

Sherman died the next day, and Dr. Beardsley performed a postmortem examination. Dr. Beardsley's suspicions were confirmed when Sherman's stomach was chemically analyzed. Sherman had died of arsenic poisoning, and Lydia was charged with his murder. The bodies of Frankie and Ada were exhumed and it was determined that they died of arsenic poisoning as well. Then Dennis Hurlburt was exhumed, and another count of murder was added against Lydia.

Trial: April 16, 1872

Lydia Sherman's trial lasted eight days; it was well attended and closely followed by newspapers throughout America. The stories often commented on how ordinary Mrs. Sherman looked. The prim and proper forty-eight-year-old defendant came to court wearing a black alpaca dress, black-and-white shawl, straw hat, and black kid gloves. She appeared calm and almost cheerful behind her thin, lacy veil.

The defense tried to convince the jury that Horatio Sherman had taken arsenic accidentally, or perhaps had committed suicide, despondent over his financial problems and the recent deaths of two of his children. But the evidence against Lydia was overwhelming. She was found guilty of second-degree murder and sentenced to life in prison.

Verdict: Guilty of second-degree murder

Aftermath:

While awaiting sentencing, Lydia Sherman dictated her confessions, in which she admitted to most of the murders she was accused of committing. The book became a bestseller.

Lydia Sherman died in Wethersfield Prison in 1878.

Ballad:

This anonymous ballad was originally published as a broadside and sold in Boston. It probably began life as a poem but has since been set to music.

Lydia Sherman

Lydia Sherman is plagued with rats
Lydia has no faith in cats.
So Lydia buys some arsenic,

And then her husband gets sick;
And then her husband, he does die,
And Lydia's neighbors wonder why.

Lydia moves, but still has rats;
And still she puts no faith in cats;
So again she buys some arsenic
This time her children; they get sick,
This time her children, they do die,
And Lydia's neighbors wonder why.

Lydia lies in Wethersfield jail,
And loudly does she moan and wail.
She blames her fate on a plague of rats;
She blames the laziness of cats.
But her neighbors' questions she can't deny—
So Lydia now in prison must lie.

Charles Silver

37.   THE BALLAD OF FRANKIE SILVER

Charlie and Frankie Silver were the ideal young married couple, so the legend goes. He was strong and handsome; she was kind and beautiful. They lived an idyllic life, with their baby daughter, in a little cabin in the woods of Burke County, North Carolina. But things changed quickly when Frankie learned that Charlie had been seeing other women. Allegedly, one night in December 1831, she methodically and brutally murdered Charlie in his sleep. That is the legend of Frankie Silver, but the reality is even darker. Frankie had endured physical abuse from Charlie throughout their marriage until, on that December night, she fought back to save her own life.

THE EXECUTION OF FRANKIE SILVER

Frankie Silver's subsequent execution was a tragic miscarriage of justice.

Date: December 22, 1831

Location: Burke County, North Carolina

Victim: Charles Silver

Cause of Death: Blows from an axe

Accused: Francis "Frankie" Stewart Silver

Synopsis:

"The Ballad of Frankie Silver" is another great old North Carolina folk song that tells a story of an actual murder, and like "Omie Wise" and "Tom Dooley," the story it tells is mostly fiction. The facts concerning the murder

174

of Charlie Silver are sparse. Charlie and Frankie (both aged nineteen or twenty in 1831) and their one-year-old daughter, Nancy, lived in a one-room cabin near Toe River. On December 23, 1831, Frankie Silver went to her mother-in-law's cabin to ask if she had seen Charlie. Frankie said that he had gone on a hunting trip with a neighbor, George Young, but she had expected him home before then. Charlie's parents had not seen him and thought Frankie was being unduly anxious. But when he was still missing on December 24, his father, John Silver, accompanied Frankie to George Young's house.

George Young told them there had been no plans for a hunting trip and, in fact, he had not seen Charlie since Thanksgiving. Frankie got angry and accused him of lying. John calmed her down and suggested they return to her cabin. There they found Charlie's dog Drum outside the cabin. They knew Charlie would not have gone hunting without his dog, and that Drum never left his master's side. Outside in the snow they found Charlie's hat, a fur cap made from an albino raccoon. Now his father suspected foul play and called in the sheriff.

The sheriff began investigating, searching the woods and river near the cabin. John Silver got impatient and sent for a "Guinea Negro conjure man"—a slave at the home of Colonel Williams, who used a glass divining ball to locate missing objects and people. In some versions of the story, it was Colonel Williams himself who had learned the skill from a slave; in others, it was just a perceptive neighbor who saw bloodstains on the floor. In any case, the locator persuaded them to lift the floorboards. There they found huge splotches of blood and hunks of charred flesh and bone. They stirred the ashes in the fireplace and found them to be thick with grease. They also found a piece of iron that Frankie identified as part of the heel of Charlie's hunting boot. The pieces of Charlie were quickly buried. As new pieces were found, the family, not wanting to disturb Charlie's buried remains, dug new graves. Charlie Silver is buried in at least three graves. Frankie was arrested, along with her mother, Barbara Stuart, and her brother, Blackstone Stuart.

The Stuarts (later changed to Stewart) and the Silvers did not get along. The Stuarts were poor; the Silvers owned a considerable amount of land and were wealthy by comparison. The land under Charlie and Frankie's cabin was a wedding gift from John Silver. The Stuart family planned to move west and had tried to persuade Charlie to sell the land and go with them. Charlie refused. This was thought to be the motive for the murder, and the reason other family members were arrested.

Frankie's father, Isaiah Stuart, knew enough about the law to obtain a writ of habeas corpus and get his wife and son released from jail. Frankie was held in the Morganton, North Carolina, jail for the murder of Charlie

Silver and would say nothing about what had happened in the cabin other than assert her innocence. Frankie's silence was offset by the Silver family who spoke volumes. Charlie's brother Alfred, who was fifteen at the time, described what happed with a level of detail that he could not possibly have known. He said that Frankie had asked Charlie to chop some firewood, knowing Charlie would soon be away hunting. Charlie cut down a hickory tree, then chopped and stacked enough firewood to last a week. Alfred continued:

> *Being tired and sleepy after the labor of chopping, my brother lay down on the floor, close by the fire with his little girl in his arms, and went to sleep. His head rested on an inverted stool for a pillow. Frankie gently took the baby from his breast, put it to bed, picked up the axe from the door, where she had placed it for the purpose, and whacked his head half off at a single blow. She intended to cut it clean off, but miscalculated and either stood too close or too far back. The first lick did not kill him instantly, for he sprang to his feet and cried: 'God bless the child!' The wife fled to the bed by the child, and covered herself up, 'til she heard Charles fall, then jumped out and finished the job with a second blow.*

Other members of the Silver family believed that Frankie's parents were behind the killing. The legend among the Silvers says that Frankie's father was in the cabin urging her to strike, saying, "If you don't kill him, I will," or "If you don't kill him, I'll kill you." Some said Isaiah Stuart struck the second blow.

Trial: March 29, 1832

Frankie Silver's trial lasted less than two days. Her attorney, Thomas Wilson, probably in consultation with her father, decided to continue denying everything, believing that the prosecution did not have enough evidence to convict Frankie of murder. The evidence was all circumstantial and it was not an easy case for the jury to decide. At one point in their deliberation, the jury was deadlocked at nine for acquittal and three for conviction. They asked if they could rehear some of the testimony, so the witnesses were called to testify again. In the end the jury found Frankie guilty of murder and she was sentenced to hang.

The case was appealed to the North Carolina Supreme Court. At issue was the reexamination of witnesses. They had been isolated before their initial testimony but afterward had been allowed to hear each other's testimony. The state's supreme court upheld the verdict. The date for Frankie's execution was set for June 28, 1833.

Verdict: Guilty of murder

Aftermath:

On May 18, 1832, with her execution just over a month away, Frankie Silver escaped from the Morganton jail. Either her father was able to pick the locks or they had help from jailer John Maguire, who was known to have signed a petition asking the governor to pardon Frankie. Outside the jail Frankie cut her hair short and dressed like a boy. She went with her father and her uncle in a wagon heading for Tennessee. Their progress had been interrupted by a flooded river, and Frankie was walking behind the wagon when they were apprehended by the law. According to Alfred Silver, the sheriff called out, "Frankie?" To which she answered, "I thank you, sir; my name is Tommy." And her uncle added, "Yes, her name is Tommy." Frankie was arrested and taken back to Morganton.

There is much folklore surrounding the hanging of Frankie Silver. It is sometimes said that she is the only woman ever hanged in North Carolina, or the first woman hanged in North Carolina. Her gravestone reads: "Only woman ever hanged in Burke County." None of these statements are true. She was not even the first woman hanged in Burke County. In 1813, a slave named Betsy was hanged as an accomplice in the murder of her master. In 1788 John and Elizabeth Wells were both hanged, probably in Morganton, for burning down a neighbor's house.

Legend says that Frankie Silver was hanged from an oak tree in Morganton—even today, residents of Morganton can show you the tree—but it is more likely that she was hanged from a gallows constructed for her execution, as prisoners before and after her were. There are no eyewitness accounts of the hanging, but secondhand stories say that as many as ten thousand people came to watch, only to find that a tall stockade fence had been built to conceal it from the public.

In a bid for clemency, Frankie confessed to the murder. She could not read or write, so the confession was dictated to her lawyer. Unfortunately there is no surviving copy of the confession, but reportedly it claimed that she swung the axe at Charlie in self-defense as he was loading his gun to kill her.

In the time between her conviction and the date of her execution, public sentiment turned in Frankie's favor. Dozens of petitions were drawn up and sent to the governor requesting a pardon. Seven of the jurors who convicted Frankie signed a petition for her pardon. Governor Stokes said he would need all twelve signatures to pardon Frankie Silver.

The most impressive petition was from the ladies of Burke and Buncombe County. It was extraordinary because of its strong wording, coming from citizens who, at the time, could not vote, serve on juries, or even hold property. In it they made the case that Frankie's lawyer did not: that Frankie acted in self-defense and the homicide was justifiable.

> *The husband of the unfortunate creature now before you we are informed, Sir, was one of that cast of manhood who are wholly dissolute of any of the feeling that is necessary to make a good Husband or parent—the neighborhood people are convinced that his treatment of her was both unbecoming and cruel very often and at the time too when female delicacy would most forbid it. He treated her with personal violence. He was said by all the neighborhood to have been a man who never made use of any exertions to support either his wife or child, which terminated as frequently the case that those duties Nature ordered and intend the husband to perform were thrown to her. His own relatives admit of his having been a lazy and trifling man.*

The governor, now David L. Swain, was moved by the petition and the confession, but not to the point of clemency. On July 12, 1833, Frankie Silver, wearing a white dress made for her by the ladies of Burke County, was hanged in Morganton, North Carolina.

Ballad:

It is said that when Frankie Silver was asked, on the gallows, if she had any last words, she responded by reciting or singing the confessional verses we now know as "The Ballad of Frankie Silver." The song (also known as "I Try that Awful Road") was collected in the 1930s, in the Toe River Valley, North Carolina. It is not known who actually wrote it or when it was written.

The Ballad of Frankie Silver

This dreadful dark and dismal day
Has swept my glories all away;
My sun goes down, my days are past,
And I must leave this world at last.

Oh! Lord, what will become of me?
I am condemmed, you all now see;
To heaven or hell my soul must fly,
All in a moment when I die.

Judge Donnell my sentence has passed,
These prison walls I leave at last;
Nothing to cheer my drooping head
Until I'm numbered with the dead.

But Oh! That awful judge I fear.
Shall I that awful sentence hear:
"Depart, ye cursed, down to Hell
And forever there to dwell."

I know that frightful ghosts I'll see,
Gnawing their flesh in misery;
And then and there attended be
For murder in the first degree.

Then shall I meet that mournful face,
Whose blood I spilled upon this place;
With flaming eyes to me he'll say,
"Why did you take my life away?"

His feeble hands fell gently down.
His chattering tongue soon lost its sound.
To see his soul and body part
It strikes with terror in my heart.

I took his blooming days away,
Left him no time to God to pray;
And if sins fall upon his head,
Must I not bear them in his stead?

The jealous thought that first gave strife
To make me take my husband's life,
For months and days I spent my time
Thinking how to commit this crime.

And on a dark and doleful night
I put the body out of sight,
With flames I tried to him consume.
But time would not admit it done.

You all see me and on me gaze.

179

Be careful how you spend your days;
And never commit this awful crime,
But try to serve your God in time.

My mind on solemn subjects rolls.
My little child, God bless its soul;
All you that are of Adam's race,
Let not my faults this child disgrace.

Farewell, good people, you all now see
What my bad conduct's brought on me;
To die of shame and disgrace
Before the world of human race.

Awful indeed to think of death,
In perfect health to lose my breath;
Farewell my friends, I bid adieu,
Vengeance on me you must now pursue.

Great god! How shall I be forgiven?
Not fit for earth, nor fit for heaven;
But little time to pray to God,
For now I try that awful road.

Amasa Sprague

38.   RHODE ISLAND INEQUITY

The body of Amasa Sprague was found shot and beaten on the road between his factory and his mansion on New Year's Day, 1844, and suspicion immediately fell on three members of Sragueville's Irish community. Nicholas Gordon was known to hold a grudge against Amasa Sprague; John and William Gordon would do whatever their older brother asked, but it was a conspiracy theory based more on bigotry and class warfare than hard evidence. The arrest of three immigrants would strain the already tense relations between Rhode Island's English and Irish communities.

AMASA SPRAGUE

Date: December 31, 1843

Location: Spragueville, Rhode Island

Victim: Amasa Sprague

Cause of Death: Beating

Accused: John, William, and Nicholas Gordon

Synopsis:

Rhode Island, in the 1840s, was awash in political and social turmoil. The Rhode Island constitution had very stringent requirements for voting—only white, male property holders had the right. This meant that only about one third of the white male population could vote. Thomas Dorr started a movement, based on the language of the Declaration of Independence, asserting that all power belonged to the people. In 1841 the Dorrites drafted the Peoples Construction that included a bill of rights and granted suffrage to all white males. It was put to a vote and overwhelmingly ratified when all were allowed to vote. In opposition, an incensed coalition of conservative Whigs and Democrats formed the Law and Order Party and had the constitution declared illegal by the state supreme court. But the Dorrites had already set up a rival government, based on the new constitution, with Thomas Dorr as governor. When they attempted to capture the state arsenal in Providence, the Dorrites were defeated and Thomas Dorr fled the state. When he returned, he was arrested and sentenced to life in prison.

At the same time, Rhode Island was experiencing a rapid influx of Irish immigrants seeking work in the state's textile mills. While the new workers were essential to the mills and to Rhode Island's economy, they were not considered equals by the ruling elite. It is no surprise that Irish immigrants overwhelmingly supported the Dorr Rebellion.

Amasa Sprague was a member of the ruling class. Together with his brother William—who in 1844 was a US senator—Amasa Sprague owned a textile business started by his father, William Sprague Sr. The Spragues owned several cotton mills in Rhode Island, but their most profitable factory was the print works in Spragueville, which printed calico patterns on cloth. The A & W Sprague Company employed most residents of Spragueville and owned the tenements they rented and the company store where they shopped.

Sprague was actively opposed to the Dorrites and was instrumental in Dorr's arrest. When Sprague's body was found shot and beaten, the murder was first thought to be a political assassination by Dorr's followers. But since the arrest of their leader, the Dorrites had been in disarray. A number of individuals had personal grudges against Amasa Sprague; the killer was believed to be one of them. One name kept coming up in the early investigation—Nicholas Gordon.

Nicholas Gordon came from Ireland in the mid-1830s with enough capital to open a general store. The store, located about a mile from the print works, proved profitable and in 1843, he built an addition on his house and sent for the rest of his family: his mother Ellen; his three brothers John, William, and Robert; his sister Margaret; and William's seven-year-old daughter.

One reason for the success of Nicholas Gordon's store was the license he obtained in 1840 allowing him to sell bottled liquor. In 1842 he was granted an ale-house license allowing him to sell drinks by the glass. The licenses had to be renewed every three months, and he had no trouble until the summer of 1843 when the town council, under the influence of Amasa Sprague, denied his request. Sprague was unhappy about his employees getting drunk during working hours and he blamed it on Nicholas Gordon's store. This was the beginning of the animosity between Sprague and Gordon and the reason Nicholas Gordon and his brothers were suspected in Sprague's murder.

An examination of the body showed that Sprague had been shot in the wrist then hit twice on the head, fracturing his skull—either blow to the head could have killed him. The following day a town meeting was held (excluding those without property) and vigilance committees were formed in several school districts to investigate. Additionally, the Sprague family offered a $1,000 reward for information leading to the conviction of the murderer.

Nicholas and John Gordon were arrested and the house and store were searched. No gun was found, though it was known that Nicholas owned a gun. Other members of the Gordon family were arrested, including the other two brothers and their mother, as well as a friend of Nicholas named Michael O'Brian. Also arrested was Nicholas Gordon's dog, because dog tracks had been found near the body, and the dog wore a collar of jagged metal that could have caused some of the wounds on Sprague's throat.

Tracks in the snow near the murder scene led to a swamp where a coat and a broken gun were found. The gun was identified as belonging to Nicholas Gordon. The coat had a hole in the elbow and a shirt found in the Gordon home had a bloody stain on the elbow corresponding to the hole in the coat. According to the *Providence Journal*:

> ...*two men were seen going to toward the fatal spot shortly before the murder. Two men were seen to emerge from the swamp on the other side after the deed had been committed; one of them without his coat.*

Nicholas, John, and William were held for the murder of Amasa Sprague, the rest (including the dog) were released.

Trials: John and William Gordon – April 8, 1844
Nicholas Gordon – October 13, 1844; April 7, 1845

The trial of John and William Gordon was taken very seriously. There would be four presiding judges, all members of the Rhode Island Supreme Court. The Irish Catholic community of Providence rallied behind the Gordons, raising a substantial fund for their defense. Thomas Carpenter, leader of the defense team, had been an ardent supporter of Thomas Dorr's suffrage movement. William Sprague resigned his Senate seat to oversee the prosecution. In the courtroom the prosecution team would be led by Rhode Island Attorney General Joseph M. Blake, a leader of the Law and Order Party. The trial would mirror the Dorr Rebellion.

John and William Gordon were tried together; Nicholas, the alleged ringleader, would be tried separately. Nicholas Gordon would also be the central figure in John and William's trial. John and William had only been in the country six months and would have no reason to murder Sprague but for their brother's grudge. The prosecutors were allowed considerable leeway in establishing the brothers' conspiracy, including testimony of alleged threats made by Nicholas against Amasa Sprague. As one observer noted:

> ...the decision...that threats made by another person in the presence of an accused prisoner are admissible as tending to prove a motive on the latter's part, without actual proof of a conspiracy or an effective response, stands unique in the annals of American trials.

This decision was not used as precedent in any later trial.

The prosecution proved that Nicholas Gordon did own a rifle and it was now missing. John Gordon had been seen holding the rifle. The coat was identified as belonging to Nicholas but had been more recently seen as the dog's bed. John had also been seen wearing the coat.

The trial lasted nine days. The jury deliberated for an hour and fifteen minutes before returning their verdicts—John Gordon, guilty; William Gordon, not guilty. When the verdict was read, John Gordon turned to his brother and said, "It is you, William, that have hung me." It would be nine months before the full import of this statement was revealed.

On October 13, 1845, Nicolas Gordon's trial began. Since he had been the focal point of his brothers' trial, his own followed much the same course. The difference was that, just as his threats were used against John and William, John's conviction was used against Nicholas. His trial also lasted nine days but ended in a hung jury—eight for conviction, four for acquittal.

Before Nicolas Gordon's second trial, and just prior to John Gordon's scheduled execution, William Gordon revealed the reason that Nicholas's rifle was missing. When he first learned of Amasa Sprague's murder, he hid the rifle and a pistol owned by Nicholas under the floorboards of the attic of their house. He thought it would keep suspicion away from Nicholas, but hiding the weapons had the opposite effect. John learned what his brother had done during the trial. It is why he blamed William for his conviction.

Regardless of the new information, John Gordon was hanged on February 14, 1845.

Nicholas Gordon's second trial began on April 7, 1845. The defense did not use the information about the hidden guns because it would have meant putting William on the stand, and his answers on cross-examination could not be predicted. Instead they attacked the credibility of the prosecution's witnesses, who were now not as sure of their stories as they had been six months earlier. But the result was much the same: hung jury, this time three for conviction and nine for acquittal.

Nicholas Gordon did not have a third trial.

Verdicts: John Gordon – Guilty of murder
William Gordon – Not Guilty
Nicholas Gordon – Hung jury

Aftermath:

Though John Gordon's execution was not public, there were more than sixty official witnesses to the hanging in the yard of the state prison in Providence. Over a thousand people had gathered on the hillside outside the prison, their view obstructed by a tall fence. John Gordon's last words were, "I hope all good Christians will pray for me."

More than 1,400 of John Gordon's countrymen joined the funeral procession to the North Burial Ground in Providence. Many had come from Massachusetts and Connecticut to protest the injustice of the execution. Instead of following a direct route to the cemetery, the procession turned down Benefit Street, where it would pass the statehouse and several aristocratic homes.

Nicholas Gordon was released on bail but lived under constant threat of another trial. He died in debt on October 22, 1846. William Gordon was sentenced to debtors' prison on June 18, 1850. The real killers of Amasa Sprague were never found.

In 2011, a resolution requesting the posthumous pardon of John Gordon was passed by the Rhode Island Senate and House of Representatives. On June 29, 2011, Governor Lincoln Chafee granted that pardon. The ceremony was held in the same room where John Gordon was tried and convicted.

Mary E. Stannard

39.   THE MADISON HORROR

A little after 1:00 p.m. on Tuesday, September 3, 1878, Charles Stannard saw his twenty-two-year-old daughter, Mary, leave their home in the Rockland, Connecticut, carrying a tin pail; she was off to pick berries, just a few hundred yards away. Mary never reached her destination. At 6:00 that evening, Mary's father found her lifeless body lying in the path leading from the house. She had been stabbed in the throat and left lying on her back with her hands folded across her stomach. As the news spread through town, so did rumors and speculations as to her killer. By Thursday all speculation pointed to one man: Mary's Methodist pastor and onetime employer, the Reverend Herbert H. Hayden.

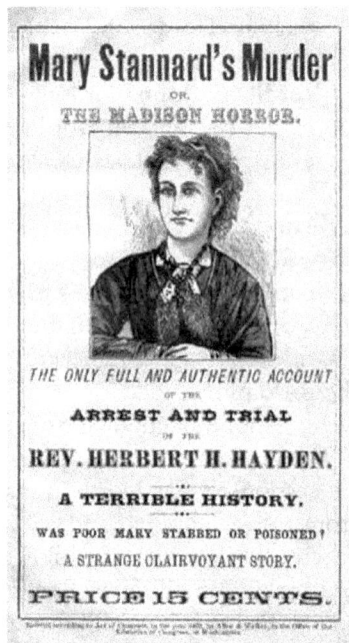

Mary Stannard's Murder
OR,
THE MADISON HORROR.

THE ONLY FULL AND AUTHENTIC ACCOUNT
OF THE
ARREST AND TRIAL
OF THE
REV. HERBERT H. HAYDEN.

A TERRIBLE HISTORY.

WAS POOR MARY STABBED OR POISONED?

A STRANGE CLAIRVOYANT STORY.

PRICE 15 CENTS.

MURDER PAMPHLET, 1879

Date: September 3, 1878

Location: Rockland, Connecticut

Victim: Mary E. Stannard

Cause of Death: Stabbing, poisoning

Accused: Rev. Herbert H. Hayden

Synopsis:

Mary E. Stannard was described as "a very simple, easy-minded girl." She was known to be honest, but easily influenced and manipulated by others. Around two years before her death, Mary gave birth to a son out of wedlock. The father was a married man living in another town. In the 1870s most women in this situation would be treated as outcasts, but Mary was more an object of pity than blame. Mary's friends and neighbors made it clear that they saw her not as a sinner, but one who had been sinned against, and did what they could to help her.

Reverend Herbert H. Hayden, the thirty-eight-year-old, newly appointed Methodist minister of Rockland, took a special interest in Mary's case. In the winter of 1877, he was preaching and teaching school in Madison, ten miles away, requiring him to be away from his family much of the week. He and his wife hired Mary Stannard to help with the chores and keep his wife company while the reverend was away.

Neighbors began to suspect that Reverend Hayden's relationship with Mary went beyond that of employer and employee. They had been seen together "in lots, and other unfrequented places, evenings." One instance that many remembered was an oyster supper to benefit the Rockland church in March 1878. The Haydens had left their three children in Mary Stannard's care as they attended the supper. The site of the supper was not far from the Hayden's home, and at one point in the evening, Reverend Hayden excused himself and went home to check on the children. It was alleged that during his absence he was engaging in improper intimacy with Mary Stannard.

In August 1878 Mary, in a despondent state, went to live with her friend, Mrs. Jane Studley, in Guilford, Connecticut. When Mrs. Studley questioned Mary as to the cause of her sadness, Mary admitted that, beginning one night in March 1878, she had been "criminally intimate" with Reverend Hayden and believed herself to be five months pregnant. Mrs. Studley told Mary she should confront Hayden and ask for assistance. Mary took her advice and wrote a letter to her half-sister, Susan Hawley, explaining her situation and included a letter to be delivered to Reverend Hayden. She told Mrs. Studley that she had requested Hayden to pick her up and take her to New Haven for an abortion, then leave her at the Studley's to recover. When Mr. Studley heard of this plan, he wanted no part of it and sent Mary packing.

Mary went to Susan Hawley's house, where she intercepted and destroyed the letter to Hayden; she had decided to see him in person. The result of this meeting, according to Susan Hawley, was that Hayden had told Mary that he had seen a doctor in Middleton and gotten some "quick medicine" to end the pregnancy. The afternoon of Tuesday, September 3, Mary had been on her way to an appointment with Hayden.

On September 9, a hearing began to determine whether there was enough evidence to try Reverend Herbert Hayden for the murder of Mary Stannard. The hearing, which lasted seventeen days, was extremely contentious. The prosecution asked for more time to continue their investigations, but the defense wanted to push ahead, with no break in the proceedings. The defense moved to have the testimony of Jane Studley and Susan Hawley disallowed as hearsay. In both instances, the judge ruled for the defense. The prosecution had a knife belonging to Reverend Hayden that, according to their expert witness, had traces of human blood. They wanted to admit it as evidence, but only if it was kept out of the hands of the defense attorney. When the judge said all should have access to the knife, the prosecution decided not to enter it, and all but directly accused the defense of wanting to tamper with evidence, resulting in a prolonged and bitter argument between opposing counsels. In the end the prosecution realized that they did not have the evidence necessary to indict Reverend Hayden for murder, and public sentiment briefly turned in the reverend's favor.

A postmortem examination had been performed on Mary Stannard's body at 3:00 a.m. on September 4, where it was determined that a blow to the head, leaving a star-shaped wound, was inflicted before her throat was stabbed. It would be the first of at least four postmortems before and after the hearing, and by the end, all of Mary Stannard's vital organs were preserved in glass jars. Two significant pieces of information had been revealed after the first hearing: Mary Stannard was not pregnant at the time of her death, and her stomach had contained enough arsenic to kill twenty people.

It was known that on September 3, the very day of the murder, Reverend Hayden had purchased an ounce of arsenic in Middleton. The new information was presented to a grand jury, who indicted the Reverend Herbert Hayden for the murder of Mary E. Stannard.

Trial: October 7, 1879

The trial of Rev. Hayden, commencing more than a year after the murder, was just as contentious as the first hearing. All of the witnesses called in the hearing were called again in the trial and subjected to intense questioning. This time the prosecution's case was dominated by medical and scientific experts. More than a hundred witnesses were called to testify, including fifteen doctors and at least four Methodist clergymen.

The defense floated a number of alternative suspects, including Mary's father Charles, sixty-year-old Ben Stevens, who had been staying at the Stannard house, and various local indigents. All had sufficient alibis and insufficient motive. At one point the judge subpoenaed every male citizen of Rockland to testify to his whereabouts on September 3, hoping to determine who could have killed Mary. It brought him no closer to the truth.

Twelve distinguished professors from Yale University, and three more from the University of Pennsylvania, were called by the prosecution to testify on the chemical and medical properties of arsenic. In the eyes of the press and public, their academic expertise was overshadowed by the arrogance and erudition of their testimony, which ran the gamut from superhuman intellectual certainty to reluctance to admit the certainty of anything. Professor Edward S. Dana (who "never used a word of one syllable when one of five would answer the purpose") during a question concerning the microscopic measurement of arsenical octahedrons stated that it was something that "no ordinary mortal could understand." At the other extreme was Prof. Moses C. White, who refused to be pinned down on anything. When asked if he had seen a certain object, he replied, "My eyes saw it," but would not state with certainty the he himself had seen it.

Hayden had admitted to buying an ounce of arsenic for killing rats and told investigators they could find it in his barn. Sure enough, they had found an ounce of arsenic, in an unlabeled tin, in Hayden's barn. What the experts proved, through microscopic analysis of the arsenic crystals, was that the arsenic in the barn was not from the same batch as the arsenic Hayden had bought in Middleton on the day of the murder.

But it was the testimony of Reverend Hayden and his wife that had the greatest impact on the jury. They were relaxed, reasonable, and poised, in a way that their accusers were not.

The trial went on longer than three months and cost the town more than $30,000. The case was given to the jury on January 16, 1880, and they deliberated for eighty-two hours before telling the judge they could not reach a unanimous verdict—they were a hung jury. It was later revealed that only one juror was not swayed by the testimony of Hayden and his wife; he believed that they were lying and could not be convinced to change that belief.

Verdict: Hung jury

Aftermath:

The state attorney agreed to release Reverend Hayden upon payment of a nominal bond. Hayden was welcomed back the Methodist ministry, where he remained briefly before returning to his original occupation of carpentry. Hayden was never retried for the crime, and no one was ever convicted of murdering poor Mary Stannard.

Betsey Van Amburgh

40.   A SAVAGE RUFFIAN!

James Fennimore Cooper recalled a day in June 1806 when he joined the population of Cooperstown, New York, to witness an eclipse of the sun. The eclipse was not the only memorable sight he saw that day, a prisoner had been brought up from his windowless dungeon to view the event. The man "with haggard face and fettered arms...the very picture of utter misery," was Stephen Arnold, convicted of beating to death his six-year-old adopted daughter Betsey Van Amburgh for mispronouncing a word.

A Savage Ruffian !

Two Hundred Dollars Reward !
ON the 10th inftant, Stephen Arnold of the town of Burlington, county of Otfego, and State of New York, returned home from a fchool he was teaching in the neighborhood, and enquired of a little orphan girl of fix years of age, who lived with him, whether fhe would fpell and pronounce GIG aright, fhe immediately replied " je, fir," but being terrified by the feverity of his manner, or not having

OTSEGO HERALD, JANUARY 31, 1805

Date: January 10, 1805

Location: Burlington, New York

Victim: Betsey Van Amburgh

Cause of Death: Beating

Accused: Stephen Arnold

Synopsis:

Stephen Arnold was the son of a wealthy Rhode Island farmer, but his family determined early on that Stephen did not have the temperament to manage a large farm. He did have an aptitude for scholarship, though, and he studied at a nearby academy. By the time he was eighteen, he had joined the faculty of the school. He went to Massachusetts to learn medicine but after five months of intensive study, Arnold suffered what could probably be called a nervous breakdown and gave up his schooling.

After a couple of shiftless years, Arnold went to stay with an uncle in the town of Burlington, in Otsego County, New York. Arnold became a teacher again; the area was still frontier country and the Yankee farmers who settled there welcomed a learned New Englander to educate their children. He was paid by the student and at its peak, Arnold's school had 150 pupils. By 1803 Stephen Arnold had earned enough to buy several hundred acres of farmland.

Around 1800 he married a farmer's daughter named Susannah Van Amburgh. Though they had no children of their own, the Arnolds adopted Susannah's niece Betsey Van Amburgh. In the winter months, Stephen would spend the day teaching his paying students, then come home and tutor Betsey.

In 1805, Stephen Arnold was described as "about thirty-four years of age, sandy hair, a little bald, speaks through his nose, has something of a down look, shews his upper teeth when speaking, [and] is very abstemious to strong drink." Teaching so many pupils who, in Arnold's words, "did not appear to be really civilized," was taking a toll on his nerves. On January 10, 1805—after a day in which Arnold would later say, "I was provoked even to madness, through the ill behavior of my pupils..."—he came home to teach Betsey.

Betsey Van Amburgh was described as a lively child, good-natured, and always dancing. She also may have had a speech impediment that Arnold was trying to remedy. In any case, on January 10 he was trying to have her correctly pronounce the word "gig" (a two-wheeled horse cart), and Betsey continually pronounced it as "jig." Arnold thought that she was just being obstinate. He and his wife had previously punished Betsey by whipping her and observed that it had a positive effect. Believing he could whip the stubbornness out of Betsey, he went outside and cut eight beechwood switches, each three feet long and the size of his little finger, and heated them over the fire to make them supple. He then took Betsey outside in the cold for her punishment.

He laid her over a post, raised her dress over her head, laying bare her backside from the ankles to the shoulders, and then proceeded to whip her with a switch. When he thought she had learned her lesson, Arnold took Betsey back inside to try the word again. But once again she pronounced it "jig" and once again he took her out for a whipping. They went outside six times and each time Betsey came back unable to pronounce the word. If Betsey screamed or cried out in pain during her punishment, it was not heard inside the house or by any of the neighbors but on the sixth time out, she was heard to say "Do, Uncle, let me thaw my feet, for they are almost froze."

The whippings had gone on for an hour with no success. When Betsey failed to pronounce the word correctly after her sixth whipping, Arnold completely lost control. He took her outside once again and beat her savagely for a half hour more. Betsey then pronounced the word correctly before becoming delirious with fever. She was taken to bed, where she would pass in and out of consciousness.

When Betsey's condition did not improve after two days, the Arnolds sent for a doctor. They explained the symptoms but not the cause and the doctor diagnosed her as having worms. On January 13 it became clear that Betsey was dying and Arnold went to Dr. Gaines Smith, saying, "I want to tell you something and can't—I'm ruined. I will tell you—I have whipped it to death, and if you will go and cure it and keep it a secret, I will give you half my property—even all."

Mrs. Arnold did not want to show the doctor the wounds, but Stephen convinced her that it was their only hope. The doctor found cuts and bruises from her legs to the middle of her back, with the bruised parts appearing "black, withered, dead, and sunk down." Dr. Smith called in two other physicians, but there was nothing to be done. Betsey died the following day. Stephen Arnold was not there to witness her death; he had already fled to the woods and was bound for Pennsylvania.

Elihu Phinney, publisher of the Otsego Herald, took an interest in the case. Under the headline "A Savage Ruffian!" he told the story of Betsey's death and announced a $200 reward, offered by the county, for the capture of Stephen Arnold. The story was picked up by nearly every newspaper in America.

A man named Thomas Cahoon of neighboring Chenango County decided to seek the reward. He tracked Arnold to Pittsburgh, Pennsylvania, and found him in a tavern. When Cahoon approached him, Arnold took out a pistol and attempted to shoot himself in the head. Before he could pull the trigger, someone knocked his arm and the shot went up, just grazing Arnold's head. Arnold was taken to jail in Pittsburgh and Cahoon claimed the reward.

Arnold was brought back to Burlington and put into the county jail. A grand jury, with Elihu Phinney as its foreman, indicted Stephen Arnold for the murder of Betsey Van Amburgh. Though they heard testimony that Susannah Arnold had abetted the beating and had attempted to hide the wounds, she was not indicted; Stephen Arnold was held solely responsible.

Trial: June 6, 1805

Stephen Arnold was tried before the Otsego County court of Oyer and Terminer in Cooperstown, New York. Interest in the case was so high that the courtroom could only accommodate half of those who desired to attend. The trial did not last long; there were only six witnesses, all testifying for the prosecution. There was no question that Stephen Arnold had killed Betsey Van Amburgh. What was at issue was whether his excessive punishment had criminally exceeded the parental right of corporal punishment. The prosecution said, "Such an outrageous correction as this can never be allowed by law."

The defense countered that the death was an accident, provoked because "the child persisted in its perverseness, when it could and had pronounced the word right."

The jury deliberated for two hours before returning a verdict of guilty.

Verdict: Guilty of murder

Aftermath:

Stephen Arnold was sentenced to be hanged on July 19, 1805. In the six weeks between the end of the trial and the scheduled hanging, Arnold received a multitude of visitors, including clergymen and other prominent citizens. As they viewed the contrite and sorrowful prisoner, shackled to the floor of his windowless stone dungeon, in nearly every case, anger gave way to pity and then to sympathy for the pathetic man's plight.

A petition was started to ask the governor for clemency in the case. Leading the drive was Elihu Phinney. Phinney had done an about-face, and his sympathies now sided with the prisoner—the "Savage Ruffian" had become "the unhappy Arnold." Two thousand residents of Otsego County signed the petition, two hundred of them from Burlington.

As impressive as those numbers sound, it became clear that public sentiment was still against Arnold when at least 12,000 people from all across New York State came to Cooperstown on July 19 to witness Stephen Arnold's hanging. The event promised to be instructive as well as entertaining, with prayer and sermons on the wages of sin, so the spectators brought along their children.

It would be the first execution in Otsego County and Sheriff Solomon Martin was determined to do it right, including all the required pomp and pageantry. At noon the sheriff, on horseback, led a procession from the jailhouse to the gallows outside of town. Behind the sheriff were "The Reverend Clergy and other gentlemen," then a band playing funeral dirges, followed by a wagon bearing the prisoner seated on his coffin. Bringing up the rear were two companies of state militia with muskets and bayonets.

After they arrived at the gallows, the Reverend Mr. Williams of Springfield Center led the gathering in prayer, Reverend Isaac Lewis of Cooperstown delivered a sermon, and Elder Ebenezer Vining of Winfield offered a prayer of forgiveness. Stephen Arnold was given the opportunity to address the crowd. He urged the people to improve by his fatal example and place strict guard upon their passions. The noose was placed around Arnold's neck. Elihu Phinney described what happened next:

> *The thousands of spectators were waiting in silent and gloomy suspense for the fatal catastrophe, when the sheriff, after a few concise and pertinent remarks to the prisoner, produced a letter from his Excellency Governor Morgan Lewis containing directions for "A Respite of the Execution" until further orders—the prisoner swooned, the countenances of the vast concourse assumed a different expression and the whole scene changed.*

Phinney reported that the crowd "dispersed without any tumultuous conduct," but George Peck, another observer, saw a different scene:

> *Wild excitement followed. Arnold fell as if he had been shot through the heart. Women shrieked; some of them wept aloud; some feinted; men raged and swore. The criminal was so detested for his cruelty that his escape from execution provoked a storm of fury. So indignant were the people that some rough fellows captured a dog, named him 'Arnold,' and hung him on the gallows, which had failed to do justice to his namesake.*

Earlier in the week, Jacob Ford of Cooperstown had taken the petition to Governor Lewis, but the governor proved hard to track down. When he was finally found, visiting the home of a friend, Governor Lewis was sympathetic, but being away from his office, he could only order a temporary stay of execution. Ford managed to make it back to Cooperstown on the morning of the hanging. Sheriff Martin, fearing a riot, decided to give the crowd all of the show except the climax. Though he has been criticized for it, the sheriff probably made the right decision.

Stephen Arnold remained in Ostego County's dank dungeon, still under sentence of death, until March 1807 when the state legislature commuted his sentence to life in prison. He was transferred to Newgate Prison in New York City, where he would at least be able to see the sun through his cell window.

James Reeves Walkup

41. THE VAMP OF NEW ORLEANS

James Walkup, a successful businessman and politician from Emporia, Kansas, met Minnie Wallace on a trip to New Orleans in December 1884 and instantly fell madly in love. He was forty-eight years old; she was fifteen. A year and a half later, they were married and a month after that, James Walkup was dead from arsenic poisoning. During her murder trial, Minnie had the help and support of other prominent businessmen and the sympathy of the all-male jury. The same was true in 1897 when her second husband, also much older, died mysteriously. And again in 1914 when a male companion died from cyanide poisoning after including Minnie in his will. What power did this New Orleans vamp have over middle-aged men?

MINNIE WALLACE WALKUP

Date:	August 22, 1885
Location:	Emporia, Kansas
Victim:	James Reeves Walkup
Cause of Death:	Poisoning
Accused:	Minnie Wallace Walkup

Synopsis:

James Reeves Walkup was successful at everything he did. He was a Civil War veteran from West Virginia who made money on coalmines before moving to Kansas, where he took up farming, railroad contracting, and buying and selling grocery stores. In Emporia, he became a city councilman and was elected president of the council, making him acting

195

mayor when the elected mayor was away. In 1884, he had outlived two wives and had three grown children.

Walkup was a man with hearty appetites, especially prone to sexual excess. Throughout his marriages he visited prostitutes and had a mistress fifteen years his junior. Two Emporia physicians would later testify that they had treated him for gonorrhea and that he had hired them to treat prostitutes as well.

In December 1884 Walkup traveled to New Orleans with his friend Eben Baldwin, ostensibly to attend a world's fair—The New Orleans World's Industrial and Cotton Centennial Exposition—but also to visit the city's famed bordellos. On the recommendation of a man they had met in Baton Rouge, Walkup and Baldwin stayed at a boardinghouse on Canal Street run by Mrs. Elizabeth Wallace.

Mrs. Wallace, divorced, had two daughters, Dora and Minnie, who played piano and sang in New Orleans's red-light district, Storyville. The Wallace girls were famous for their beauty and had caught the eye of Judge William T. Houston. He tried to persuade Mrs. Wallace to let Minnie live with him and his wife, saying, "She's too beautiful to be stuck in a boardinghouse." Judge Houston escorted Dora Wallace to a Mardi Gras ball, though she was married to someone else. He would later kill a newspaper man who criticized in print his public affection for the Wallace girls.

On his first night at Mrs. Wallace's boardinghouse, James Walkup met fifteen-year-old Minnie Wallace and became hopelessly infatuated with her. He spent the evening chatting with her and listening to her play the piano while her sister sang. The next morning Walkup told Mrs. Wallace that he was in love with her daughter and wanted to marry her. Mrs. Wallace laughed and said, "Minnie has many such admirers." Walkup would not be dissuaded and for the rest of the trip, he spent as much time as he could with Minnie. He asked if he could write to her when he returned to Emporia and Mrs. Wallace finally agreed, provided the letters were addressed to her rather than to her daughter.

After a couple of token letters to her mother, Walkup began writing directly to Minnie. He remained so obsessed with her that he could not concentrate on his business. The following April Walkup took his daughter Libbie to see the fair and they stayed at Mrs. Wallace's. Walkup spent the week showering Minnie with attention. He finally offered her mother $4,000 to let him marry Minnie. Mrs. Wallace refused the money and left the decision to Minnie. Then Walkup made offers to Minnie herself, promising to support her mother and buy her a house. He would give Dora's husband a job in one of his enterprises, and he would see that her cousin Willie had a good education. Minnie said maybe.

In May, Walkup was in New Orleans again, pleading with Minnie, and this time she relented. She agreed to an October wedding in New Orleans but first she and her mother would visit Emporia and see if they approved of where Minnie would be living. They decided to travel to Emporia in July, and then go to Cincinnati to visit Mrs. Wallace's sister. When Minnie, her mother, and her nephew Milton came to Emporia in July, Minnie liked what she saw. Walkup couldn't wait and wanted to get married immediately. Mrs. Wallace finally agreed, provided they were married near Cincinnati so her sister could attend the ceremony. After the wedding, they hurried back to Emporia so Walkup could show off his sixteen-year-old bride.

Walkup kept his promises and in Emporia, Minnie lived a life of ease, spending most of her time shopping. She began buying clothing and merchandise and shipping them to her family in New Orleans. She also began a series of visits to drug stores. First she had a druggist analyze some powder she had purchased in Cincinnati. She told him it was a remedy given to her by a friend and she wanted to be certain what it was. He told her it was quinine. She had, in fact, purchased strychnine in Cincinnati but the druggist had given her quinine by mistake. At another drugstore Minnie bought eight grains of strychnine—half a grain is enough to kill a person. He had her sign the "poison book," a legal requirement when buying strychnine, but did not notice that she had left the purpose blank. At another drugstore she was refused strychnine because she would not state the purpose.

On Saturday, August 15, James Walkup had returned from a trip to Topeka and that evening was taken ill. The symptoms were nausea, diarrhea, and a tightening in his leg muscles—classic symptoms of strychnine poisoning. Dr. Luther Jacobs treated Walkup for what he thought was either indigestion or cholera. Walkup recovered on Sunday morning.

On Sunday, Minnie went downtown and purchased some arsenic. This was much easier to purchase because it was common for women to use arsenic to lighten their complexion. Though Minnie's complexion was naturally quite pale, she had no trouble buying arsenic and stating "complexion lightening" as the reason.

On Tuesday Walkup was deathly ill again with similar symptoms. Dr. Jacobs was surprised, though, that there was no fever. He began treating Walkup with morphine and by Thursday Walkup was well enough to be eating canned oysters and drinking soda pop. Shortly after eating he began vomiting again and Minnie blamed the oysters.

Dr. Jacobs was beginning to suspect arsenic poisoning and wanted to take a urine sample, but Walkup's kidneys had ceased functioning. The doctor had confided his suspicions with Dwight Bill, Walkup's business partner, who went to see Walkup. He told his partner that the doctor suspected arsenic poising and it was known that Minnie had recently purchased arsenic. Walkup, on his deathbed, was ready to have his wife arrested. On Saturday August 22, exactly one month after his wedding, James Walkup was dead. Minnie Wallace Walkup was placed under house arrest.

Trial: October 1885

On hearing the news of Minnie's arrest, Judge William T. Houston hurried from New Orleans to Emporia to help with the defense. Mrs. Wallace, worried that Judge Houston would try to marry her daughter if she were acquitted, proposed that, since Minnie was a minor, a legal guardian be appointed by the court. The judge disagreed, saying her marriage had made her an emancipated minor and he was perfectly capable of handling her affairs. In the end, the court appointed sixty-five-year-old ex-mayor of Emporia William Jay as Minnie's guardian. Judge Houston left in a huff.

An inquest was held and Minnie Wallace Walkup was indicted for the murder of her husband. One witness at the inquest signaled what would be the defense's strategy at the trial. Dr. Charles W. Scott of Kansas City testified that in the fall of 1884, James Walkup had visited him complaining of abdominal pains. Walkup volunteered that he was taking prescribed pills that were a combination of arsenic and opium. He took them for two reasons: treatment for a chronic disease (for which he was also taking mercury) and he believed that arsenic was a male enhancement drug. The implication was that Walkup was a chronic user of arsenic and was being treated for syphilis.

An autopsy was performed that revealed what everyone knew: James Walkup had died of arsenic poisoning. However, a thorough examination showed no sign of syphilis and no indication of chronic arsenic use.

For Minnie's trial, the largest courtroom in Emporia was modified to seat 300 people and the witness stand was placed on a platform so all could see the testimony. At times as many as two-thirds of the spectators were women. When the trial started, the public was evenly divided for and against Minnie. Newspapers cautioned against rushing to judgment and seemed to relish any news that might exonerate the poor teenager.

Between the medical testimony and the testimony of druggists who sold Minnie strychnine and arsenic, the prosecution had a fairly tight circumstantial case against her. The defense contended that Walkup's chronic arsenic use had caught up with him. In what the *New Orleans Daily Picayune* called "a carnival of filth," James Walkup's prodigious sex life was paraded before the court. Pimps, fellow cavorters, and doctors who treated Walkup and his whores for sexually transmitted diseases told all.

Dr. Scott and others testified to Walkup taking arsenic as treatment for disease and to "keep up." The problem for the defense was that all of these witnesses were from out of town. There is no record of Walkup buying arsenic—which, as Minnie's experience showed, would have required signing the poison book—and no local doctor had prescribed it. The solution to this came with the testimony of William Jay, Minnie's new guardian.

William Jay was Minnie Walkup's most ardent supporter. As she did with all older men, Minnie had thoroughly charmed him—so much so that the testimony he gave was almost certainly perjury. Jay testified that in July 1885 Walkup had come to his office to transact business. He claimed he was not feeling well and asked Jay for a knife and a glass of water. He put some white powder on the knife and poured it into the water, then he drank it. He told Jay he had better wipe off the knife because the powder was arsenic.

The most controversial claim of the defense was that the arsenic Walkup had taken in Toledo killed him nearly a week later. To support this they cited a case where a woman had tried to kill herself with arsenic but failed. When she succeeded a year later, an autopsy showed that the original arsenic had not killed her because it formed a cyst in her stomach. The same, the defense said, happened to Walkup.

The jury deliberated for fifty-two hours, finding Minnie Walkup not guilty. The reason for the verdict was probably their reluctance to send a sixteen-year-old girl to the gallows. As one juryman said later, "If I had voted for that little girl's conviction, her face would haunt me to my dying day."

Verdict: Not Guilty

Aftermath:

The trial of Minnie Walkup had gotten national publicity, and there was talk of Minnie going into show business. Nothing ever materialized and she moved back to New Orleans. She traveled for a while with US senator and former Louisiana governor, William Pitt Kellogg. Kellogg, Minnie's senior by thirty-nine years, was, according to observers, acting like a "decidedly 'gone' lover." They traveled the Southwest together and may have travelled to Europe as well. Kellogg financed Minnie's move to Chicago.

In Chicago, though she was probably not a prostitute, Minnie associated with known courtesans and kept a separate room where she entertained men salon-style. Just as her money was running out, Minnie met wealthy (and married) John Berdan Ketcham. After his wife divorced him, Ketcham moved into Minnie's house, where she kept him a virtual prisoner. In 1897, Ketcham was dying of alcoholism. Minnie took him to Wisconsin for a secret marriage ceremony. On November 1, 1897, Ketcham signed a will that left everything to Minnie. Twelve days later he was dead.

Because of Minnie's background, an autopsy was performed, specifically looking for signs of poison. None were found and the cause of death was listed as "acute alcoholism." Though the Ketcham family challenged the will and the marriage, Minnie inherited $250,000, the same amount her first husband had left her.

In 1900, Minnie began a relationship with DeLancy Horton Louderback—twenty years her senior and a married man. Louderback and Minnie would travel together while he was still married. After his wife died, he updated his will to leave a quarter of his estate to Minnie. Soon after, he died of cyanide poisoning. The official cause of death was "overdose of cyanamide, taken medicinally." Since there is no medicinal use of cyanamide, the death had to have been either suicide or murder. Minnie could not have been directly responsible because Louderback died in Chicago and Minnie was in Europe at the time, though there are theories that she or an accomplice could have poisoned his food or medicine.

Minnie died in 1957 at the age of eighty-eight in San Diego, California, where she was living under the name Estelle Minnie Keating.

Mansfield Walworth

42.   THE WALWORTH PARRICIDE

The name Walworth was an old and venerable one in the state of New York. William Walworth arrived there from London in 1689, during the American Revolution, Benjamin Walworth fought in the Battle of White Plains; Reuben Hyde Walworth, in 1828, was named chancellor of New York, the state's highest judicial office. But in 1873 the name Walworth was forever tarnished when Frank Walworth murdered his father, Mansfield Walworth.

THE MURDER OF MANSFIELD WALWORTH

Date: June 3, 1873

Location: New York, New York

Victim: Mansfield Walworth

Cause of Death: Gunshot

Accused: Frank Walworth

Synopsis:

Stephen Reuben Walworth was an up-and-coming young attorney when he married Maria Avery of Plattsburg, New York. They settled in at Pine Grove, outside of Saratoga Springs, which would become the Walworth estate. Maria died in1848 leaving Reuben a widower with five children. Two years later, on a trip to Louisville, Kentucky, he met a thirty-nine-year-old widow named Sarah Hardin. After only one meeting, he proposed to her and she accepted. That is when the trouble began.

201

Sarah and her children, two sons and a daughter, moved in with Reuben's family at Pine Grove. Reuben's youngest son, nineteen-year-old Mansfield, became infatuated with Sarah's daughter Ellen, also nineteen, and they began courting in secret. In 1852 Mansfield and Ellen revealed their romance and were married in a lavish ceremony at Pine Grove.

Reuben Walworth had educated his son to follow in his footsteps, but Mansfield had no love for the law and instead became a novelist. Though prolific, as an author Mansfield Walworth was not particularly successful either critically or financially and had to rely on his father's money to support his family. Reuben Walworth had little respect for the life his son had chosen and on his death, he left Mansfield a small portion of his fortune, to be held in trust by his older brother, to support Mansfield's wife and children. Mansfield felt emasculated by this disinheritance and took out his frustrations on his wife.

The marriage had always been tumultuous, and Mansfield Walworth was an abusive husband. He spent extended periods away from his wife and had affairs with other women. At the time of Reuben's death, Mansfield and Ellen were separated; she had taken their children back to Kentucky. They tried several times to reconcile, in Kentucky and at Pine Grove, and though they always began with the best of intentions, the meetings invariably would end with Mansfield beating Ellen over some perceived insult or jealousy. Ellen would leave again, bruised physically and emotionally, and often pregnant.

In January 1871, while Ellen was pregnant with their eighth child, she and Mansfield tried one last time to reconcile. While they were in Ellen's New York City apartment, calmly discussing where and how they would live, Mansfield went into a rage and accused Ellen of conspiring with his family to drag him back to Saratoga. Ellen raised her arms to shield herself from Mansfield's blows, and he grabbed her hand and bit one of her fingers to the bone. Her screams awakened everyone in the household, and their seventeen-year-old son, Frank, broke up the fight. Two weeks later Ellen filed for divorce and never saw her husband again.

Frank Walworth assumed the role of protector for his mother, who was now living at Pine Grove. Though Mansfield could no longer physically abuse Ellen, he would send her abusive and threatening letters. Frank was able to intercept these letters before they could disturb his mother. But Frank had his own problems; he was subject to spells where he would lie stiff and pallid, his face unnaturally "convulsed." He became absentminded and forgetful and would sometimes cry out in his sleep.

Frank never forgave his father for the way he treated Ellen. During a chance meeting with his father in Saratoga, Frank told him that if he did not leave his mother alone, he would shoot him.

"There are bounds," Frank told him, "which I will not allow any man to go beyond with impunity, especially when my mother is being insulted."

On June 2, 1873, Frank intercepted another letter from his father to his mother. In it Mansfield accused Ellen of turning his children against him. He said that unless she convinced him that she had not taught their children to hate him, he would kill her and himself. This was the last straw for Frank; he took the train to New York City and went to the boardinghouse where his father was living. His father was out, so he left a note with the landlady: "I want to settle some family matters. Call at the Sturtevant House. If I am not there, I will leave word with the clerk. Frank Walworth."

Mansfield did not return until midnight, so he did not go to the Sturtevant House until six o'clock the next morning. The bellman escorted Mansfield to room 267, where his son was waiting for him. After the door was shut, guests in adjoining rooms heard shouting, then four gunshots fired in quick succession. Frank walked out of the room, went quickly to the front desk, and told the clerk that he had shot his father and wanted a policeman.

Trial: June 24, 1873

Frank Walworth's trial was a sensation in an era when murders always generated headlines in New York City. His fellow inmates in the Tombs prison included other famous murderers, such as Edward Stokes and William Sharkey, whose stories, like Frank Walworth's, had been followed in daily papers throughout America. All of the Walworth family's dirty linen—though hardly a secret in Saratoga—would be exposed by the New York press.

There was no question that Frank Walworth had murdered his father; what was at issue was whether the murder was in self-defense, and whether or not Frank Walworth was insane at the time. There was some debate over the extent that Mansfield Walworth's letters constituted direct threats, and the judge hesitated to include them. He finally allowed all to be read except those that were "entirely too filthy to be repeated." If nothing else, the letters made the trial as much about Mansfield's behavior as about Frank's.

The defense brought out evidence of Frank Walworth's deteriorating mental health. They examined an expert witness who declared that Frank Walworth was epileptic. The prosecution countered with its own experts, who asserted that Frank was not having a fit when he committed murder.

This would be the first murder case tried under a new state law that distinguished between first- and second-degree murder—both were intentional murder but first-degree murder required "deliberation and premeditation." The jury took advantage of the new law and found Frank Walworth guilty of second-degree murder. It meant life in prison rather than execution.

Verdict: Guilty of second-degree murder

Aftermath:

Frank Walworth was taken first to Sing Sing prison, and then, within the first year, he was transferred to Auburn Prison, where fellow inmates there included murderers Kate Stoddard and Henrietta Robinson. In 1877, after four years in prison, Frank was pardoned by newly elected governor Lucius Robinson who, as a young lawyer, had served before Chancellor Walworth. Frank returned to Pine Grove, where he lived until his death in 1886 from a lung condition contracted in prison.

The death of her husband had been liberating for Ellen Hardin Walworth; she became an author, a lawyer, and an educator. She was one of the founders of the Daughters of the American Revolution.

Another of her sons, Clarence Augustus Walworth, wrote *The Walworths of America*, a history of the Walworth family. The book makes no mention of the murder.

Freda Ward

43. "GIRL SLAYS GIRL"

Alice Mitchell and Freda Ward, aged nineteen and seventeen, had become close friends at the Higbee School for Girls in Memphis. So close, in fact, that they declared their love for each other and planned to elope to St. Louis to live together as husband and wife. When Freda's family stopped the relationship, forbidding Freda from seeing Alice, events took a dreadful turn. On the afternoon of January 25, 1892, Alice Mitchell met Freda Ward on Front Street and cut her throat with a straight razor. Was Alice driven by insanity, by jealousy, or by "an unnatural love?"

ALICE MITCHELL

Date: January 25, 1892

Location: Memphis, Tennessee

Victim: Freda Ward

Cause of Death: Slashing

Accused: Alice Mitchell

Synopsis:

Freda Ward and her sister Jo, daughters of a wealthy planter and merchant, met Alice Mitchell and Lilly Johnson, also from prominent families, at the Higbee School for Girls in Memphis, Tennessee. They became very close friends, with Freda especially close to Alice. It was not uncommon in 1892 for girls to form close relationships and express undying love for each other in letters and diaries. These relationships were considered "a rehearsal in girlhood of the great drama of a woman's life,"

FREDA WARD

something the girls would outgrow when they reached adulthood. It was not considered unusual that Alice and Freda were seen kissing and embracing.

After Freda's family moved several miles south to the town of Gold Dust, Arkansas, they began to see Freda's relationship with Alice as unhealthy. One night in August 1891, Freda's older, married sister, Ada Volkmar, caught Freda, with her suitcase packed, ready to leave for Memphis. Freda said that Alice had given her a ring and the two considered themselves engaged. They had planned to elope to St. Louis where Alice would be the man, changing her name to Alvin J. Ward, and Freda would be the wife. Mrs. Volkmar stopped the elopement and forbade any further contact or correspondence between her sisters and Alice Mitchell and Lillie Johnson.

The following January, when the Ward sisters were visiting a family friend, Mrs. Kimbrough, in Memphis, Alice and Lillie had attempted to visit them but were turned away. On January 25, Alice arrived at Lillie's house with a horse and buggy and they went for a ride. They drove past Mrs. Kimbrough's house and saw Freda and Jo leaving for the ferry to take them back to Gold Dust. As the sisters were heading to the dock on Front Street, Alice jumped out of the buggy saying, "I'll fix her!"

She ran to Freda, grabbed her by the arm, and slashed her face with a straight razor she had concealed in her hand. Jo Ward knocked Alice down and hit her with an umbrella as Freda ran away. Alice jumped up and ran after her. She caught up with Freda and slashed her face again. Then Alice grabbed Freda by the hair, pulled her head back, and slit her throat from ear to ear. Alice went back to the buggy, and Freda was carried to a nearby office where she bled to death. Alice was arrested that night at her parent's home, and Lillie was arrested at her home the next morning.

Hearings: Lillie Johnson – February 23, 1892
Alice Mitchell – July 18, 1892

Lillie Johnson's habeas corpus hearing was held first, to determine whether there was enough evidence to try her for murder. Though it would not determine anyone's ultimate fate and was far less important than the pending murder trial of Alice Mitchell, it would be the most significant trial held in Memphis to date. The anticipated crowd would be so large that Judge Julius DuBose delayed the opening so that construction could be done to enlarge the courtroom until it had a seating capacity to rival Memphis's largest theatres. On the day the trial opened, Judge Dubose was overwhelmed by a crowd of more than a thousand people of all races and nationalities, about half of them women. Women were drawn to the hearing in numbers unprecedented for a criminal trial. In an effort to stem the confusion, the judge issued a "ballroom order": "Ladies to the right, gents to the left."

All of the salient evidence came out in this hearing—the "unnatural love" of Alice for Freda, the attempted elopement, Lillie's intimacy with Alice and with the Ward sisters, and vivid descriptions of the murder scene. The defense argued that Lillie had no idea of Alice's intention that day and in no way assisted her. But Judge Dubose ruled that "[t]he proof is evident that the defendant aided and abetted in the commission of the crime, a crime the most atrocious and malignant ever perpetrated by a woman." Lillie Johnson was released on $10,000 bail.

Alice Mitchell pled not guilty to murder but also entered a plea of "present insanity," which meant that before she could be tried for murder, a hearing would be held to determine if she was mentally fit to stand trial.

To show a genetic predisposition to madness, Alice's father testified that her mother, who had borne seven children, suffered from "puerperal insanity" after the birth of her first child and had to be committed to a lunatic asylum for several months. After the death of the child, she became increasingly unstable. Other testimony brought by the defense stressed Alice's boyish behavior growing up as an indication of her insanity. The engagement ring, inscribed "From A to F" was entered as evidence and the story of the elopement was retold. Frank Mitchell, Alice's brother, testified that Alice had once tried to commit suicide by taking laudanum over Freda's infidelities.

The prosecution argued that though Alice's behavior was strange, it was not insane. Her tomboyish behavior was not even unusual, just a normal part of growing up. However, the defense brought in a number of psychologists who unanimously thought Alice insane, probably incurably so. Her predisposition to insanity was triggered by an "exciting cause"—the emotional disturbance of love and jealousy. Alice's belief that she could marry Freda was a manifestation of her insanity.

207

Throughout the trial, Alice seemed docile and unconcerned, which, to some observers, seemed further evidence of her insanity. On the witness stand, she remained calm and indifferent as she told of her love for Freda and detailed their intended elopement. Then she told of her plan to kill Freda:

I wanted to cut her because I knew I could not have her, and I did not want anyone else to have her...My intention was to cut Freda's throat and then my own, but Jo's interference made me cut Freda again.

The trial lasted ten days, and the jury returned the verdict of insanity. She was committed to the Tennessee State Insane Asylum at Bolivar, Tennessee. Charges against Lillie Johnson were later dropped.

Verdicts: Lillie Johnson – Sufficient evidence to try for murder; charges later dropped.
Alice Mitchell – Present insanity, not competent to stand trial.

Aftermath:

Officials at the Tennessee State Insane Asylum could have, at any time, declared Alice Mitchell competent to stand trial, but she never left the institution. In 1898, she reportedly died of tuberculosis; however, one of her attorneys later stated in an interview that she committed suicide by jumping into a water tower.

In 1892, the terms "lesbian" and "homosexual" were not commonly used in America. At that time, the medical term for Alice's condition was "sexual inversion," the condition where a person inappropriately took on the characteristics of the opposite sex.

While much was said about the "unnatural love" of Alice Mitchell for Freda Ward, there was never a suggestion that their relationship was sexual. The public also had trouble accepting Alice's sexual inversion as the driving force behind the murder. Though Alice never wavered from her assertion that she killed Freda for love, two other stories were told as a motive for the murder:

- Alice, Lillie, and the Ward sisters were "fast" girls, always flirting with men. Freda was prettier than Alice and had more luck with men. Alice was jealous of Freda's beauty and was only trying to disfigure, not murder, her.

- A mysterious man was involved. He followed Alice's buggy and disappeared after the murder. The murder was the result of a rivalry for the love of this man.

Ballad:

The folk song "Alice Mitchell and Freddy Ward" (sung to the tune of "The Boston Burglar") expresses the view that Alice and Freddy were rivals for the same man.

Alice Mitchell and Freddy Ward

You-all have heard of Freddy Ward,
Who lived many miles from town.
While walking down the stone pavement,
Alice Mitchell cut her down.

She says she killed her because she loved her,
But love was not the thing,
For Alice and Freddy both loved the same man,
And she taken her life for him.

They put her on an eastbound train,
With arms strong tightly bound down.
And every town that she would pass through,
You could hear those people say:

"There goes that Alice Mitchell,
With arms strong tightly bound down,
For the crime she did in Memphis,
She's bound for Bolivar now.

"And they won't do anything to her--
She has two of the best lawyers in town--
But if they served Alice Mitchell right,
They would simply cut her down."

Christie Warden

44.   MURDER IN THE VALE OF TEMPE

George Abbott was a young child when he began his career as a thief and by his thirtieth birthday, he had spent a third of his life in jail. When he left prison, he changed his name and tried to change his evil ways, traveling and taking honest employment. While working as a farmhand in Hanover, New Hampshire, he fell in love with the farmer's daughter, Christie Warden. When Christie did not return his love, Abbot went back to his old ways and tried to take her love at gunpoint in the shady hollow known as the Vale of Tempe.

CHRISTIE WARDEN

Date: July 17, 1891

Location: Hanover, New Hampshire

Victim: Christie Warden

Cause of Death: Gunshot

Accused: Frank Almy (George Abbot)

Synopsis:

George Abbott came from a prosperous New England family. His grandfather, Eliphalet Abbott, the owner of Abbott's Mills, dominated the town of North Thetford, Vermont. His father, Harris Abbott, owned a small business in Salem, Massachusetts. George Abbott's mother died three days after his birth in 1857 and he was adopted by his uncle and aunt, Israel and Mary Abbot. In 1867, they moved from Salem to the family estate in North Thetford.

Young George was handsome and intelligent and did well in school, but he had a habit of taking things that did not belong to him. He was an avid reader, but his taste in literature tended toward dime novels, which "…only served to stimulate his evil intentions."

He was soon stealing jewelry, tools, and farm implements from his neighbors and stashing the loot in a cave overlooking the Connecticut River. At age fourteen he stole a stove from the house of Daniel P. Prescott. The theft was traced to George, but his family's considerable influence allowed the matter to be settled out of court. Sometime later George Abbot saw Prescott out walking his dog and without a word, he pulled out a revolver and shot Prescott's dog, then pointed the gun at Prescott, saying, "Stop where you are or I'll treat you just as I did the dog." Prescott did not report the incident.

In the early 1870s, Abbott teamed up with one of his uncle's employees, Peter Duplissy, to commit a series of house burglaries in the Connecticut River Valley between Barnet, Vermont, and Lyme, New Hampshire. He was eventually caught holding a pocketbook containing a number of stolen watches, two revolvers, a dirk, a bottle of chloroform, a bottle of strychnine, and a bottle of arsenic. On his person he was carrying another revolver and another dirk. This time his family could not help him and George Abbot was sentenced to four years in the New Hampshire State Prison. His father was so ashamed that he hanged himself in his barn.

When he left prison, Abbot expressed a desire to go straight, but he soon took up where he left off, with a new gang of thieves, burglarizing homes in the Connecticut River Valley and hiding the swag in a cave. His cave was discovered and after a gunfight in which Abbott reportedly received at least twenty gunshot wounds, he was arrested and sentenced to fifteen years in Windsor Prison.

Abbott was a model prisoner, but he had no intention of serving his full term. Over the course of seven years, he accumulated pieces of string and cord and sections of iron pipe, which he managed to fashion into a crude rope ladder. On September 30, 1887, Abbott used the ladder to make his escape.

Then Abbott drifted through the South, working as a ranch hand in Texas, an oysterman in Baltimore, an engineer in Savannah, and a riveter in Edgemoor, Delaware. He changed his name to Frank Almy, the name by which he would be known for the rest of his life.

In July 1890, Abbott/Almy drifted back to New England and got a job at the farm of Andrew H. Warden in Hanover, New Hampshire. After a

211

week's trial, Warden hired him through the following March. Andrew and Louisa had two sons and five daughters—the two oldest daughters had already left home. Fifteen-year-old Fanny Warden took an instant dislike to the new farmhand, but Frank Almy did much better with twenty-eight-year-old Christie.

Christie Warden was attractive, intelligent, and vivacious, described as a "medium-blonde type" with a "fine rounded form and discrete manners." She was secretary of the Grafton Star Grange and worked part time as a secretary for Professor Charles H. Pettee of the State Agricultural College in Hanover. Christie and Frank Almy began a courtship of sorts; they went on sleigh rides, attended church together, and exchanged Christmas presents. They had sessions of reading aloud to each other from Edward Bulwer-Lytton's *The Last Days of Pompeii.*

But Christie was bothered by Almy's refusal to talk about his past. That, together with his violent temper and other habits and actions, made her view him as someone in need of reform—a task that she did not wish to undertake. Frank Almy had become infatuated with Christie, but she did not return his affections. In early 1891, when she was away in Manchester at a shorthand class, Christie wrote him of her feelings:

> *…but to be honest with you and true to myself, I think you should know how I feel toward you. You already know, for I have told you, the sort of man I wish to love…You have set yourself in defiance to God and man. I believe you have suffered the misery that must follow. You surely would not wish me, who you love, to share that misery…I would never think of marrying a man to reform him. The reformation must come first.*

But she left the door open just wide enough to give him hope:

> *Frank, I shall test the strength of your love. Can you open your heart to all good influences, practice rigid self-control, and wait patiently? If it ever so, I believe you must win in the end, for you have many fine qualities that I admire, and I cannot help liking you for all your faults.*

But in March 1891, his hopes were dashed; Andrew Warden did not renew Frank Almy's contract. Christie's brother Johnny reported that Almy wept when he said good-bye to the family.

Almy went back to Massachusetts for two months. While there he showed his landlady a photograph of the girl he loved, Christie Warden, saying, "If I don't have her, then no other fellow will either."

In June 1891, Frank Almy took a train back to New Hampshire and late one night he went to the Warden farm. Behind the house they had three interconnected barns filled from wall to wall with hay. He went inside one and dug out a space to sleep, next to a wall with a knothole through which he could see the yard. He had brought with him some presents for Christie, a copy of Rudyard Kipling's *The Light that Failed* and two revolvers.

He waited there for an opportunity to talk with Christie alone, but that opportunity never came. At night he would go out and steal eggs, milk, fruit, and canned goods from neighboring farms. One night he broke into the Warden's house trying to find Christie, but she was not there. After learning that she was staying at Professor Pettee's house, he broke in there but found, instead, another houseguest, Miss Amelia Thompson. He grabbed her by the throat and threatened to kill her if she told of his visit.

On July 17 Almy learned that Christie would be going to a grange meeting, so he went out to meet her coming home. Around 9:15 that evening, Almy saw Christie, Fannie, and Louisa Warden with their friend Louisa Goodell walking down Lyme Road near a spot known locally as the Vale of Tempe. Almy jumped into the road brandishing a .44 caliber revolver. He was now wearing a full beard and was not instantly recognized by the women. "You know me, Mrs. Warden," he said. "I am Frank Almy. I only want to talk to Christie. The rest of you run along. You go and I won't hurt you. If you interfere with me, I will shoot you like dogs."

Then he grabbed Christie by the arm and said, "Christie, I have come a thousand miles to see you."

Fannie grabbed Christie's other arm and tried to pull her back. Almy dragged both of them toward the fence by the road until Fannie stumbled and had to let go. He dragged Christie through the fence to a meadow near a brook. Fannie picked herself up and followed after. She heard her sister shout, "Oh Fannie, come and help me. He is tearing my clothes all off!"

As Fannie approached, Almy fired three shots at her but all missed. Fannie ran back to get help. She returned with Emmitt Marshal, a local farmer, arriving in time to hear two more gunshots then see Almy dart into the brush. They found Christie lying dead, shot pointblank in the head. It would be impossible to tell whether he raped her because the second shot went through her vagina.

A large-scale manhunt was undertaken to find Almy and a $5,000 reward was offered for his capture. Almy was spotted in locations throughout New England. However, he had not fled the scene; Almy went back to his hole in the hay in Warden's barn. He lived there for more than a month until Louisa Warden found a hole in the barn concealed by a piece of wood. Inside were a jelly jar, empty beer bottles, and empty tin cans. She told the sheriff what she found, and on August 19, he and another man staked out the barn. Around two in the morning, they saw a barefoot man in tattered clothing enter the barn.

The following day, hundreds of Hanover residents flocked to the Warden farm to help with the capture. The *Lebanon Free Press* described them as the "curious, the do-nothings, and the fault-finders." They attacked the hay with pitchforks trying to find Almy and eventually succeeded. Almy started shooting at them. Everyone backed off and for two hours negotiated with Almy, trying to get him to surrender. Finally a group of men rushed the barn and captured him, dragging him to a waiting wagon. There were calls to lynch Almy, but cooler heads prevailed. Since Hanover lacked a secure jail, he was taken to the Wheelock House Hotel.

More than a thousand angry people gathered around the hotel, and there were fears that a lynching would occur after all. But the crowd was placated when each was given the opportunity to view the prisoner. That day 1,500 people filed past the room where Almy was being held, just to get a glimpse of the murderer.

Trial: November 16, 1891

Almy pleaded guilty and opted to take his case to a panel of two judges who would determine whether the charge would be first-degree murder or second-degree murder—whether or not it was a hanging offense. Since his capture, Almy had been identified by a number of people, including the warden of Windsor Prison, as George Abbott. Almy vigorously denied this. Not wanting to muddy the waters, the judges refused to allow any testimony relating to George Abbott and tried the prisoner as Frank Almy.

The most powerful testimony came from Louisa and Fannie Warden describing what happened at the Vale of Tempe that night. The two doctors who had performed the postmortem examination concurred that there was no way the shot to the head had been accidental—as Almy now claimed—and the second shot had been fired after he knew Christie was dead.

Frank Almy spoke for several hours in his own defense. He spoke of his undying love for Christie and claimed that she had agreed to marry him. Unfair treatment of him by the Warden family had been the cause of the trouble. He said, "…had Mrs. Warden only spoken one pleasant word to me, I should not be here today."

The judges ruled the charge was first-degree murder, and Almy was sentenced to hang in December 1892. Due to some technical problems with the trial, such as the fact that Almy was not present for the sentencing, the case had to be retried. The outcome was the same in the second trial in April 1892 and the verdict was upheld by the New Hampshire Supreme Court in July 1892.

Verdict: Guilty of first-degree murder

Aftermath:

On May 16 1893, Frank Almy was hanged in front of an invitation-only crowd of 150 people. He is buried in the prison's potter's field in Blossom Hill Cemetery.

Christie Warden is buried in Dartmouth Cemetery.

Several months after the murder, a reporter visited the Vale of Tempe and found that every leaf and twig within reach had been taken by souvenir hunters. Today the murder site is part of a golf course.

John Whipple

45.   ALBANY GOTHIC

Cherry Hill, the stately mansion overlooking the Hudson River near Albany, New York, was already forty years old in 1827 when it sheltered a vibrant household of seventeen people. They were aristocrats mostly, scions of the Van Rensselaer and Lansing families. And there was John Whipple, the young upstart who had married Elsie Lansing, the

CHERRY HILL

erratic niece of Catherine Van Rensselaer. At least five servants, including itinerant workman Jesse Strang, were living in the basement rooms. Domestic tranquility at Cherry Hill would be disrupted forever when Elsie and Jesse failed to observe the distinction between upstairs and downstairs.

Date: May 7, 1827

Location: Albany, New York

Victim: John Whipple

Cause of Death: Gunshot

Accused: Jesse Strang (Joseph Orton)

Synopsis:

Cherry Hill was built in 1787 for Philip Van Rensselaer, who made his fortune as a merchant and a farmer. He died in 1798 but in 1826, his wife Maria was still living there. She occupied the north side of the house and their son, Philip P. Van Rensselaer, occupied the south side with his wife Catherine and four of their seven children. The southwest bedroom was rented to John and Elsie Whipple and their son. Elsie was the daughter of Abraham Lansing, Catherine's deceased brother.

216

Elsie Whipple had a reputation for being hysterical and undisciplined. Her father had died when she was very young and Elsie was raised and pampered by a mother and grandmother who had the same characteristics. At age fourteen she eloped with John Whipple, who lived next door. He was nine years her senior. Elsie's grandfather, Captain Abraham Lansing, was livid because he had given her Elsie's father money and property that had passed to Elsie and now, by law, would be controlled by John Whipple. Captain Lansing viewed Whipple as a fortune hunter and went to court trying to get his gifts back but he lost the suit. Lansing died before there was any reconciliation but the rest of the family eventually warmed to John Whipple; he was a shrewd businessman and grew his wife's inheritance into a small fortune.

Living in one of the basement rooms of Cherry Hill was a workman who went by the name of Joseph Orton—called "Doctor" by the rest of the household because he wore glasses and knew how to read and write. He did farm work, chopped wood, tended the stable, and made general repairs to the house. His real name was Jesse Strang and he had a wife and four children in Fishkill, New York, whom he had deserted 1825. He moved to Sandusky, Ohio, then in the spring of 1826, to western New York where Jesse Strang faked his own death and became Joseph Orton.

Strang first saw Elsie Whipple when he was working at a tavern near Albany owned by Otis Bates. She came into the tavern with Philip P. Van Rensselaer's daughter, Maria. The girls got a little bit rowdy and Elsie, who Strang described as "sprightly, playful, and giddy" caught his eye. That night he commented to Bates's son that he would like to sleep with her.

Soon after, Strang went to work at Cherry Hill and his amorous feelings for Elsie continued to grow. He would see her often and they would sometimes talk, but he had no indication that she was interested in him. But Elsie could sense Strang's interest, and she told him to write her a letter and tell her his feelings. Strang was perplexed. He knew Elsie was married and he did not want trouble, but he did not want to pass up the opportunity. The original letter he wrote and delivered to her was destroyed, but this is how he reconstructed it ten months later:

Dear Elsie,

I have seriesly considered on it as you requested of me yesterday and I have concluded two compose a few lines two You and I thought that it was not my duty two right very freely not nowing Your object perhaps it is two get sum of my righting two show two your husband as you ar a marid woman, and If that is your intenshin It is my whish fore you two let me know it fore it is a thing that I skorn two make a disturbance between you and your husband but If on the outher hand It is out of pure offections I should be quite hapy for two have the information in your hand riting and I hope that you will not tak any offen in my manner of riting two you as we ar pirfect strangers two each other, but hop that those few lines may find free exceptan with you and after I find out your motive I can right mour freely on the subject and as for my offections thay are quite favorable I shall expact an answer from you If that is you motive, sow I remain your well whisher, Joseph Orton.

Half an hour after receiving the letter, Elsie handed Strang her response. She did not mince words: "My motive is out of pure love for you," she said. Several times in the letter she expressed her love for Strang and ended the letter with, "I remain your true and affectionate lover until death separates us."

This began a series of daily love letters between the two, delivered by servants or the Van Rensselaer children. Their desire for each other was heightened by fact that it was next to impossible to be alone together with so many people in the house. However, they did occasionally find the opportunity for, in Strang's words, "criminal intercourse."

In their correspondence Elsie expressed her willingness to flee with Strang. He was agreeable to this but said they would need $1,200 to get established somewhere else. Elsie had a fortune worth much more than $1,200 but by the laws of the time, it all belonged to her husband; she could not touch any of it while he was alive. Strang and Elsie decided they could live together only on John Whipple's death, and they were determined to make that happen. They made a pledge that neither would inform on the other, and if one were caught, the other would confess and they would hang together.

In the spring of 1827, they began to take action. First they tried poison—Sprang bought some arsenic in Albany and Elsie put it in a tonic that her husband took every day. She did not give him enough, and though it gave him stomach cramps, the poison did not kill him. Next they thought of using a hitman. Strang believed he could hire a man in Montreal for $300, but they did not have the money. Finally they decided that Strang would have to shoot Whipple himself. Elsie suggested he use one of her husband's dueling pistols, but Strang preferred rifles and bought a $25 flintlock.

They spread rumors that some men were out to kill Whipple over a business matter. Sprang said he had seen strange men lurking around the house. He and Elsie tested the rifle to see how much kick it had and whether it would be accurate when fired through glass. They planned to shoot through the window of Whipple's room.

The evening of May 7, 1827, Jesse Strang took off his coat and boots and climbed, with the rifle, onto the shed attached to the back of Cherry Hill. Standing in the dark, he could see into John Whipple's window without being seen himself. Whipple was in the room talking with Phillip Van Rensselaer's son, Abraham. Whipple stood up with his back to the window and Strang fired the rifle, hitting Whipple under his left arm.

Strang jumped off the shed and ran to a ravine behind the house, where he buried the rifle. He put his coat and boots back on and returned to the house, where he learned that John Whipple had been shot and killed. No one in the household suspected that Strang was responsible, and he was sent into town to fetch the coroner. When he returned he was sworn in as a member of the coroner's jury.

The next morning the jury convened and, though a member of the jury, Strang also gave testimony. He spoke vehemently about prowlers he had seen outside the night before. But Strang had overplayed his hand and his zeal to place the blame on the prowlers made the coroner suspicious. The following afternoon Strang was arrested for murder. Two weeks later Elsie Whipple was arrested as well.

Trials: Jesse Strang – July 25, 1827
Elsie Whipple – July 30, 1827

In June Jesse Strang confessed to the murder and told prosecutors where to find the rifle. He believed that if Elsie was convicted as well, her powerful family connections would get them both pardoned, so he tried to lay the blame on her. But when his lawyer and the prosecutor told him that nothing he said against Elsie would lighten his punishment, he withdrew his confession.

Strang's trial generated intense excitement. It had to be held in the assembly chamber of the state capital because no other building was large enough for the crowd. Even then, the streets outside the chamber were packed with people who could not get in.

Members of the household testified that they had heard Strang spread the stories of prowlers out to kill Whipple. The merchants who sold him the rifle and the arsenic testified, as did hotelkeepers who had seen Strang and Elsie together. But it was Sprang's confessions, admitted over the objection of the defense, that sealed his fate. The jury deliberated for fifteen minutes before returning a verdict of guilty.

Elsie's trial followed the same course as Strang's, except the prosecution tried to call Strang as a witness. There was much debate over his eligibility to testify because he had been convicted but not yet sentenced. In the end the judge would not allow his testimony. The prosecution rested, and the jury, without leaving their seats, acquitted Elsie Whipple. The Albany establishment had closed ranks to save one of their own from a public hanging.

Verdicts: Jesse Strang – Guilty of first-degree murder
               Elsie Whipple – Not guilty

Aftermath:

Between 30,000 and 40,000 people turned out August 24, 1827 to witness the hanging of Jesse Strang. In the crowd were hucksters selling a pamphlet entitled, *The Confession of Jesse Strang Made to C. Pepper, Esq.* On the scaffold, holding a copy of the confession, Jesse Strang advertised the pamphlet, saying: "This contains a full confession of the great transaction for which I am about to die, and every single word that it contains, to the best of my knowledge, is true; if there is a single word in it that is not true, it has been inserted by mistake and not by design."

The hanging was botched; the fall did not break Strang's neck and he swung for half an hour before suffocating. It was the last public hanging in Albany.

Elsie married Nathanial Freeman in New Brunswick, New Jersey, and on his death, she moved to Onondaga, New York, where she died in 1832.

Cherry Hill is still standing; it is fully restored and open to the public. It's claimed that the house is haunted, but whether the ghost is John Whipple or Jesse Strang is an ongoing debate.

Captain Joseph White

46.   "A MOST EXTRORDINARY CASE"

Joseph Knapp expected a sizable inheritance on the death of his great-uncle, eighty-two-year-old Captain Joseph White, but he hadn't the patience to wait for the old man's natural death. In 1830, he and his brother John hired a hitman to murder their benefactor. They might have gotten away with their scheme if they hadn't been prosecuted by the great orator Daniel Webster, whose

THE MURDER OF CAPT. JOSEPH WHITE

courtroom skill and persuasive argument set legal precedent and won their convictions.

Date: April 6, 1830

Location: Salam, Massachusetts

Victim: Captain Joseph White

Cause of Death: Clubbing and Stabbing

Accused: Richard Crowninshield, John F. Knapp, Joseph J. Knapp Jr.

Synopsis:

Captain Joseph White, a wealthy, retired merchant, lived in a fine house in Salem, Massachusetts, with a manservant and his niece, Mrs. Beckford, who served as housekeeper. Mrs. Beckford's daughter was married to Joseph J. Knapp Jr. and lived in nearby Wenham, Massachusetts. Knapp learned that Captain White had just completed his will, leaving $15,000 to Mrs. Beckford. But Knapp believed that if his great-uncle died without a will, his mother-in-law would, instead, inherit half his fortune: $200,000. He set out to guarantee this would happen.

221

Joseph Knapp conspired with his brother John Francis Knapp to hire a local criminal, Richard Crowninshield, to murder Captain White. They planned the deed for the night of April 6, 1830 when they knew Mrs. Beckford would be in Wenham, staying with her daughter. As a relative, Joseph Knapp had free access to Captain White's home and on April 6, he entered the house, stole the captain's will, and left the back parlor window unlatched.

That night, while the two brothers waited outside, Richard Crowninshield entered the house through the window. He went to the bedroom where Captain White was sleeping, fractured his skull with a club, and stabbed him thirteen times with a long dagger.

The people of Salem were shocked by the news that a prominent citizen had been murdered in his sleep and organized a committee of vigilance to investigate the crime. Adding to the confusion, the Knapp brothers falsely reported to the vigilance committee that they had been robbed by three men on the road from Salem to Wenham. This led to the belief that a gang of assassins was working in the area.

The committee had no clues in the case until a pickpocket in the New Bedford jail, seventy miles away, testified that his friend Richard Crowninshield had told him that he had killed Captain White. Crowninshield was arrested in Salem but would say nothing about the murder.

Around the same time, Joseph J. Knapp Sr., father of the Knapp brothers, received a letter from a Charles Grant of Belfast, Maine, demanding a large sum of money to avoid "ruinous disclosures." Joseph Sr. could make no sense of the letter, because it had been intended for his son. He showed it to Joseph Jr., who called it "a devilish lot of trash" and told his father to take it to the vigilance committee. Then, to muddy the waters further, Joseph Jr. wrote two letters, both purporting to be from Charles Grant. One was written to the committee claiming that he (Grant) had been hired to murder Captain White by the captain's nephew, Steven White. The second was to Steven White from Grant, demanding payment for the murder.

The committee dispatched a messenger to Belfast, Maine, and arranged to have Grant arrested at the post office when he came to pick up his mail. His real name was Palmer; he was an associate of Richard Crowninshield and was privy to the whole plot, including the instigating role of the Knapp brothers whom he was attempting to blackmail. To avoid prosecution himself, Palmer told all. The news reached Salem and when the false letters were found to be in Joseph Knapp Jr.'s handwriting, Joseph and John Knapp were taken into custody.

On his third day of imprisonment, Joseph Knapp Jr. made a full confession to his role in planning the murder, fabricating the story of the robbery, and forging the letters. After learning of Knapp's confession, Richard Crowninshield realized he had no hope and hanged himself in jail with a handkerchief tied to the bars of his cell.

Crowninshield's death complicated matters even further. The Knapps were to have been tried as accessories to murder, but under existing law, accessories could not be convicted unless the actual murderer was first convicted. Crowninshield's suicide made this impossible. It appeared that the Knapp bothers would get away with murder.

Trials: John Francis Knapp – July 1830
                       Joseph Jenkins Knapp – November 1830

The Commonwealth of Massachusetts employed the distinguished Daniel Webster to prosecute the case. Though better known as a defense attorney, Webster occasionally served as prosecutor. He described Captain White's murder as:

> *...a most extraordinary case. In some respects, it has hardly a precedent anywhere; certainly none in our New England history. This bloody drama exhibited no suddenly excited, ungovernable rage. The actors in it were not surprised by any lionlike temptation springing upon their virtue, and overcoming it, before resistance could begin. Nor did they do the deed to glut savage vengeance, or satiate longsettled and deadly hate. It was a cool, calculating, moneymaking murder. It was all 'hire and salary, not revenge.' It was the weighing of money against life; the counting out of so many pieces of silver against so many ounces of blood.*

The defense in the first trial argued that John Knapp could not be considered an accessory in the murder because the legal requirement said that an accessory must be present during the murder. The Knapps had been standing in the street, 300 feet away from the room where the murder was being committed.

Webster's response was:

> *To constitute a presence, it is sufficient if the accomplice is in a place, either where he may render aid to the perpetrator of the felony, or where the perpetrator supposes he may render aid. If they selected the place to afford assistance, whether it was well- or ill-chosen for that purpose, is immaterial. The perpetrator would derive courage and confidence from the knowledge that his associate was in the place appointed.*

With the letter of the law seemingly supporting the defense, it was not an easy case for a jury to decide. But in the end, they sided with Webster. John Knapp was convicted of murder. Four months later his brother Joseph was convicted as well.

Verdicts: John Francis Knapp – Guilty of murder
Joseph Jenkins Knapp – Guilty of murder

Aftermath:

On September 28, 1830, thousands of people witnessed the hanging of John Francis Knapp and Joseph Jenkins Knapp in Salem. The brothers were hanged together from the same gallows.

Ballad:

This ballad about the murder of Joseph White, sung to the tune of "Auld Lang Syne," was originally ten stanzas long. Olive Woolley Burt, in her book *American Murder Ballads* selected only the most pertinent:

The Ballad of Joseph White

O what a horrid tale to sound
In this our land to tell,
That Joseph White of Salem Town
By ruffian hands he fell!

Perhaps for money or for gain
This wicked deed was done;
But if for either, great the pain
This murderer must be in

Oh the infernal of the damn'd,
To murder in the night;
With cruel arm and bloodstain'd hand
Which pierc'd the side of White.
Thou harden'd hearted monster devil,
To thrust the dirk of death,
You will be plac'd upon the level.
For time will stop your breath!

(three stanzas omitted)

Calmly he laid in sweet repose,
The ruffian forced the room,
And with his dirk he did dispose
Of him who'd done no harm.
Great God, how can these things be so,
When man is left alone?
Poor feeble wretch, he does not know
How wicked he has done.

(Last four stanza's omitted)

Naomi Wise

47.   LITTLE 'OMIE

The haunting folk ballad "Omie Wise" has kept the story of Naomi Wise's murder alive for more than two hundred years. According to legend, Naomi Wise, a poor but beautiful orphan girl, was courted by Jonathan Lewis, son of a wealthy farmer. His mother persuaded him to stop the courtship but not before Naomi became pregnant with Jonathan's child. To avoid

THE MURDER OF NAOMI WISE

marriage and scandal, Jonathan Lewis drowned Naomi Wise in Deep River. That is the traditional tale of Naomi Wise, but how much of it is true?

Date: Spring 1807

Location: Randolph County, North Carolina

Victim: Naomi Wise

Cause of Death: Drowning

Accused: Jonathan Lewis

Synopsis:

Naomi Wise was extraordinarily beautiful, so the story goes. "Her size was medium, her figure beautifully formed, her face handsome and expressive, her eyes keen yet mild, her words soft and winning," wrote nineteenth century author Braxton Craven. She was an orphan, indentured as a child to William and Mary Adams, farmers in Randolph County, North Carolina, who raised Naomi as a daughter.

Jonathan Lewis lived in Guilford County but worked in Asheboro as a clerk in a store owned by Benjamin Elliot. He boarded with his employer on workdays, but each Saturday night he would ride fifteen miles back to his family's home. And each Sunday night he would ride back to Asheboro.

His route took him past the Adams's farm. Craven described Lewis as "a large, well-built, dignified-looking man. He was young, daring, and impetuous...His smile was like sunbeams bursting through a cloud [and] illuminated every continence upon which it fell." Naomi would watch in admiration as he rode by each week.

Once, as Naomi was carrying water from the spring, Jonathan stopped and asked if he could have a drink of water. She obliged, then he dismounted and helped her carry her buckets to the house. Naomi fell in love with Jonathan Lewis then, and he seemed smitten as well. He would stop on each journey and they would spend time together by Adams's spring.

Naomi thought that she and Jonathan would soon marry and began to prepare for the wedding. But Jonathan's mother had other ideas. His employer, Mr. Elliot, had a daughter, Hattie, who Mrs. Lewis thought would be a perfect match for her son. At his mother's insistence, Jonathan began courting Hattie Elliot and would ride by Adams's farm without stopping.

Naomi's heart was broken. She thought she had been engaged to Jonathan Lewis, but he proved faithless. When this news reached Hattie Elliot, she confronted Jonathan. He said the rumors were untrue, that he was never engaged to Naomi, and that he loved only Hattie.

One April afternoon Naomi picked up the pails and went to the spring to fetch some water. She never returned. By the spring a search party found a woman's footprints leading to a tree stump. On the other side of the stump were hoof prints. Naomi had used the stump to climb onto a horse, behind Jonathon Lewis. She thought he had come to marry her and got on his horse willingly. They stopped near a ford in Deep River; he dismounted and helped Naomi down. Then he strangled her and threw her into the river. When he knew she had drowned, he rode away.

Naomi's body was found tangled in weeds growing near the shore of Deep River. Her neck had been bruised and the coroner gave the cause of death as "drowning by violence." His examination also revealed that Naomi had been pregnant when she died.

There was little question who was responsible. The sheriff and his deputy rode off to arrest Jonathan Lewis. He was captured and jailed, but they did not hold him long enough for a trial. He escaped after being held only thirty days.

That is the traditional story of Naomi Wise, first published in 1851 by Braxton Craven (under the name Charlie Vernon) and reprinted many times since. Craven's version is a somewhat romanticized version of the true story.

In her 2003 book, *Naomi Wise, Creation, Re-Creation and Continuity in an American Ballad Tradition*, Eleanor R. Long-Wilgus included a long poem entitled "A True Account of Nayomy Wise." The poem was handwritten by Mary Woody not long after the murder but was unknown until the 1980s. Mary Woody's very detailed account of the murder is quite different from Braxton Craven's. Not a beautiful orphan girl, Naomi Wise was quite a bit older than Jonathan Lewis and already had two illegitimate children when they met. She was not seeking marriage from Lewis but a payment so she would not name him as the father of her child, which, by the laws of North Carolina, would have required him to pay a sizeable bastardy bond to support the child.

In reality, facts in the case are sparse. Contrary to Craven's story (and Naomi's tombstone), she died in 1807, not 1808. Jonathan Lewis was arrested for the murder of Naomi Wise on April 8, 1807. His trial was scheduled for October 26, but he escaped from jail on October 9 and fled Randolph County. He was recaptured in 1811 but did not go to trial until two years later. He was tried and found guilty of escaping from jail. He was never tried for the murder of Naomi Wise.

Trial: October 4, 1813

Jonathan Lewis was found guilty of breaking jail. He was fined "ten pounds and cost" and sentenced to thirty days in jail.

Aftermath:

In Craven's version, Lewis was acquitted of Naomi's murder because the evidence was circumstantial and on his deathbed, Jonathan Lewis admitted to drowning Naomi Wise, providing the story's needed closure. While this is the story that lives on in song and legend, in fact, no one knows for sure who killed Naomi Wise.

Ballad:

This song, called "Omie Wise" or "Little Omie" tells the traditional story of Naomi Wise's murder. There have been many versions sung throughout America. This is how it is usually sung today.

Little Omie

Come all good people, I'd have you draw near,
A sorrowful story you quickly shall hear;

228

A story I'll tell you about Omie Wise,
How she was deluded by Lewis's lies.

She promised to marry and use me quite well;
But conduct contrary I sadly must tell,
He promised to meet me at Adams's spring;
He promised me marriage and many fine things.

Still nothing he gave, but yet flattered the case.
He says, "We'll be married and have no disgrace,
Come get up behind me, we'll go up to town.
And there we'll be married, in union be bound."

I got up behind him, and straightway did go
To the bank of Deep River where the water did flow;
He says, "Now Naomi I'll tell you my mind,
I intend here to drown you and leave you behind."

"O pity your infant and spare me my life;
Let me go rejected and be not your wife;"
"No pity, no pity," this monster did cry;
In Deep river's bottom your body shall lie."

The wretch then did choke her, as we understand,
And threw her in the river below the milldam;
Be it murder or treason, O! what a great crime,
To drown poor little Omie and leave her behind.

Omie was missing they all did well know,
And hunting for her to the river did go;
And there found her floating on the water so deep,
Which caused all the people to sigh and to weep.

The neighbors were sent for to see the great sight,
While she lay floating all that long night;
So early next morning the inquest was held;
The jury correctly the murder did tell.

The Woolfolk Family

48.   BLOODY WOOLFOLK

In the early hours of August 6, 1887, nine members of the Woolfolk family of Bibb County, Georgia—ranging in age from eighteen months to eighty-four years—were hacked to death in their home. The only surviving member of the household was twenty-seven-year-old Tom Woolfolk, who quickly became the prime suspect. The press called him "Bloody Woolfolk" and it was all the sheriff could do to keep him out of the hands of a lynch mob. But when the trap sprung on Tom Woolfolk's legal hanging, had the State of Georgia finished the work of the real killer?

TOM WOOLFOLK

Date: August 6, 1887

Location: Bibb County, Georgia

Victims: The Woolfolk family (nine people)

Cause of Death: Blows from an axe

Accused: Tom Woolfolk

Synopsis:

Around two o'clock on the morning of August 6, 1887, neighbors were awakened by dogs barking at the home of Captain Richard Woolfolk (pronounced WUL-fork) in Bibb County, near Macon, Georgia. Tom Woolfolk, the captain's oldest son, wearing just his socks and underwear, ran to the house of Green Lockett, a black sharecropper who worked on the captain's plantation, crying, "Get a gun; they're killing Pa." Lockett refused to go back with him, but sent his son to alert the white families in the area. Soon a crowd of men, both black and white, had amassed at the Lockett shack.

Tom told them someone had entered the house and killed his entire family. Tom himself escaped death by climbing out the window. He did not see who the killer was. The crowd went with him back to the captain's house and watched as Tom went back inside to make sure everyone was dead. No one else would go inside while it was still dark; they stood there waiting until daybreak.

When it was light enough to see, the men entered the house and saw that Tom was correct—the entire Woolfolk family had been murdered. Amid thick pools of blood and spattered brains, nine bodies lay hacked to death: Tom's father, Richard F. Woolfolk, age 54; his stepmother, Mattie Woolfolk, age 41; his half-brother, R. F., age 20, his half-sister, Pearl, age 17; his half-sister, Annie, age 10, his half-sister, Rosebud, age 7; his half-brother, Charlie, age 5; his half-sister, Mattie, age 18 months, and his stepmother's aunt, Mrs. Tempe West, age 84. Their heads had been smashed by blows from an ax, some wounds from the blade, some from the end—a fact that led some to believe there were two killers. There was one set of bloody footprints made by Tom in his stocking feet.

News of the murders spread quickly and by midmorning hundreds of people had gathered around the home of Richard Woolfolk, who had been a leader in the community. That afternoon a coroner's jury was formed to investigate the crime. Tom, who had since put on pants and a shirt, was asked to strip so they could see the clothes he had been wearing. They noticed a bloody handprint on Tom's thigh; he could not explain it. Under Tom's bed someone found his bloodstained undershirt. The jury suggested that Sheriff Westcott take Tom to Macon for further questioning. They went out the back door. Out front, the crowd had already grown impatient with the wheels of justice and when they learned Tom had been taken away, a group of men took off after them. Tom arrived in Macon just barely ahead of a mob bent on lynching him.

Richard Woolfolk had married Tom's mother Susan in 1854, the year he graduated from the University of Georgia. They had two daughters, Flo and Lillie, before Tom was born in 1860. Susan never fully recovered from Tom's birth and died in 1865. Richard Woolfolk went to war, fighting for the Southern Confederacy, and became captain of Company A, Ross's battalion of the Georgia state troops. He returned to find his home in a state of economic disarray. In 1867, he married Mattie Howard, daughter of a wealthy man, allowing him to regain his position as a gentleman farmer.

At twenty-seven, Tom Woolfolk had yet to find his place in the world. He had failed as a farmer and as a merchant. He was married, but his wife left him three weeks after the ceremony. He had a reputation for being unstable and eccentric; he was suspicious and irritable. After his arrest, several people came forward remembering threats Tom made against his father, and claiming he had more right to his father's land than his half-siblings had.

His motive for the murder was to inherit his father's land. To that end, the order of the deaths would be important. If his father died before his stepmother, she would inherit the land and on her death, it would go to her surviving family. If she died first, Tom would be in line to inherit his father's property. In fact, the property was not worth as much as people thought; the captain was in bad financial straits and was heavily in debt.

Tom Woolfolk was the only person the authorities looked at for the murder, but another name kept popping up. A black vagrant named Jackson Dubose had been arrested on suspicion of being an escaped convict. He began talking in detail about the Woolfolk murders. He claimed he did not participate but was there when they happened. He was eventually released when it was learned that he had a reputation for lying about crimes, a dangerous game he used to get free room and board at local jails.

Trials: December 5, 1888
March 4, 1889
March 11, 1889
May 29, 1889
June 8, 1889

The morning of December 5, 1887, there were more spectators trying to get into Tom Woolfolk's trial than there were seats in the courtroom. Tom Woolfolk's defense was handled by Colonel John C. Rutherford, the former solicitor general for the Southwestern court circuit. He moved for a continuance because a number of his subpoenaed witnesses, including Jackson Dubose, were not present. Judge George W. Gustin denied the motion. The prosecution presented all of the circumstantial evidence and testimony of witnesses who had heard Tom Woolfolk threaten his father. The defense tried to admit statements of witnesses who heard others claim they killed the Woolfolks, but because the speakers themselves were not in the courtroom, they were disallowed as hearsay.

On December 14, 1887, as prosecutor John L. Hardeman was giving his closing arguments, he had worked up the crowd to such an extent that several spectators began shouting, "Hang him." Judge Gustin was not effective in restoring order. The following day the jury returned a verdict of guilty.

The case was appealed to the Georgia Supreme Court, who considered the shouts of "hang him" sufficient cause to overturn the verdict. On

March 4, 1889, Tom Woolfolk was tried again. Rutherford believed his client could not get a fair trial in Bibb County, so he moved for a change of venue. Judge Gustin denied the motion. On the close of the first day of trial, it was reported that one of the jurors had said he would cause a mistrial before allowing the prisoner to be found not guilty. Judge Gustin learned this and had little choice but to declare a mistrial.

On March 11 they began proceedings again but only got to eleven jurors before running out of eligible men to serve. Judge Gustin was forced to try again in a new venue.

On May 29, a new trial began in Houston County. This time several people reported that one of the jurors stated he did not believe in convicting a man on circumstantial evidence. Another expressed doubt about some of the evidence. Another mistrial was declared.

Tom Woolfolk's fifth trial was held on June 8, 1889. This time the trial went to completion, and again the verdict was guilty. The verdict was appealed but this time was not overturned.

Verdicts: Guilty; verdict overturned on appeal
Mistrial
Unable to empanel a jury
Mistrial
Guilty of first-degree murder

Aftermath:

While Tom Woolfolk awaited hanging, Jackson Dubose was arrested as an accomplice in the Woolfolk murders. On July 5 Dubose met with Judge Gustin, and they talked for an hour. The judge dropped the charge of murder entered against Dubose and tried him on a writ of lunacy. He was found guilty and sent to an insane asylum.

On October 29, 1890, they took Tom to the gallows in Perry, Georgia, where the atmosphere resembled a circus, with photographers and street vendors hawking souvenirs to the enormous crowd. Tom maintained his innocence to the end, reading this statement to the crowd:

> *I, Thomas G. Woolfolk, realizing the existence of an infinite, wise, and holy God, and so as to meet Him, knowing all that I have ever done, and fully understanding that I must stand before the judgment bar of God, and that today, in a few hours, I shall be called into his presence, do solemnly declare my innocence, and I leave as my last declaration that I did not take the life of my father or any member of his family, or have any knowledge of*

the person or persons who did the murderous deed. Signed, Thomas G. Woolfolk.

At 1:31 p.m., they sprung the trap. But the fall did not break his neck, and Tom Woolfolk slowly strangled to death. He was pronounced dead at 2:11.

Shortly after the Woolfolk murders, Simon Cooper, son of London and Luana Cooper, black farmworkers who lived nearby, left Bibb County. In 1898, Simon was lynched in Sommerville, South Carolina. On his body was found a notebook with the following lines: "Tom Woolfolk was mighty slick, but I fixed him. I would have killed him with the rest of the damn family, but he was not at home."

This entry has caused some to speculate that Simon Cooper was the real killer of the Woolfolk family.

Verse:

Like the Borden murders, the Woolfolk murders spawned a children's rope-skipping rhyme.

Woolfolk, Woolfolk, look what you've done
You killed your family and didn't fire a gun.

Dr. William York & nine others

49. THE BLOODY BENDERS

HOW THE BENDERS MURDERED THEIR VICTIMS

In the early 1870s, the counties of Labette and Montgomery in Kansas were experiencing an alarming number of missing persons. Investigators passed several times through the cabin of the Benders, a family of German immigrants who ran a small grocery store and restaurant outside of Cherryvale, Kansas, but the Benders appeared completely innocent. When authorities found the cabin abandoned one day, the picture changed. A closer look revealed ten murdered corpses, the handiwork of the "Bloody Benders."

Dates: 1870-1873

Location: Cherryvale, Kansas

Victims: Dr. William York and nine others

Cause of Death: Blows from a hammer; suffocation

Accused: The Bender family

Synopsis:

Around 1870 the Bender family built a small cabin outside of Cherryvale, Kansas, about fifty miles north of the Oklahoma border. William Bender and his wife (sometimes referred to as "Ma" Bender) were in their sixties; Thomas and Joanna (better known as Kate) were in their twenties. They were German immigrants; all spoke with accents, and the elder Benders spoke little English. It is unclear exactly how these four were related—most accounts say that Thomas and Kate were the son and daughter of William Bender and his wife, but Thomas was also known as John Gebhardt and is sometimes referred to as Kate's husband. Other accounts say that none of them were actually named Bender and that only the mother and daughter were related. The men were described as "large, coarse-appearing men." The descriptions of Kate range from "a large, masculine, red-faced woman" to "good-looking, well formed, rather bold in appearance." A number of sources agree that she had a ruddy complexion and may have been a redhead.

The Benders kept a small grocery store in the front of the cabin, selling staples such as tobacco, crackers, sardines, candles, powder, and shot. They also provided meals for travelers. Though they kept to themselves, the Benders attended church and town meetings and seemed to be an ordinary rural family. The only exception was Kate, who professed to being clairvoyant, giving public lectures on spiritualism and advertising in local newspapers her ability to "heal disease, cure blindness, fits, and deafness."

In 1873, citizens of Labette County became concerned over the inordinate number missing persons in their community. Neighboring counties were experiencing losses as well. In March 1873, Dr. William York from Onion Creek, Montgomery County, came in search of a man named Loucher and his infant daughter, who had travelled in the region the previous winter and were never heard from again. Dr. York never made it home either.

Dr. York was from a very prominent family and in April his brother, Col. A. M. York, came to Labette County leading a party of fifty citizens of Montgomery County. They searched unsuccessfully for the missing doctor, stopping several times at the Benders' cabin. On one occasion they asked Kate to use her clairvoyant powers to help with the search, but she had no information for them.

The next time someone stopped at the Benders' cabin, they found it deserted. Their wagon was missing and a calf they were raising had died of neglect. The authorities in Cherryvale were notified and went back to check on the house. Everything seemed to be in order, nothing was missing but clothes and bedding. But a thorough search of the house began to reveal the Benders' horrible secret. Near the table where guests were served was a trapdoor, and the foul-smelling hole beneath the door was clotted with blood.

The ground in an orchard near the house had been carefully plowed, but one small section was noticeably indented. The ground was dug up, revealing the decomposed body of Dr. York. His skull had been crushed and his throat had been cut. Before nightfall seven more bodies were extracted and another was found the next day. Most were badly decomposed, but some could be identified by clothing and jewelry. They were:

- W. F. McCrotty of Cedarville.
- D. Brown of Cedarville.
- Henry F. McKenzie of Hamilton County, Indiana.
- Mr. Loucher and his baby daughter from Independence.
- Two unidentified men.
- One child believed to be an eight-year-old girl.

Another body previously found in Drum Creek was also attributed to the Benders. All but the baby had fractured skulls and slit throats. It was believed that the baby was suffocated when buried alive with her father. The eight-year-old girl's body had been badly mutilated.

The travelers were murdered for their money. The amounts stolen by the Benders ranged from forty cents to $2,600, along with horses and wagons.

From the condition of the bodies and the arrangement of the house, the authorities were able to surmise how the killings were done. The table where customers took their meals was in a small booth formed by cloth partitions on both sides. The partitions were close enough to the back of the chairs that, when sitting upright, the heads of the diners would indent the cloth. The male Benders would wait behind the cloth partitions and, when the opportunity presented itself, would smash their victims' skulls with stonebreaker's hammers. The bodies were thrown through the trapdoor—into what one book called the "slaughter-pen"—where the throats were cut to guarantee death. After dark the bodies were removed and buried in the orchard.

This speculation was verified to an extent by a Mr. Wetzell of Independence, Kansas, who had read Kate's advertisement and travelled to the Benders' with his friend, Mr. Gordan, seeking a cure for neuralgia. Kate examined Wetzel and expressed confidence in her ability to affect a permanent cure but invited them to dine first. For some reason the two men rose from the table and decided to eat their dinners at the counter instead. This caused a change in Kate's behavior; she became caustic and abusive toward them. They saw the two Bender men emerge from behind the partitions. Wetzell and Gordan became suspicious then and decided to leave—a decision that probably saved their lives.

When the news of the murders spread through Labette County, it whipped the citizens into a frenzy. They demanded vengeance and formed vigilance committees to hunt down the Benders. The vigilantes went first to the home of a man named Brockman, another German immigrant who had briefly been a partner of Mr. Bender's. They put a rope around his neck and threatened to hang him if he would not confess. When Brockman swore he knew nothing, they hanged him from a tree. But when he was at the point of death, they lowered him down and questioned him again. When he still had nothing to tell them, they hung him again. This torture was repeated three times before the posse left him semiconscious, lying on the ground.

Aftermath:

The search for the Benders continued, but though the governor of Kansas offered a $2,000 reward for their capture, the Benders were never brought to justice. One investigation determined that they took a train from Thayer to Chanute, where John and Kate got off and took the MK&T train south to Red River in Indian Territory. Here they met up with the elder Benders and travelled through Texas and New Mexico.

Other residents of Labette County told a different story. While researching the Benders' story for his 1910 book, Celebrated Criminal Cases of America, San Francisco captain of police Thomas S. Duke contacted police chiefs of Cherryvale and Independence, Kansas. This is how they responded:

Cherryvale, Kansas
June 14, 1910

Dear Sir:
Yours just received. It so happened that my father-in-law's farm joins the Bender farm and he helped locate the bodies of the victims. I often tried to find out from him what became of the Benders, but he only gave me a knowing look and said he guessed they would not bother anyone else.
There was a vigilance committee organized to locate the Benders, and shortly afterward old man Bender's wagon was found by the roadside riddled with bullets. You will have to guess the rest. I am respectfully yours,
J. N. Kramer
Chief of Police

Independence, Kansas

June 14, 1910
Dear Sir:
In regard to the Bender family, I will say that I have lived here forty years, and it is my opinion that they never got away.

A vigilance committee was formed and some of them are still here, but will not talk except to say that it would be useless to look for them, and they smile at the reports of some of the family having been located.
The family nearly got my father. He intended to stay there one night, but he became suspicious, and although they tried to coax him to stay, he hitched up his team and left.
Regretting that I cannot give you more information, I am yours respectfully,
D.M. Van Cleve
Chief of Police

Though some have speculated that the Benders were killed by vigilantes, most believe that their escape was successful. Several times suspected members of the Bender family were arrested in other parts of the country and brought back to Kansas to be tried. Most notably, in 1890 two women were arrested in Michigan and alleged to be Ma Bender and Kate. There attorney had affidavits proving they were Mrs. Almira Griffith and Mrs. Sarah E. Davis and were in Michigan between 1870 and 1874. After a habeas corpus hearing, they were released from the Labette County jail.

The true fate of the Bender family remains a mystery.

Mabel H. Young

50. THE BOSTON BELFREY TRAGEDY

In the early 1870s, the city of Boston experienced a rash of gruesome murders. In 1872, the dismembered body of Abijah Ellis was found floating in the Charles River. In 1874, Jesse Pomeroy killed two children and tortured several others. And, perhaps most disturbing to the people of Boston, a series of violent sexual assaults committed between 1871 and 1875 resulted in the deaths of two young women. These crimes remained unsolved until a Sunday in May 1875 when the body of five-year-old Mabel Young was found in the bell tower of the Warren Avenue Baptist Church shortly after Thomas W. Piper was seen leaping from the belfry.

THOMAS PIPER LEAPING FROM THE BELFRY

Date: May 23, 1875

Location: Boston, Massachusetts

Victim: Mabel H. Young

Cause of Death: Blows to the head

Accused: Thomas W. Piper

Synopsis:

When Sunday school classes at the Warren Avenue Baptist Church let out around 3:30 on May 23, 1875, Miss Augusta Hobbs was at the church

240

to meet her five-year-old niece, Mabel Young. Mabel stood by her aunt's side as Miss Hobbs conversed for several minutes with Rev. Pentecost but when the conversation was over, Mabel was nowhere to be found.

While Miss Hobbs and some other women of the church were searching for Mabel, they heard an agonized cry coming from the church belfry. Three men broke down a locked door and rushed up the stairs into the tower. At the first landing, they saw a fresh puddle of blood, and under a loose floorboard, they found a bloodstained cricket bat. They hurried up to the next level and pushed open a heavy trapdoor. Dozens of pigeons flew out of the way as the men entered the belfry and found Mabel Young lying on the floor. Her skull was crushed and her hair and clothes were covered with blood, but she was still alive. The men carried her down from the belfry, and though she never regained consciousness, Mabel managed to live until eight o'clock the following evening.

A young boy outside the church had seen a man leap from the belfry and run away. When Chief of Police Savage heard of the attack, he had a good idea who that man was. Savage lived not far from the Warren Avenue Baptist Church and knew that the sexton of the church had been a suspect in a similar murder a year and a half earlier. On December 5, 1873, near Dorchester, a man heard a noise in the bushes and when he investigated, a cloaked figure jumped from the bushes and ran away. He had interrupted the rape of a woman who was later identified as a domestic servant named Bridget Landregan. Her skull had been crushed and she was naked from the waist down. Nearby was a bloody "bat-like" club. A few hours later, the rapist accomplished his goal with the assault and rape of Minnie Sullivan. Though she survived the attack, Miss Sullivan could give no description of her attacker. The police were able to trace the club to a shop where Thomas W. Piper was working, buy they did not have enough evidence to arrest him.

Not long after this, Piper was hired as sexton of the Warren Avenue Baptist Church on the recommendation of his brother, a member of the church who was studying for the ministry. Even without knowing his suspicious past, members of the church had reason to be wary of their new sexton. The twenty-six-year-old Piper was described as melancholy but quiet and agreeable until the sixteen-year-old daughter of a minister met him in the vestry one Sunday evening. It was not revealed what he proposed to her, but she hurried home to tell her parents "she thought he was a very bad man indeed, and was afraid of him."

Reverend Pentecost had caught Piper reading a racy adventure novel called *Cord and Creese*. The prosecutor at Piper's trial would later say that the book's publishers "ought to be sent to the House of Correction for the rest of their lives." It was also discovered that Piper kept bottles of whiskey in his room and had one hidden in the pews at the church, laced with laudanum.

Thomas Piper was already in police custody when Mabel Young died. At least three more little girls came forward to say that Piper had tried to lure them into the belfry, offering to show them the pigeons. The cricket bat, used on church outings, was usually kept in the sexton's room. Piper had deliberately brought it out in preparation for the crime.

Trials: December 11, 1875
             January 31, 1876

While Piper was being questioned in police custody, assistant deputy chief of police John Hamm told him, "It would go better if you confessed." He then brought Reverend George Pentecost into Piper's cell, and Piper apparently complied, making some incriminating statements to his spiritual advisor.

When the prosecution tried to enter the confession as evidence, Piper's attorney vehemently objected, saying that Hamm had deliberately brought Pentecost to encourage Piper to confess. The judges sitting on the trial first ruled for the defense, but the prosecutor argued that he was not offering the testimony as evidence of a confession but to show the defendant's "consciousness of guilt." On this fine point of law, the testimony was allowed. Nonetheless, Piper's first trial ended in a hung jury.

In his second trial, prosecutors entered evidence of the "evil literature" that Piper enjoyed reading. This seemed to be enough to sway the jury to convict Thomas Piper of first-degree murder.

Verdicts: Hung jury
             Guilty of first-degree murder

Aftermath:

Throughout his trials, Thomas Piper maintained that he was innocent of the murder of Mabel Young. However, on May 7, 1876, he sent for his attorney and confessed to the crime. In addition, he confessed to the murder of Bridget Landregan and the attack on Minnie Sullivan. He also confessed to the murder of Mary Tynam, a crime for which he had not been a suspect. Mary Tynam was a prostitute, and Piper had spent the night with her. In the morning, he smashed her head with the blunt end of an axe so he could get his money back. He told the police where they could find the murder weapon.

Thomas W. Piper was hanged on May 26, 1876 inside Suffolk County Jail in front of a crowd of 400 people. Tickets to the hanging had been selling for as much as $50. Outside the jail another thousand people waited for the announcement of Piper's death. At 10:35, the sheriff said to the hushed crowd, "I proceed to execute the sentence of the law, and may God in his infinite mercy have pity on his soul." The trap was sprung; Piper fell eight feet and died instantly.

In 1920, the congregation of the Warren Avenue Baptist Church joined the First Baptist Church on Commonwealth Avenue and sold the church building on the corner of Warren and Canton Streets. In 1969, it was razed by the city and eventually replaced by Hayes Park. Today the small, but beautifully landscaped park includes an original sculpture called West Canton Street Child by former West Canton Street resident Kahil Gibran. Though not specifically intended as a memorial to Mabel Young, it is a fitting monument for the site of her death.

Poem:

"Verses Composed on the Confession and Execution of Thomas W. Piper, The Convicted Belfry Murderer" was published in 1876 and attributed to George Gordon Byron DeWolfe, known as "The Wandering Poet of New Hampshire." However, DeWolfe died two years before the murder was committed. The publisher explained that verses were composed from beyond the grave and transferred through a spirit medium named Miss Lillie. The printed poem included an advertisement for Miss Lillie's services.

Verses Composed on the Confession and Execution of Thomas W. Piper, The Convicted Belfry Murderer.

It was on the twenty third of may
In eighteen seventy five,
When little Mabel went to church
Led at her aunty's side!

But ah alas they little thought
As they to church did go,
The sexton of that holy house
Would lay dear Mabel low

They listened to the word of God
The music soft and sweet,

243

But when the services were out,
Her aunt, a friend did meet?

She stopped to press her goodly hand
And pass the time of day,
And while thus talking to her friend
Sweet Mable strayed away!

She strayed back to that holy place
That house of God and prayer.
The innocent and living child
She met her murderer there!

He led her by her little Hand
Into the Belfry High.
And with the bat he dealt a blow
That made dear Mabel Die.

For one who'd been a lovely child,
Was lying nearly dead!
And near her was a pool of blood
From the blow upon her head!

Beside her lay the dreadful bat
Had left the murderous hand!
Ah that was There!—also the wretch
That Justice did demand?

Ah soon the child is recognized,
And bitter tears are shed?
The beautiful, the musical
Sweat Mabel was quite dead!

Boston looked sad with the dawning of morning;
The lifeless girl's body was laid in the Hall;
And many fierce words full of vengeance were spoken,
And Piper was hated, cursed, loathed in them all!

From many a village the people did gather
To look on the form that in death did repose;
And many a merciful mother and father
Had hearts that to Piper the murderer froze.

244

O'er gentle little Mabel's grave
When grass is growing green.
Many fond ones weep—a nobler child.
The earth has seldom seen!

Strew flowers over Mabel's form,
Which now the earth does cover.
Her spirits free from every harm!
God is her kindest lover!

Now in the dark embracing earth,
Does sleep sweet Mabel's form;
But she the mild and beautiful.
No more can feel the storm!

Sleep, mangled form, in the cold earth be sleeping;
Rest, gentle spirit, in sunshine and love;
Mother afflicted, O, answer though weeping,
Don't Mable now wait for your coming, above?

An angle she seem'd when on earth she was living,
Made her beautiful home al sunshine within;
An angle she is, with "Our Father" in Heaven,
And free from surroundings of sorrow and sin.

Is human life so frail a thing,
That fiends can murder so,
And through the land from North to South
One day unpunished go?

O, watch and wait, and trust and pray!
To sweet hope fondly cling!
Till he, whose hands have known her blood,
Shall on the gallows swing!

Pity for fiends such as Thomas Piper,
His cruelty to a kind mother and mild,
Who wishes some spot neath the beautiful Heaven.
That's safe for her darling and innocent child!

Pity there can be in one does illumine

With sunshine and earth and the breast of the sea,
But pity for fiends,—O it never was human,
And never through the coming ages can be!

Fiend in the prison cell, who would remove you
From it to be free on this bright earth again?
Who, when that deed more than devil does prove you,
What mother would plead your freedom obtain?

There's not a spot in the far arctic regions,
AS cold and as pitiless as thou hast been!
There's not a devil amid countless legions,
So wicked—so cruel—so abject—so mean!

Some parties were working for his commutation,
Thinking possibly he might innocent be.
When his council, one Sunday, called and told him;
He feared he could never again be free!

He then confessed all to his good faithful counsel,
Telling him of the tree murders he'd done.
And for the first one he named little Mabel,
Then Bridget Landregan and Mary Tynan!

CHAPTER NOTES

1. The Corpse in the Shipping Crate

"The Adams-Colt Murder Sad Coincidence." *The New York Times*, October 23, 1872.

Colt, John Caldwell. *Trial of John C. Colt for the murder of Samuel Adams*. New York: The Sun, 1842.

"John Colt Trial: 1842," *Encyclopedia.com*, < http://www.encyclopedia.com/doc/1G2-3498200057.html>.

Lawson, John Davison. *American State Trials*. St. Louis: Thomas Law Books, 1914.

Tucher, Andie. *Froth and Scum: Truth, Beauty, Goodness, and the Ax Murder in America's First Mass Medium*. Chapel Hill: University of North Carolina, 1994.

2. The Raven Stream Crime

"Cartoons and Comments." *Puck*, September 19, 1883.

"History of a Crime." *Truth*, September 16, 1883.

"Looking for Bad Lewis." *New York Times*, September 23, 1883.

"The Mystery Unsolved." *New York Times*, September 6, 1883.

"Norman Ambler's Story." *Troy Times*, October 4, 1883.

"The Raven Stream Crime." *New York Times*, September 24, 1883.

"Rose Ambler." *Aurora Daily Express*, September 6, 1883.

"Rose Ambler's Assassin." *New York Times*, September 8, 1883.

"Rose Ambler's Murder." *New Haven Register*, April 5, 1885.

"Rose Clark Ambler." *Find A Grave*, <http://www.findagrave.com/cgi-bin/fg.cgi?page=gr&GRid=59409275>.

"Rose Clark Ambler." *Harvard University Library*, <http://via.lib.harvard.edu/via/deliver/deepcontent?recordId=olvwork362878>.

"Rose Clark Ambler." *Kalamazoo Gazette*, August 12, 1892.

"The Rose Clark Ambler Mystery." *Trenton Evening Times*, September 14, 1883.

"The Rose Clark Murder Mystery." *New York Tribune*, September 7, 1883: 5.

"The Stratford Tragedy." *New Haven Register*, September 4, 1883.

Twain, Mark. *Mark Twain's Notebooks & Journals, Volume 3*. San Francisco: University of California Press, 1878.

"The Verdict in the Rose Ambler Case." *New York Herald*, September 30, 1883.

"Who Killed Rose Ambler?" *New York Times*, September 11, 1883.

7. The Sleepwalking Defense

Cohen, Daniel A. *Pillars of Salt, Monuments of Grace: New England Crime Literature and the Origins of American Popular Culture, 1674-1860*. New York: Oxford University Press, 1993.

---. "The Murder of Maria Bickford: Fashion, Passion, and the Birth of a Consumer Culture."
<https://journals.ku.edu/index.php/amerstud/article/viewFile/2899/2858>

Hobson, Barbara Meil. *Uneasy Virtue: The Politics of Prostitution and the American Reform Tradition*. New York: Basic Books, 1987.

4. Lizzie Borden Took an Axe...Or Did She?

Chaney, Karen Elizabeth. *Lizzie Borden (New England Remembers)*. Beverly, MA: Commonwealth Editions, 2006.

Kent, David and Robert A. Flynn. *The Lizzie Borden Sourcebook*. Boston: Branden Books, 1992.

Linder, Doug. "The Trial of Lizzie Borden." *UMKC School of Law*, <http://www.law.umkc.edu/faculty/projects/ftrials/LizzieBorden/borden account.html>

Lizzie Andrew Borden Virtual Museum and Library. <http://www.lizzieandrewborden.com/>.

"Lizzie Borden." *Find A Grave*. <http://www.findagrave.com/cgi-bin/fg.cgi?page=gr&GRid=115>.

Lizzie Borden Bed and Breakfast. <http://www.lizzie-borden.com/>.

Lizzie Borden: Warps and Wefts. <http://lizziebordenwarpsandwefts.com/>.

Masterton, William. *Lizzie Didn't Do It!* Boston: Branden Books, 2000.

5.   He Done Her Wrong

"Allen Britt." *Find A Grave*, <http://www.findagrave.com/cgi-bin/fg.cgi?page=gr&GRid=23212>.

"Frankie and Johnnie." *Mudcat*, <http://mudcat.org/@displaysong.cfm?SongID=2122>

"Revisiting the Ballad 'Frankie and Johnny'." *NPR Music*. <http://www.npr.org/templates/story/story.php?storyId=4185374>.

Slade, Paul. "It's a Frameup: Frankie and Johnny." *Planet Slade*, http://www.planetslade.com/frankie-and-johnny1.html.

Spaeth, Sigmund Gottfried. *Read 'Em and Weep: The Songs You Forgot to Remember.* New York: Doubleday, Page & company, 1926.

Wilentz, Sean, and Greil Marcus. *The Rose & the Briar: Death, Love and Liberty in the American Ballad.* New York: W.W. Norton, 2006.

Wright, John A. *Discovering African American St. Louis: a guide to historic sites.* Saint Louis: Missouri Historical Society, 2002.

6. "Old Shakespeare"

Casebook: Jack the Ripper - http://www.casebook.org/

Douglas, John E., and Mark Olshaker. *The Cases That Haunt Us.* New York: Pocket, 2001.

"Jack the Ripper in Queens Jail?" Greater Astoria Historical Society, <http://www.astorialic.org/starjournal/1800s/1891may_p.php>

"Witness Against Frenchy," *New York Times,* June 30, 1891.

7. A Balance of Probabilities

Budge, Henry H., *The Entire and Unabridged Evidence, Given on the Second Inquest, Concerning the Death of Mrs. Priscilla Budge.* Lowville, N.Y.: Printed at the Lewis County Banner Office, 1860.

Conkling, Alfred Ronald. T*he Life and Letters of Roscoe Conkling: Orator, Statesman, Advocate,* New York: C.L. Webster & Company, 1889.

Gedge, Karin E. *Without Benefit of Clergy: Women and the Pastoral Relationship in Nineteenth-Century American Culture (Religion in America),* Oxford: Oxford University Press, 2003

Swinburne, John. *A Typical American: Or, Incidents In The Life Of Dr. John Swinburne, Of Albany, The Eminent Patriot, Surgeon, And Philanthropist.* Albany: The Citizens' Association, 1888.

8. The Bond Street Tragedy

"Dr. Burdell, or the Bond Street Murder." *Library of Congress,* <http://www.loc.gov/item/amss003279/>

Duke, Thomas Samuel, *Celebrated Criminal Cases of America*, San Francisco, The James H. Barry company, 1910.

Feldman, Benjamin. *Butchery on Bond Street - Sexual Politics and The Burdell-Cunningham Case in Ante-bellum New York*, New York: Green-wood Cemetery Historic Fund in association with the New York Wanderer Press, 2007.

"The Most Celebrated Crime Of The 19th Century, The Murder Of Dr. Harvey Burdell." *The History Box*, http://www.thehistorybox.com/ny_city/nycity_crime_19th_century_dr._b urdell_article00427.htm

Newman, Andy, "A Lurid Tale from 1857 Is Revived in Granite", *New York Times*, September. 19. 2007.

Sutton, Charles, James B. Mix, and Samuel Anderson Mackeever. *The New York Tombs; Its Secrets and Its Mysteries. Being a History of Noted Criminals, With Narratives of Their Crimes*. New York: United States Pub. Co., 1873.

9.   The Smuttynose Murders

"Celia Thaxter's 'Murder Letter.'" *SeacoastNH.com* <http://seacoastnh.com/smuttynose/letter.html>.

Faxon, David. *Cold Water Crossing: An Account of the Murders at the Isles of Shoals*. David Faxon, 2009.

"Graves of Smuttynose Victims." *SeacostNH.com*, <http://seacoastnh.com/smuttynose/graves.html>.

Spooner, Emeric. *Return To Smuttynose Island: And Other Maine Axe Murders*. On Demand, 2009.

"Testimony of Mary S. Hontvet." *SeacostNH.com*, <http://seacoastnh.com/smuttynose/marentestimony.html#1>.

Thaxter, Celia. "A Memorable Murder." *SeacostNH.com*, <http://seacoastnh.com/smuttynose/memo.html>.

10. The Minister and the Mill Girl

Avery, Ephraim K. *A Report of the Trial of the Rev. Ephraim K. Avery, Before the Supreme Judicial Court of Rhode Island, On an Indictment for the Murder of Sarah Maria Cornell.* Providence: Marshall and Brown, 1833.

Clarke, M. Sarah. *Maria Cornell, or the Fall River murder: a domestic drama in three acts.* New York: No. 5 Chatham Square, 1833.

Kasserman, David Richard. *Fall River Outrage: Life, Murder, and Justice in Early Industrial New England.* Philadelphia: University of Pennsylvania Press, 1986.

"The Minister and the Mill Girl" *American Heritage,* October 1961.

"She is more to be pitied than censured. " *Brown University Library,* <http://www.brown.edu/Facilities/University_Library/exhibits/RLCexhibit/avery/averyms.html>.

11. Found Drifting with the Tide

The Beautiful victim of the Elm City being a full, fair, and impartial narrative of all that is known of the terrible fate of the trusting and unfortunate Jennie E. Cramer: giving all the particulars that can be ascertained about Miss Annie Blanche Douglas. New York: M.J. Ivers, 1881.

"Jennie Cramer's Death; Arguments For and Against the Malleys." *New York Times,* October 22, 1881.

McConnell, Virginia A. *Arsenic Under the Elms: Murder in Victorian New Haven.* Westport, Conn.: Praeger, 1999.

12. The Woman in Black

Adams, Charles F. *Murder by the Bay: Historic Homicide In and About the City of San Francisco.* Sanger, Calif.: Quill Driver Books/ Word Dancer Press, 2005.

Marsh, Andrew J., and Samuel Osbourne. *Official report of the trial of Laura D. Fair, for the murder of Alex. P. Crittenden including the testimony, the arguments of counsel, and the charge of the court, reported verbatim, and the entire correspondence of the parties, with portraits of the defendant and the deceased.* San Francisco: San Francisco Co-operative Print. Co., 1871.

"The Sensational Murder Trial of Laura D. Fair." *Holy Hormones Journal,* <http://holyhormones.com/womens-health/menstrual-cycle/premenstrual-syndrome/pms/was-female-hysteria-a-viable-legal-defense-for-a-victorian-woman/>

"Murderess Laura D. Fair." *YesterYear Once More,* <http://yesteryearsnews.wordpress.com/2009/07/13/murderess-laura-d-fair/>.

13. Clan-na-Gael

Duke, op. cit.

"Fenian Dynamiters The Clan na Gael." *Esoteric Philosopher: Study of the Endless Path of Wisdom,* <http://logos_endless_summer.tripod.com/id237.html>.

Hunt, Henry M. *The Crime of the Century Or, the Assassination of Dr. Patrick Henry Cronin* (Chicago: H. L. & D. H. Kochersperger, 1889).

McEnnis, John T., *The Clan-Na-Gael and the Murder of Dr. Cronin.* San Francisco: G. P. Woodward, 1889.

"The Murder of Dr. Patrick Henry Cronin." *Eneyclopedia.com,* http://www.encyclopedia.com/doc/1G2-2536601671.html

Pearson, Edmund, ed. Gerald Gross, *Masterpieces of Murder: An Edmund Pearson True Crime Reader.* Boston: Little, Brown & Co., 1924.

14. The Boston Boy Fiend

Duke, op. cit.

Pomeroy, Jesse Harding. *Autobiography of Jesse H. Pomeroy,* Boston: J.A. Cummings & Co, 1875.

Reynolds, Arthur, et. al. "Jesse Harding Pomeroy 'The Boy Fiend." Department of Psychology, Radford University, Radford, VA.

Schechter, Harold. *Fiend: The Shocking True Story Of Americas Youngest Serial Killer.* New York: Pocket, 2000.

15. The Druse Butchery

Hill, David Bennett. *Public Papers of David B. Hill, Governor. 1885-[1891].* Albany: The Argus Company, printers, 1886.

Mrs. Druse's case, and Maggie Houghtaling An innocent woman hanged. The truth revealed at last. A startling confession. Dying innocent to save those she loved. Philadelphia: Old Franklin Pub. House, 1887.

Tippetts, William Henry. *Herkimer County murders this book contains an accurate account of the capital crimes committed in the County of Herkimer, from the year 1783 up to the present time. Among those of recent date are the Wishart murder, the Druse butchery, and the Middleville tragedy.* Herkimer, N.Y.: H.P. Witherstine & Co., Steam Book and Job Printers, 1885.

"William Druse: Murdered, Chopped Up, Burned, Thrown in a Swamp." *YesterYear Once More,* <http://yesteryearsnews.wordpress.com/2009/03/09/william-druse-murdered-chopped-up-burned-thrown-in-a-swamp/>

16. The Assassination of Jim Fisk

"Edward S. Stokes Dead." *New York Times,* November 3, 1901.

Fuller, Robert H. *Jubilee Jim: From Circus Traveler to Wall Street Rogue: The Remarkable Life of Colonel James Fisk, Jr.* New York: MacMillan 1928.

Gordon, John Steele. *The Scarlet Woman of Wall Street: Jay Gould, Jim Fisk, Cornelius Vanderbilt, the Erie Railway Wars, and the Birth of Wall Street.* New York: Weidenfeld & Nicolson, 1988.

"Jim Fisk, or, He Never Went Back on the Poor." *The Lester Levy Sheet Music Collection.* http://levysheetmusic.mse.jhu.edu/catalog/levy:058.021

Swanberg, W. A. *Jim Fisk: the Career of an Impossible Rascal.* New York: Charles Scribner's Sons 1959.

17. Hang Down Your Head Tom Dula

"Laura Foster." *Find A Grave,* <http://www.findagrave.com/cgi-bin/fg.cgi?GRid=5915&page=gr>.

"Tom Dooley: A Wilkes County Legend." *Wilkes Playmakers,* <http://www.wilkesplaymakers.com/contente.asp?page_id=dooleye>.

"Tom Dooley" *Mudcat* <http://mudcat.org/@displaysong.cfm?SongID=7374>

"'Tom Dooley' Dula." *Find A Grave,* <http://www.findagrave.com/cgi-bin/fg.cgi?GRid=2473&page=gr>.

Wellman, Manly Wade. *Dead and Gone.* New York: University of North Carolina, 1980.

West, John Foster. *The Ballad of Tom Dula: The Documented Story Behind the Murder of Laura Foster and the Trials and Execution of Tom Dula.* New York: Parkway, 2002.

18. Delia's Gone, One More Round

Kodish, Debora G. *Good Friends and Bad Enemies: Robert Winslow Gordon and the Study of American Folksong (Music in American Life),* Urbana: University of Illinois, 1986.

Wilentz, Sean. "The Sad Song of Delia Green and Cooney Houston." *Princeton Alumni Weekly,* January 26, 2005.

Wilentz & Marcus, op. cit.

19. The Arsenic Tragedy

Burt, Olive Woolley. *American Murder Ballads and Their Stories*. New York: Oxford University Press, 1958.

Green, Henry G. *Trial of Henry G. Green, for the murder of his wife*. New York: Printed for the publisher, 1845.

Jones, Louis C. *Three Eyes on the Past: Exploring New York Folklife* (York State Books), Syracuse, N.Y.: Syracuse University Press, 1982.

Mysteries of Crime as Shown in Remarkable Capital Trials. Boston: S. Walker, 1870.

"Henry Green and His Bride of One Week." *Stephentown Genealogy*, <http://www.stephentowngenealogy.com/hometowntales.html>.

"DTStudy: Henry Green/The Arsenic Tragedy." *The Mudcat Café*, <http://www.mudcat.org/thread.cfm?threadid=96283&messages=11>.

20. The Girl in Green

Cohen, Patricia Cline. *The Murder of Helen Jewett*, New York. New York, N.Y: Vintage, 1999

"The Sensational Murder of Helen Jewett." *Crime Library*, <http://www.trutv.com/library/crime/notorious_murders/classics/helen_jewett/index.html>.

21. Temporary Insanity

Brandt, Nat. *The Congressman Who Got Away With Murder*, Syracuse, Syracuse University Press, 1991.

"Dreadful Tragedy." *The New York Times*, February 28, 1859.

"General Daniel E. Sickles." *Find A Grave*, <http://www.findagrave.com/cgi-bin/fg.cgi?page=gr&GSln=sickles&GSfn=dan&GSbyrel=in&GSdyrel=in&GSob=n&GRid=7381&>.

"Phillip Barton Key." *Find A Grave*, <http://www.findagrave.com/cgi-bin/fg.cgi?page=gr&GRid=9458197>.

Sickles, Daniel Edgar and Felix Gregory De Fontaine, *Trial of the Hon. Daniel E. Sickles for Shooting Philip Barton Key, Esq., U.S. District Attorney, of Washington, D.C., February 27th, 1859*, New York: R.M. De Witt, 1859.

"The Sickles Tragedy." *New York Times*, April 12, 1859.

"Teresa Bagioli Sickles." *Find A Grave*, <http://www.findagrave.com/cgi-bin/fg.cgi?page=gr&GSln=Sickles&GSfn=Teresa&GSbyrel=in&GSdyrel=in&GSob=n&GRid=16926340&;>

Thomas, Keneally. *American Scoundrel: The Life of the Notorious Civil War General Dan Sickles*. New York: Nan A. Talese/Doubleday, 2002.

"The Washington Tragedy." *Illinois State University*, <http://my.ilstu.edu/~ftmorn/cjhistory/casestud/washingt.html>.

22.   The Demon of the Belfry

Adams, op. cit.

"Blanche Lamont." *Find A Grave*, <http://www.findagrave.com/cgi-bin/fg.cgi?page=gr&GRid=6944365>.

"Blanche Lamont's Sister Testifies." *New York Times*, September 12, 1895.

"'Demon of the Belfry' Goes to the Gallows." SFist Daily, <http://sfist.com/2009/01/07/today_in_san_francisco_history_-_de.php>.

Duke, op. cit.

McConnell, Virginia A. *Sympathy for the Devil: The Emmanuel Baptist Murders of Old San Francisco*. Lincoln: University of Nebraska, 2005.

"Minnie Williams." *Find A Grave*, <http://www.findagrave.com/cgi-bin/fg.cgi?page=gr&GRid=6944373>.

23. The Three Thayers

Cutrona, Sue, and Amy Vilz. "Hanging of the Thayer Brothers - 1825 Featured at Downtown Library." *The Buffalo Downtoner*, May 2010: 5.

Lawson, op. cit.

Severance, Frank H. *Publications of the Buffalo Historical Society*. Buffalo, N.Y.: Buffalo Historical Society, 1907.

24. The Sausage Vat Murder

Loerzel, Robert. *Alchemy of Bones: Chicago's Luetgert Murder Case of 1897*. New York: University of Illinois, 2007.

Duke, op. cit.

"Forensics Story." *Scienceray*, <http://scienceray.com/biology/human-biology/forensics-story/>.

25. That Bad Man Stagolee

Brown, Cecil. *Stagolee Shot Billy*, Cambridge: Harvard University, 2004

McCulloch, Derek. Stagger Lee, Image Comics, 2006. *Planet Slade*, < http://www.planetslade.com/stagger-lee1.html>.

Slade, Paul. "A Christmas Killing: Stagger Lee." *Planet Slade*, < http://www.planetslade.com/stagger-lee1.html>.

"'Stack' Lee Sheldon." *Find A Grave*, <http://www.findagrave.com/cgi-bin/fg.cgi?page=gr&GRid=13558138>.

"Stagger Lee / Stag-O-Lee / Stagolee/ Stack-A-Lee / Stack O'Lee." *Harry's Blues Lyrics*, <http://blueslyrics.tripod.com/dictionary/stagolee.htm>.

26. Startling Parallelisms

"Bertha M. Manchester." *Find A Grave*, < http://www.findagrave.com/cgi-bin/fg.cgi?page=gr&GRid=11502090>.

Douglas & Olshaker, op. cit.

Martins, Michael, and Dennis A. Binette. *Parallel Lives: A Social History of Lizzie A. Borden and Her Fall River. Fall River, Mass.*: Fall River Historical Society, 2010.

"Startling Parallelisms." *Boston Daily Globe*, June 1, 1893: 1.

27. The Meeks Family Murder

Conard, Howard Louis. *Encyclopedia of the history of Missouri, a compendium of history and biography for ready reference*. New York: The Southern History Company, 1901.

"Meeks Family Murder" *Mudcat*, <http://www.mudcat.org/@displaysong.cfm?SongID=3939>

"Meeks Murder Summary." *Linn R-1 Libraries*, < http://www2.linnr1.k12.mo.us/LIB1/meeks.htm>.

"The Meeks Murders." *Pickler Memorial Library*, <http://library.truman.edu/scpublications/Chariton%20Collector/Spring%201982/The%20Meeks%20Murders.pdf>.

Murder of the Meeks family, or, Crimes of the Taylor brothers the full and authentic story of the midnight massacre, by Bill and George Taylor, of the Meeks family, father, mother and three little children ... the gruesome story of little Nellie Meeks, Kansas City, Mo.: Ryan Walker, 1896.

28. The Man of Two Lives

Bailey, Richard W. *Rogue Scholar: The Sinister Life and Celebrated Death of Edward H. Rulloff*. Ann Arbor: University of Michigan Press, 2003.

Crapsey, Edward. *The Man of Two Lives*. New York: American News Co., 1871.

"Edward Rulloff, Philologist and Murder", *New York Times*, January 12, 1871

Freeman, E. H. *The veil of secrecy removed the only true and authentic history of Edward H. Rulloff: his biography, trials and execution, the mysteries of his life revealed, his confessions of the murder of his wife and the killing of Myrrick, the motives and ambition which governed him, the sequel of a remarkable career.* Binghamton, N.Y.: Carl & Freeman, 1871.

"The Genius Killer." *Crime Library*, <http://www.trutv.com/library/crime/serial_killers/history/john_rulloff/1_index.html>.

29. The Hart-Meservey Murder

Dunton, Alvin R. *The true story of the Hart-Meservey murder trial: in which light is thrown upon dark deeds, incompetency, and perfidy: and crime fastened upon those ... should have commanded honest dealing*, Boston: Published by the author, 1882.

Snow, Edward Rowe. *Mysterious Tales of the New England Coast*. New York: Dodd, Mead, 1961.

30. Who Killed Benjamin Nathan

Byrnes, Thomas. *Professional Criminals of America*. New York: Castle & Company, Ltd, 1886.

Clemens, Will M. "The Murder of the Rich Banker." *The Era Magazine*: January 1905.

Crapsey, Edward. *The Nether Side of New York*. New York: Sheldon & Co., 1872.

"A Death in the Family." *Tablet*. <http://www.tabletmag.com/jewish-life-and-religion/23461/a-death-in-the-family>.

"The Latest Horror." *Daily Enquirer* 1 Aug 1870: 4.

Murphy, Cait N. *Scoundrels in Law*. New York: Harper Collins, 2010.

Pearson, Edmund Lester. *Studies in Murder.* New York: The Macmillan Co., 1924.

Walling, George W. *Recollections of a New York Chief of Police.* New York: Caxton Book Concern, Ltd., 1887.

31. The Pedestrian

"George Parkman." *Crime Library*, <http://www.trutv.com/library/crime/notorious_murders/classics/george_parkman/1.html>.

Schama, Simon. *Dead Certainties: Unwarranted Speculations*, New York: Knopf, 1991.

Sullivan, Robert. *The Disappearance of Dr. Parkman*, Boston: Little, Brown, 1971.

Thomson, Helen. *Murder at Harvard.* Boston: Houghton Mifflin, 1971.

"The Webster-Parkman Case." *Forensic Science*, <http://jimfisher.edinboro.edu/forensics/webster2.html>.

32. "I Was Born with the Devil in Me"

Borowski, John, (adapter). *The Strange Case Of Dr. H.H. Holmes.* West Hollywood, Calif: Waterfront Productions, 2005.

"H. H. Holmes (Herman Mudgett)." *Find A Grave*, <http://www.findagrave.com/cgi-bin/fg.cgi?page=gr&GRid=2415>.

Larson, Erik. *The Devil in the White City: Murder, Magic, and Madness at the Fair that Changed America.* New York: Vintage, 2004.

Schechter, Harold. *Depraved: The Definitive True Story of H.H. Holmes, Whose Grotesque Crimes Shattered Turn-of-the-Century Chicago*, New York: Pocket Star Books, 2004.

33. The St. Louis Trunk Tragedy

"Charles Arthur Preller." *Find A Grave*, <http://www.findagrave.com/cgi-bin/fg.cgi?page=gr&GSln=preller&GSiman=1&GScid=27534&GRid=27905782&>.

Duke, op. cit.

"Ewing Brooks" *Mudcat*, <http://mudcat.org/@displaysong.cfm?SongID=1873>

"The St. Louis Murder." *Paperspast*, <http://paperspast.natlib.govt.nz/cgi-bin/paperspast?a=d&d=OW18860730.2.38&l=mi&e=-------10--1----0-->.

"Hugh Mottram Brooks." *Find A Grave*, <http://www.findagrave.com/cgi-bin/fg.cgi?page=gr&GSln=+Brooks+&GSfn=hugh&GSmn=m&GSiman=1&GSbyrel=in&GSdyrel=in&GSob=n&GRid=15103468&df=all&>.

"Victorian Gay Lovers Tragedy in St. Louis Recalled." *The St. Louis LGBT History Project*, <http://stlgayhistory.livejournal.com/14009.html>.

Wagner, Allen Eugene. *Good Order and Safety: A History of the St. Louis Metropolitan Police Department, 1861-1906*. Saint. Louis, Mo.: Missouri History Museum, 2008.

34. The Richardson-McFarland Tragedy

Cooper, George. *Lost Love: A True Story of Passion, Murder, and Justice in Old New York*, New York: Pantheon, 1994.

"Richardson, Albert D." *The House of Beadle and Adams*, <http://www.ulib.niu.edu/badndp/richardson_albert.html>.

The Richardson McFarland Tragedy. Philadelphia: Barclay & Co. 1870.

Sutton & Mix, op. cit.

Twain, Mark. "Our Precious Lunatic." *Buffalo Express*, May 14, 1870.

35. The Massachusetts Borgia

"Against All Precedent." *New York Times*, March 6. 1888: 1.

"The Awful Crimes of one Woman." *Chariton Herald*, August 19, 1886.

Defenders and Offenders. New York: D. Buchner & Co., 1888.

Jones, Ann. *Women Who Kill*. New York: Holt, Rinehart, and Winston, 1980.

"A Massachusetts Borgia." *Decatur Daily Republican*, August 13, 1886: 2.

"Mrs. Robinson. Commutation to be Asked Today." *Boston Daily Globe* October 13, 1888: 4.

"Notorious Prisoner Dead." *Logansport Daily Reporter*. January 6, 1906.

"Only Woman in 'Solitary'." *Boston Sunday Globe*, December 24, 1905: 18.

Robinson, Sarah Jane, and J. M. W. Yerrinton. *The Official Report of The Trial of Sarah Jane Robinson for The Murder of Prince Arthur Freeman, in The Supreme Judicial Court of Massachusetts, From Notes of Mr. J.M.W. Yerrinton*, Boston: Wright & Potter Print. Co., State Printers, 1888.

"They Find her Guilty." *New York Times*, February 12, 1888: 1.

36. The Poison Fiend

Jones, op. cit.

"Lydia Sherman," *Find A Grave*, <http://www.findagrave.com/cgi-bin/fg.cgi?page=gr&GRid=8890048>.

Lydia Sherman: confession of the arch murderess of Connecticut : bloody deeds perpetrated with a cold heart, numerous poisonings, trial and conviction, Philadelphia: T.R. Callender, 1873.

Schechter, Harold. *Fatal: The Poisonous Life of a Female Serial Killer*, New York: Pocket Star Books, 2003.

37. The Ballad of Frankie Silver

Burt, op. cit.

Davenport, Tom. *The Ballad of Frankie Silver*, 47 min., Folkstreams, 1996, videocassette.

"Frankie Silver." *Find A Grave*, <http://www.findagrave.com/cgi-bin/fg.cgi?page=gr&GRid=8567288>.

"'Give Me the Truth!': The Frankie Silver Story in Contemporary North Carolina." *Folkstreams.net,* <http://www.folkstreams.net/context>.

Patterson, Daniel W. *A Tree Accurst: Bobby McMillon and Stories of Frankie Silver*, Chapel Hill, NC: University of North Carolina Press. 2000.

Wellman, op. cit.

Young, Perry Deane. *The Untold Story of Frankie Silver: Was She Unjustly Hanged?* Lincoln, NE: iUniverse, 2005.

38. Rhode Island Inequity

"A Brute Witness", *Bangor Daily Whig and Courier*, January 17, 1844.

"Amasa Sprague." *Find A Grave*, <http://www.findagrave.com/cgi-bin/fg.cgi?page=gr&GRid=5563>.

"The Exoneration of John Gordon." *Stacy House*, <http://www.stacyhouse.com/District_75/John_Gordon/mainpage.htm>.

Hoffmann, Charles and Tess Hoffmann. *Brotherly Love: Murder and the Politics of Prejudice in Nineteenth-Century Rhode Island*. Boston, University of Massachusetts Press 1993.

"Sprague Mansion." *Dread Central*, <http://www.dreadcentral.com/story/sprague-mansion>.

39. The Madison Horror

Hayden, Herbert H. *The Rev. Herbert H. Hayden: An Autobiography*, Hartford: Press of the Plimpton Mfg. Co., 1880.

Minot, George E. *Murder will out*, Boston, Mass.: Marshall Jones Co., 1928.

Poor Mary Stannard! A Full and Thrilling Story of The Circumstances Connected With Her Murder, New Haven: Stafford Print. Co., 1879.

"Mary Stannard's Murder." *New York Times*, October 7,1879.

40. A Savage Ruffian!

Arnold, Stephen. *The trial of Stephen Arnold for the murder of Betsey Van Amburgh, a child six years of age: before the Court of Oyer and Terminer and General Goal Delivery, for the county of Otsego, at the court house in Cooperstown, June 4th, 1805*. Hartford: Printed by Lincoln & Gleason, 1806.

Cooper, James Fennimore "The Eclipse." Putnam's Monthly Magazine of American Literature September 1869: 352.

Hoffman, Ronald, Mechal Sobel, and Fredrika J. Teute. *Through a glass darkly: reflections on personal identity in early America*, Chapel Hill: Published for the Omohundro Institute of Early American History & Culture, Williamsburg, Virginia, by the University of North Carolina Press, 1997.

Jones, Louis C. "The Crime and Punishment Stephen Arnold." *New York History*, July 1966: 248.

Phinney, Elihu. "A Savage Ruffian!" *Otsego Herald* [Cooperstown] January 31, 1805.

41. The Vamp of New Orleans

McConnell, Virginia A. *The Adventuress: Murder, Blackmail, and Confidence Games in the Gilded Age*. Kent, Ohio: Kent State University Press, 2010.

"Minnie Walkup's Trial." *New York Times*, October 23, 1885.

French, Laura M. *History of Emporia and Lyon County, Kansas*, Westminster, MD: Heritage Books, 2008.

The Kansas City medical index-lancet, Volume 6, Kansas City, Mo: 1885.

42. The Walworth Parricide

Brien, Geoffrey. *The Fall of the House of Walworth: A Tale of Madness and Murder in Gilded Age America*, New York: Henry Holt and Co., 2010.

Walworth, Clarence A. *Walworths of America; comprising five chapters of family history, with additional chapters of genealogy*, Albany, N.Y: Weed-Parsons Printing, 1897.

Walworth, Frank H. *The Walworth Parricide, a full account of the astounding murder of Mansfield T. Walworth by his son, Frank H. Walworth, with the trial and conviction of the parricide and his sentence for life to the state penitentiary at Sing Sing*, New York: Thomas O'Kane, 1873.

43. "Girl Slays Girl"

"Alice Mitchel and Freddy Ward" *Lyons College*
<http://web.lyon.edu/wolfcollection/songs/scruggsalice1269.html>

Duggan, Lisa. *Sapphic Slashers: Sex, Violence, and American Modernity*, New York: Duke UP, 2000

Lindquist, Lisa J. "Images of Alice: Gender, Deviancy, and a Love Murder in Memphis." *Journal of the History of Sexuality*, Vol. 6, 1995.

"A Most Shocking Crime." *New York Times*, January 26, 1892.

"She Loves Men, Too." *San Francisco Call*, June 23, 1895.

44. Murder in the Vale of Tempe

Bellamy, John Stark. *Vintage Vermont Villainies: True Tales of Murder & Mystery from the 19th and 20th Centuries*. Woodstock, Vt.: Countryman Press, 2007.

"The Christie Warden Murder." *Rauner Special Collections Library*,
<http://raunerlibrary.blogspot.com/2011_01_30_archive.html>.

Holbrook, Stewart Hall. *Murder Out Yonder: An Informal Study of Certain Classic Crimes in Back-Country America*, New York: Macmillan Co., 1941.

Life, Trial, and Confession of Frank C. Almy, Laconia, N.H.: J.J. Lane, 1891.

45. Albany Gothic

Hamblin, P. R. *United States Criminal History: Being a True Account of the Most Horrid Murders, Piracies, High-Way Robberies, &c.*, Fayetteville: Mason & DePuy Printers, 1836.

Jones, Louis C. *Murder at Cherry Hill: The Strang-Whipple Case*, 1827. Albany, N.Y.: Historic Cherry Hill, 1982.

Historic Cherry Hill, <http://www.historiccherryhill.org/index.htm>.

Strang, Jesse, and William Brittainham Lacey. *The authentic confession of Jesse Strang, executed at Albany, Friday, August 24, 1827, for the murder of John Whipple as made to the Rev[erend] Mr. Lacey, rector of St. Peter's Church, Albany, from the time of Strang's imprisonment down to the hour of his execution : published to the world at Strang's dying request! : together with the account of his execution and conduct under the gallows.* New-York: Printed and published by E.M. Murden & A. Ming, Jr., 1827.

Trial of Jesse Strang for the murder of John Whipple. Albany, NY: D. M'Glashan, 1827.

46. "A Most Extraordinary Case"

Burt, op. cit.

"Commonwealth v. John Francis Knapp." *Massachusetts Cases,* <http://masscases.com/cases/sjc/26/26mass496.html>.

"Commonwealth versus Joseph Jenkins Knapp." <http://plaza.ufl.edu/edale/Knapp.htm>.

"Gardner-Pingree House." *Hawthorn in Salem,* <http://www.hawthorneinsalem.org/images/image.php?name=MMD2245>.

Knapp, Joseph Jenkins, and George Crowninshield. *Trials of Capt. Joseph J. Knapp, Jr., and George Crowninshield, Esq for the murder of Capt. Joseph White, of Salem, on the night of the sixth of April, 1830*, Boston: Charles Ellms, 1830.

Shurter, Edwin Du Bois. *Masterpieces of Modern Oratory*, Boston: Ginn and company, 1906

Duke, op. cit.

47. Little 'Omie

Burt, op. cit.

Craven, B. *Naomi Wise, or, The wrongs of a beautiful girl: a true story, enacted in North Carolina 80 years ago*, Randleman, N.C.: [W.P. Brooks], 1884. Print.

Long-Wilgus, Eleanor R. *Naomi Wise: Creation, Re-Creation, and Continuity in an American Ballad Tradition*. New York: Chapel Hill, 2003.

"Naomi Wise." *Find A Grave*, <http://www.findagrave.com/cgi-bin/fg.cgi?page=gr&GRid=15846775>

"Naomi Wise." *Notes on the History of Randolph County, NC*, <http://randolphhistory.wordpress.com/2009/06/03/naomi-wise>.

"A True Account of Nayomy Wise." *Wikisource*, <http://en.wikisource.org/wiki/A_true_account_of_Nayomy_Wise>.

Wellman, op. cit.

48. Bloody Woolfolk

DeLoach, Carolyn, *Shadow Chasers: The Woolfolk Tragedy Revisited*, Newman, Ga.: Eagles Pub Co, 2000.

---, *The Woolfolk Tragedy: The Murders, the Trials, the Hanging & Now Finally, the Truth!* Douglasville, Ga.: Anneewakee River Press, 1996.

"Family Woolfolk." *Find A Grave*, <http://www.findagrave.com/cgi-bin/fg.cgi?GRid=6722879&page=gr>.

"Perhaps Not Guilty; New Light on the Killing of the Woolfolk Family." *New York Times*, September 20, 1887.

"Thomas G. 'Tom' Woolfolk." *Find A Grave*, <http://www.findagrave.com/cgi-bin/fg.cgi?page=gr&GRid=10690460>.

"Woolfolk Murder Case." *New Georgia Encyclopedia*, <http://www.georgiaencyclopedia.org/nge/Article.jsp?id=h-2882>.

49. The Bloody Benders

"The Bloody Benders of Labette County." *Kansas Mediocrity*, <http://kansasmediocrity.wordpress.com/2009/10/09/the-bloody-benders-of-labette-county-a-true-ghost-story/>.

Case, Nelson. *History of Labette County, Kansas: From the First Settlement to the Close of 1892*, Topeka, Kan.: Crane & Company, 1893.

Duke, op. cit.

James, John T. *The Benders in Kansas*. Washington, D.C.: Photoduplication Service, Library of Congress, 1913.

"The Kansas Murders." *New York Times*, May 13, 1873

"Says They're Not the Benders." *New York Times*, January 11, 1890

50. The Boston Belfry Tragedy

"The Belfry Murder." *Boston Daily Advertiser*, May 25, 1875.

deMille, James. *Cord and Creese: A Novel* (Classic Reprint), New York: Harper & Bros, 1869.

DeWolfe, George G. B. (spirit) *Verses composed on the confession and execution of Thomas W. Piper, the convicted belfry murderer*. Boston: s.n., 1876?

Dempewolff, Robert F. *Famous Old New England Murders: And Some That Are Infamous.* Brattleboro: Stephen Daye Press, 1942.

"The History of Hayes Park." *The Friends of Hayes Park,* <http://www.hayespark.org/History.html>.

"The Murder of Mabel H. Young." *Boston Daily Advertiser,* December 11, 1875.

Piper, Thomas W., and J. M. W. Yerrinton. *The Official Report of the Trial of Thomas W. Piper for the Murder of Mabel H. Young, in the Supreme Judicial Court of Massachusetts, from Notes of Mr.J.M.W. Yerrinton,* Boston: Wright & Potter, 1887.

"Piper's Punishment." *National Aegis* [Worcester], May 27, 1876.

"Piper's Threefold Confession." *Boston Journal,* May 8, 1876.

Rogers, Alan. *Murder and the Death Penalty in Massachusetts.* Amherst: University of Massachusetts Press, 2008.

Sammarco, Anthony Mitchell. *Boston's South End* (MA) (Then & Now), Dover, N.H.: Arcadia, 1998.

"Two Executions." *Boston Traveler,* May 26, 1876.

Wilson, Colin, and Damon Wilson. *A Plague of Murder: the rise and rise of serial killing in the modern age,* London: Robinson, 1995.

INDEX

Borden, Abby Durfee, 13

Borden, Andrew Jackson, 13

Borden, Lizzie Andrew, 13, 120

Boston, MA, 9, 62, 146, 152, 167, 201

Boston, NY, 106

Britt, Allen, 17

Brooklyn, NY, 31, 73, 131

Brooks, Hugh Mottram, 154

Brown, Carrie, 21

Budge, Priscilla, 25

Budge, Rev. Henry, 25

Buffalo, NY, 106

Burdell, Dr. Harvey, 30

Burke County, NC, 174

Burlington, NY, 190

Burt, Olive Woolley, 93, 224

Byrnes, Thomas F., 23, 144

California, 52, 102

Cambridge, MA, 146, 165

Cause of Death

Beating, 5, 124, 181, 190

Blows from an axe, 13, 36, 67, 95, 120 ,174, 230

Blows from a hammer, 1, 235

Blows to the head, 139, 240

Burning, 151

Clubbing, 221

Drowning, 226

Gunshot, 17, 52, 71, 83, 99, 106, 116, 129, 160, 201, 210, 216

Poisoning, 46, 89, 154, 165, 169, 186, 195

Slashing, 9, 25, 205

Stabbing, 5, 30, 62, 78, 146, 186, 221

Strangulation, 21, 30, 41, 102, 134

Unknown, 112

Cherry Hill, 216,

Cherryvale, KS, 235

Chicago, IL, 57, 112, 151, 199

Choate, Rufus, 9

ABOUT THE AUTHOR

Robert Wilhelm is the author of *Murder and Mayhem in Essex County* (History Press), a history of capital crimes in Essex County, Massachusetts from the 1600s to the turn of the twentieth century. He blogs about historical true crime at Murder by Gaslight (www.MurderByGaslight.com) and The National Night Stick (nightstick.azurewebsites.net). Robert lives and works in Boston, Massachusetts.

www.ingramcontent.com/pod-product-compliance
Lightning Source LLC
Chambersburg PA
CBHW062048270326
41931CB00013B/2988